Stock Picking

Stock Picking

The 11 Best Tactics for Beating the Market

Richard J. Maturi

McGraw-Hill, Inc.

New York   San Francisco   Washington, D.C.   Auckland   Bogotá
Caracas   Lisbon   London   Madrid   Mexico City   Milan
Montreal   New Delhi   San Juan   Singapore
Sydney   Tokyo   Toronto

Library of Congress Cataloging-in-Publication Data

Maturi, Richard J.
   Stock picking : the 11 best tactics for beating the market /
Richard J. Maturi.
      p.   cm.
   Includes index.
   ISBN 0-07-040937-4 —ISBN 0-07-040938-2 (pbk.)
   1. Stocks.   2. Investments.   I. Title.
HG4661.M37   1993
332.63'22—dc20   93-96
                                       CIP

    6 7 8 9 0 DOC/DOC 9 9 8 7

ISBN 0-07-040937-4 (hc)
ISBN 0-07-040938-2 (pbk)

*The sponsoring editor for this book was David Conti, the editing supervisor
was Mitsy Kovacs, and the production supervisor was Pamela A. Pelton. It
was set in Palatino by McGraw-Hill's Professional Book Group composition
unit.*

Printed and bound by R. R. Donnelley & Sons Company.

To my father, Mario, and my Uncle Rudy who inspired me in the investment field with their good common sense, attitude of fair play, and belief in plain, old hard work

To my wife, Mary, who has continually supported my writing efforts and often comes up with my best ideas

Contents

Preface

Plenty of theories and strategies abound in the investment world. Some work well, while others don't deliver what they promise. In addition, some strategies work their magic only in specific investment climates and fall flat on their faces when the economic scenario changes.

Stock Picking explains why these specific strategies work, when best to implement them, and when to shift your focus to more promising strategies within the group.

Today's investor must be flexible enough to capitalize on new opportunities as the market moves through its cycles. In the compilation of this book, I researched the current body of knowledge supporting each strategy, discussed the strategies with dozens of experts, evaluated how current market conditions and projected future changes in the overall market impact each strategy, and compiled numerous examples to clearly illustrate these strategies in action.

Over many months, I contacted a number of well-known investment managers, analysts, and specialists, such as Sir John Templeton, Charles Neuhauser, Elliott Schlang, Binkley Shorts, and Matthew Weatherbie whose insights and contributions to this work proved invaluable.

The book's in-depth analysis provides investors with a clear explanation of how these strategies can be put to work to increase the value of their own portfolios and reduce their investment risk.

Of the thousands of investment strategies that exist, the eleven stragegies presented in this book were chosen because they provide the individual investor with the opportunity to get on an even playing field with institutions and other professional investment managers. All the information required to implement them is readily available to individuals.

These investment strategies are not mutually exclusive. The information presented on topics such as value investing and cashflow also apply when analyzing investment alternatives such as small-cap stocks and spin-offs. Refer to earlier chapters as often as required to perfect your use of these investment strategies.

At the end of the book is a handy glossary of important investment terms pertinent to each strategy to further educate the investor.

This is a hands-on book for the savvy investor serious about beating the market. Sit back, read about these strategies, and then go to work using them to increase your wealth.

RICHARD J. MATURI
Cheyenne, Wyoming

Acknowledgments

I extend my thanks to the following who were kind enough to allow reprint of charts and illustrations:

Ibbotson Associates

The Leuthold Group

Standard & Poor's Corporation

Value Line Investment Survey

About the Author

Richard J. Maturi is a widely respected business and invest-
ment writer whose more than 800 articles have appeared in
such distinguished publications as *Barron's*, *The New York
Times*, *Kiplinger's Personal Finance Magazine*, *Investor's
Business Daily*, *Your Money*, *Industry Week*, *Institutional
Investor*, and others. In addition, he writes a regular column,
"Talking Shop," in *Entrepreneur* and is a nationally syndi-
cated investment writer for Rocky Mountain Features
International. Mr. Maturi is the author of *Wall Street Words*
and publisher of *Utility and Energy Portfolio*.

1

Value Investing

From Graham to Templeton

Approaches to Value Investing

While the premise of value investing stands on its own, it also forms a solid foundation for many of the investment strategies in the chapters to follow. For example, the lucrative investment returns available from turnaround investing and small-cap opportunities can be enhanced by firmly rooting them within the value investing principles.

Basically, the value investing approach attempts to determine the intrinsic value of a stock in terms of earning power and future dividends and yield and then compare that value with the price the stock commands in the market. Value investors strive to make above-average investment returns by ferreting out those companies that the market underprices in relation to the underlying "value" of their earnings and yield potential.

Any number of reasons can contribute to a stock's undervaluation, including general economic conditions, a cyclical firm's downturn, unappreciated assets and unrecognized market opportunities for the company due to new technologies, innovative marketing strategies, or a change in management.

The three main approaches to stock analysis and valuation consist of relative value, performance anticipation, and intrinsic value analysis.

The relative value method attempts to analyze a stock by its value in relation to other benchmarks such as its specific industry groupings, various indices like the Standard & Poor's (S&P) 500, or comparable groupings of similar companies such as high-growth firms.

It compares the attractiveness of an individual stock in relation to others in terms of earnings power, dividends, and yield.

To illustrate, a value investor may decide that a particular stock out-ranks the S&P 500 stocks in both earnings and dividends and, therefore, deserves a higher market multiple in comparison to the S&P 500 bench-mark.

The performance anticipation approach tries to uncover those stocks that promise to outperform the market 6 to 18 months in the future and that have a present price level that does not take into account favorable circumstances.

Finally, the intrinsic valuation approach attempts to place a value on the stock based on the underlying circumstances of the firm. It tries to determine what price the stock should be selling at if properly valued in the marketplace, completely disregarding its current market price. This involves analysis of the firm's assets, earnings, dividends, future prospects, and management talent.

One method of seeking intrinsic value looks at the value of the company if it were to be liquidated and the net assets distributed to share-holders. The fallacy of this method lies in the fact that the value of a go-ing concern usually varies greatly from that of a firm being liquidated. Future earnings prospects, market share, proprietary information and techniques, etc., possess a value that cannot be liquidated as such.

Another method of seeking intrinsic valuation lies in "arm's length" transaction analysis. In other words, what would an independent party pay for the business? Taken together the values of the individual business assets or business entities total up to the firm's intrinsic value. Corporate raiders often analyze a business in this way, at least in part, to determine which assets can be sold off for cash after the takeover. However, they also take into account the synergies and benefits of con-solidations and streamlining of corporate operations in the value they place on the business.

The major components of stock valuation include expected future earnings, expected future dividends, capitalization rates (multipliers of earnings and dividends), and asset values.

The obvious advantage of using the value investing approach lies in lessening the downside risk. By determining the firm's proper valua-tion, you reduce the risk of overpaying for a stock. This works to reduce the downside risk of stock ownership while also increasing the upside potential.

Benjamin Graham

Perhaps the original bargain hunter in the value investing arena, Benjamin Graham devised numerous methods for determining the intrinsic value of a firm. In his book, *The Intelligent Investor*, published back in 1949, Graham presented a macro value investing approach using a basic earnings-yield formula based on a valuation computed from the Dow Jones Industrial Average and the yield on Aaa corporate bonds.

Graham calculated this value by capitalizing the average earnings over the past 10 years on a basis equivalent to twice the yield on high-grade Aaa bonds. According to Graham's formula, you purchased stocks when the Dow Jones Industrial Average dropped to 80 percent of this benchmark valuation and sold stocks when the average rose to 120 percent of the benchmark valuation.

For example, for the 10-year period ended December 31, 1955, annual average earnings totaled $25.25. In 1955, Moody's Aaa bonds yielded 3.3 percent. Using Graham's formula of 2 times the 3.3 percent yield provided a 6.6 capitalization factor and a benchmark valuation of 383 for the Dow Jones Industrial Average.

According to Graham, when the Dow dropped below 306 (383×0.8), it was time to buy stocks. Likewise, when the Dow rose above 460 (383×1.2), it was time to bail out of the market. During 1955, the Dow ranged from a low of 388.20 to its closing high of 488.40. In other words, Graham's earnings-yield formula would have kept you from purchasing stock in 1955 since the Dow never dropped to 306 and would have also prompted you to sell as the Dow rose above 460—probably not a good move since the Dow rose to a new high of 521.05 in 1956.

As time passed and average earnings, bond yields, and the Dow fluctuated, the failure of this value indicator became even more pronounced. Even Graham recognized the failings of this formula and revised it during 1960–61. In discussing this revision Graham said, "To be quite frank, if there are to be new standards, they cannot be reliably established in advance but can be recognized as such only after they have been validated by fairly long experience."

It's extremely valuable to keep in mind that even such noted investment analysts as Benjamin Graham have theories that go haywire after a while. The plain fact is, economic realities change and many stock theories and strategies work only within certain economic and time parameters.

Other Graham value investment gems imply that a stock is a bargain when its price equals:

- The company's book value per share or less
- 50 times the earnings per share, divided by the AAA bond rate
- 150 times the dividends per share, divided by the AAA bond rate

Whatever the current validity of specific Graham value indicators, his overall value approach contains a great deal of merit and deserves careful study.

Graham stressed the importance of considering both the quantitative and qualitative aspects of a potential investment. For a common stock, the quantitative factors include capitalization, earnings, dividends, assets, liabilities, and operating performance. On the qualitative side of the coin, Graham recommended serious study of the nature and prospects of the business, the trend of future earnings, the inherent stability of the company, and the quality of top management.

He cautioned against valuing the management factor twice in the stock analysis. Stock valuation takes into consideration the good earnings performance already delivered by management, and if another substantial incremental valuation boost gets attributed to the excellent management team, overvaluation may result. So, unless significant changes in management have taken place, be careful of placing too much additional weight for the management factor in the stock valuation process.

To Graham, the standard valuation approach for individual companies consisted of capitalizing the expected future earnings and/or dividends at an appropriate rate of return, using a time frame of 5 to 10 years. The capitalization rate, or multiplier, varied with the quality of the business under valuation, much as a bank adjusts the interest rate at which it will lend to a business depending on the firm's financial stability and expected ability to repay the loan on time.

Graham emphasized that his valuation approach was but one of several acceptable valuation methods, and analysts and investors must determine which methods work best for them.

Other Methods

Modern proponents of value investing use a variety of barometers to measure when a stock may be improperly valued. Among the most popular are price-earnings ratios, price–to–book value ratios, price-to-cash-flow ratios, dividend yields, cash per share–to–price per share ratios, debt ratios, financial strength, and asset valuations.

The trick is to narrow the list of potential candidates using various ratios indicating an undervaluation and then perform further study to determine if the company is truly undervalued or just another dog whose past performance and dismal future prospects warrant its discounted stock price. Many a company whose stock had been battered by the stock market continued to languish with lackluster earnings, mounted increasing losses, or even took a disastrous plunge into the ranks of the bankrupt.

Don't let the enticing ratios blind you to the true fundamentals of the firm and its realistic future prospects.

The Leuthold Group, an investment advisory firm in Minneapolis, Minnesota, provides a set of criteria for searching out undervalued and unloved stocks. These criteria are:

1. *Book value.*   Preferably less than 80 percent of the S&P 400 and never over 1.5 times

2. *Price-earnings.*   Using 5-year average earnings, must be less than 70 percent of the S&P 500 and never over 12 times

3. *Ratio of cash per share to price per share.*   At least 15 percent

4. *Dividend yield.*   At least equal to the S&P 500 yield and never below 3 percent

5. *Price to cashflow.*   Less than 75 percent of S&P 500 cashflow ratio

6. *Ratio of long-term debt plus unfunded pension liabilities to total capital.* Under 50 percent

7. *Financial strength.*   Must be adequate

Value investing is not a panacea for all investment and economic scenarios. Like almost all other investment strategies, it also can go out of favor. For the decade from 1975 through 1985, value investing outperformed the broad market average. However, beginning in 1986, value investors were hard-pressed to show a decent return in comparison to the overall market indices. The 1990s look to be a different story, however, with value investing coming back in vogue.

Why Companies Are Undervalued

A number of reasons exist for undervalued companies. Investors routinely undervalue companies in cyclical industries as the doom and gloom of the present economic or industry cycle overtakes the firm's long-term prospects. The stocks of automotive, real estate, and natural resources companies routinely get sideswiped by the preponderance of declining earnings releases and negative news prior to a turnaround in their fortunes.

Unrecognized and unappreciated assets also contribute to the undervaluation of some firms. In many cases, it's hard to determine proper valuation for certain corporate assets not used in the firm's mainline business operations.

For example, the true value of Burlington Northern's real estate holdings got lost in the analysis of the firm as a transportation company. Not until Burlington Northern spun off its real estate operations as Burlington Resources in July 1988 did the real value of the real estate operations come to light. Burlington Resources' stock more than doubled from its initial price of $25.50 per share to $53⅝ per share in late 1989. (See Chap. 7, "Spin-Off Successes.")

Accounting standards also work to shade the difference between real or intrinsic value and book value. While machinery and equipment do depreciate in value over time, the accounting value carried on the books rarely coincides with the real economic value. In addition, intangible assets such as trademarks, brand names, and patents often possess an economic value not recognized on the firm's books.

According to Arnold Kaufman, editor of Standard & Poor's *The Outlook*, a low market-to-book ratio serves as a buffer against market declines and should be viewed positively.

"We look for neglected assets worth enough to push stock price gains when finally recognized," says Kaufman.

Kaufman considers as other value stock candidates stocks whose prices are down even though earnings prospects look decent, stocks that have low price-earnings multiples but that provide good yields, and stocks with good value whether or not rapid growth is expected.

Price-Earnings Ratio Analysis

One of the most prevalent attempts to uncover value lies in price-earnings (P/E) ratio analysis. This consists of dividing a stock's price per share by earnings per share to get its P/E ratio. For example, a firm that earned $6 per share last year and whose stock price is $60 per share has a P/E ratio of 10 ($60/$6). In other words, investors are willing to pay $10 for every $1 in earnings.

Of course, investors also calculate P/E multiples on future expected earnings. Assume the same stock trades at $60 per share and it is projected to earn $9 per share next year. In this case, its P/E would be calculated to be 6.67 ($60/$9).

Investors search out companies with P/Es significantly lower than those of its peer group (industry, growth stocks, or other classification) as a starting point on their trail of undervalued situations.

Early research provided evidence of the validity of using the P/E as a value finder. Graham's revised 1973 edition of *The Intelligent Investor*

Table 1-1. Average Annual Percentage Gain, 1937–1969

Period	10 low-P/E stocks	10 high-P/E stocks	30 DJIA stocks
1937–1942	−2.2	−10.0	−6.3
1943–1947	+17.3	+8.3	+14.9
1948–1952	+16.4	+4.6	+9.9
1953–1957	+20.9	+10.0	+13.7
1958–1962	+10.2	−3.3	+3.6
1963–1969	+8.0	+4.6	+4.0

SOURCE: Benjamin Graham, *The Intelligent Investor*, 4th ed., 1973

cited a study by Paul Miller of Drexel & Company covering 30 Dow Jones price-to-earnings-ratios stock groupings over the 32-year period from 1937 through 1969.

As indicated in Table 1-1, low-P/E stocks outperformed the Dow Jones Industrial Average (DJIA) in 25 of the 34 years under study. In the remaining nine years, the low-P/E stocks nearly matched the performance of the Dow Jones in six of the years and lagged the Dow Jones only three times on an annual basis.

David Dreman and Price-Earnings

More recently, David Dreman, author of *Contrarian Investment Strategy* and chairman and chief investment officer of Dreman Value Management, L.P. in Jersey City, New Jersey, conducted extensive low-P/E research in conjunction with the academic community.

Using his own low-P/E value investment approach, Dreman has achieved an enviable track record. For the 11-year period ended December 31, 1991, Dreman Value Management, L.P. earned a compound annual return of 16.3 percent, versus only 15.2 percent for the S&P 500 Index.

According to Dreman, more than 80 percent of all investment managers have failed to perform as well as the popular averages in any 10-year period since such records were first kept beginning in 1965. A major reason for this failing lies in the fact that many managers do not adhere to a consistent strategy.

"Our low-P/E research and track record speak for themselves. In one of our major studies measuring the performance of the 1800 largest companies in the nation from 1968 through 1977, we found that stocks with the lowest 10 percent of P/E multiples increased 241 percent versus stocks with the highest 10 percent of P/E multiples falling 10 percent. During that same time frame, the market average as measured by the S&P 500 Index rose only 55 percent," says Dreman.

Another Dreman study covering the time period of July 1, 1963, to June 30, 1985 (the longest time frame and greatest number of stocks in any study to date), included three major bull-bear markets, a Dow Jones Industrial Average range from a low of 550 to a high of 1500, and market P/Es stretching from a bottom of 7 to a peak of 21.

This study found that the lowest-P/E stocks returned 20.7 percent annually, while the highest-P/E group returned only 10.4 percent annually. An investment of $10,000 in the lowest-P/E group in 1963 and switched annually would have grown to $630,042, compared with $88,169 for the highest-P/E group.

A third Dreman study covering the 25-year period from January 1, 1966, through December 31, 1990, showed an annual return of 13.9 percent for the low-P/E stocks versus 9.6 percent for the third P/E quartile, 8.9 percent for the high-P/E stocks, and 10.8 percent for the market.

Dreman fortifies his P/E value investment strategy with analysis of low price–to–book value relationships and debt-to-capital ratios usually less than 40 percent. Above-average dividend yields provide stronger protection on the downside. He prefers companies with low or sharply declining institutional ownership, indicating the stocks are currently out of favor with Wall Street.

"It's important to maintain a firm selling discipline as well. `Overstaying' a stock position only to see its price dive is a common mistake for investors. As stocks' P/Es rise, we replace them with other low-P/E stocks which meet our investment criteria," says Dreman.

P/E ratio analysis does have several drawbacks. If the company under evaluation is currently undergoing tough times and has suffered losses, there are no earnings with which to calculate the P/E ratio. Likewise, the earnings of cyclical firms and new growth companies often exhibit fluctuating earnings patterns, making P/E comparisons a less reliable valuation barometer.

John Slatter and Price-to-Sales Ratio

John Slatter, senior vice president and senior portfolio manager with Hickory Investment Advisors in Cleveland, Ohio, solves these problems by calculating the firm's price-to-sales ratio. Using this tack, Slatter doesn't encounter the infinity problem and avoids the effect of widely varied earnings performance.

Slatter's research on A++, A+, and A from *Value Line Investment Survey* found that the stocks of companies with low price-to-sales ratios performed much better than those with higher ratios.

Using Cashflow and Other
Criteria to Determine Value

Others such as Robert L. Renck, Jr., managing director of the New York City investment firm of R. L. Renck & Co., Inc., beef up their search for undervalued firms with a close analysis of corporate cashflow. (See Chap. 2, "Cashing in on Corporate Cashflow").

Kenneth Hackel, president of the Fort Lee, New Jersey, investment firm of Systematic Financial Management seeks out companies that can pay off their entire debt load from free cashflow within five years. In addition, Hackel prefers firms with ratios of price to free cashflow below that of the S&P investments while meeting other valuation analysis criteria.

Graham also places an emphasis on capitalization. He recommended buying stocks selling at a one-third discount to their net working capital. To calculate net working capital, take the firm's current assets (cash, receivables, and inventory) and subtract its total liabilities (payables and debt).

Fortunately, a lot of the calculations needed to find undervalued stock candidates has already been done for you. The "Summary and Index" section of *Value Line* contains several listings of potential undervalued investments. Check out the following *Value Line* tabulations: "Widest Discounts from Book Value," "Lowest P/Es," "Bargain Basement Stocks," "Highest Annual Total Returns," "Highest Estimated 3-to-5 Year Dividend Relative to Current Price," "Highest Percentage Earned on Capital," and "Biggest `Free Flow' Cash Generators."

Other business and investment publications such as *Business Week, Forbes, Fortune,* and *The Outlook* also periodically provide listings and articles on companies that appear to be undervalued according to one or more investment valuation yardsticks.

Michael Kassen

Michael M. Kassen with the investment firm of Neuberger & Berman in New York City looks for companies with the potential to generate a total return between 30 and 50 percent over the next two- to three-year time horizon in a flat to slightly upward stock market.

"There must be limited downside risk evidenced by asset strength plus earnings and dividend track record," says Kassen.

In early 1992, Neuberger & Berman held extensive holdings in the cable television area. Kassen particularly liked the prospects of Comcast Corporation. Negative market sentiment against leverage and fears of cable television regulation and industry competition contributed to buying opportunities in Comcast stock. From an all-time high of nearly $20 per share in 1989, Comcast's common share price dropped to less than $8 per share in late 1990.

As the fifth or sixth largest owner of cable television franchises plus a growing cellular telephone operation, Comcast represented a classic undervalued asset play. Although the firm's stock price rebounded to the $15 per share level in early 1992, Kassen estimated the sale value of the firm at a conservative $23 per share. By 1993, he estimates the asset value of Comcast to approach the $28 to $29 per share level.

To date, Comcast, like many cable television companies, has failed to generate any profits, but revenue growth remains strong. The increasing number of customers promises to boost revenues without a proportionate increase in costs, helping to narrow Comcast's losses and eventually deliver profits.

Using both asset valuation and cashflow multiple analysis, Neuberger & Berman projected fully diluted values of $23.87 per share for 1992 and $28.94 per share for 1993. In the analysis, cellular values of $180/potential customer (POP), $215/POP, and $250/POP were used for 1991, 1992, and 1993, respectively. This compares favorably with the $193/POP price Comcast paid for Metromedia's Philadelphia operations and the more than $380/POP McCaw paid in late 1989.

Another plus, Neuberger & Berman considers Comcast to be among the best-managed firms in the industry, both operationally and financially.

William Miller

Another value hunter, William Miller, a mutual funds manager for Legg Mason Wood Walker, Inc., in Baltimore, Maryland, concentrates on picking up companies that satisfy three major investment criteria. First of all, he must be able to acquire them at a large discount to their real worth. Next, they must be generating extra cash from operations so they will have enough cash to bail them out of inevitable mistakes. Finally, Miller seeks firms with top management exhibiting a demonstrated interest in maximizing shareholder value.

"You have to concentrate both on what you're paying for a company's stock and on what you're getting back in return. We look for low price-to-book ratios, low price to free cashflow, and low P/Es. We also analyze the value of the firm's assets in terms of what they can produce in future periods, in other words, the value of that earnings stream," says Miller.

When Miller acquires stocks at a discount, he operates with a strict time frame within which the stocks should reach their intrinsic value.

"Before we purchase, we thoroughly document why we anticipate the value will change and what needs to take place to make that happen. You can't accurately value a business without taking into account a time factor," stresses Miller.

Miller cites Tyco Toys, Inc., as a company suffering through a depressed business climate in the toy industry. Bankruptcy of a major customer resulted in a $5 million charge to increase its reserve for uncollectible accounts in 1990. In addition, restructuring its newly acquired Nasta subsidiary caused another 1990 write-off to the tune of $11.2 million.

The fifth largest toy company took a tumble in 1990, with earnings dropping to $0.50 per share from a record $2.33 per share in 1989. Wall Street didn't like the earnings decline one bit. Tyco's stock price dropped from an all-time high of nearly $28½ per share in May 1990 to $7¼ per share by the end of that year. In fact, including intangible assets, book value nearly doubled its stock price. Miller purchased the stock at around $8 per share with a target value of $25 per share.

Other evidence hinted at an undervalued situation. Tyco was working hard at improving its balance sheet from a highly leveraged company to one of financial strength. Its move into the European markets with the establishment of Tyco Toys Ltd. in the United Kingdom, Tyco Toys France, S.A., and projected subsidiaries in Spain, Belgium, and Germany positioned the firm well for capturing international market share.

The Helm acquisition boosted Tyco to the number two ranking in direct toy imports, second only to Mattel. In addition, during the first half of 1992, Tyco announced plans to acquire Universal Matchbox Group Ltd., one of the world's leading makers of toy vehicles with 1991 revenues of $167 million.

By the end of 1991, Tyco prospects were back on track. Revenues rose $80 million to $548 million, and earnings surged to $2.28 per share. Wall Street took notice and the stock price rebounded, closing out 1991 at a record high of $34⅝ per share. (See Chart 1-1.)

Signaling its confidence in the company's future, the board of directors initiated a 5 cent quarterly cash dividend plus voted a 3-for-2 stock split effective in May 1992.

In early 1992, Tyco competitors Mattel and Hasbro traded at approximately 15 times 1992 estimated earnings, while Tyco only commanded a P/E of 13 or less. With its improving financial strength, well-balanced and diverse product line, and growing international presence (Tyco's international operations account for 13 percent of company revenues versus 54 percent for Mattel, 41 percent for Hasbro, and 27 percent for Fisher Price), many analysts believe Tyco's P/E should match, if not exceed, that of its toy industry peers.

TYCO TOYS INC. NYSE-TTI

RECENT PRICE	P/E RATIO		RELATIVE P/E RATIO	DIV'D YLD	VALUE LINE
23	14.8 (Trailing: 17.8 / Median: NMF)		0.90	0.5%	1557

TIMELINESS 1 Highest
(Relative Price Perform-ance Next 12 Mos.)

SAFETY 4 Below Average
(Scale: 1 Highest to 5 Lowest)

BETA 1.35 (1.00 = Market)

1995-97 PROJECTIONS
	Price	Gain	Ann'l Total Return
High	45	(+95%)	19%
Low	25	(+10%)	3%

Insider Decisions
	M	J	J	A	S	O	N	D	J
to Buy	0	0	0	0	0	0	0	0	0
Options	0	0	3	0	0	4	0	0	0
to Sell	1	0	2	0	0	6	0	0	0

Institutional Decisions
	2Q'91	3Q'91	4Q'91
to Buy	15	33	49
to Sell	12	22	12
Hld's(000)	8608	12796	19858

Percent shares traded	60.0 40.0 20.0

High: 4.5 7.7 8.8 12.6 14.2 17.3 23.4
Low: 2.5 3.5 4.3 5.9 3.6 3.8 16.8

8.0 x "Cash Flow" p/sh
2-for-1 split

Relative Price Strength

Shaded areas indicate recessions

Options: PHLE

Target Price Range 1995 | 1996 | 1997: 50 40 32 24 20 16 12 10 8 6 4 3

©VALUE LINE PUB., INC.	1982	1983	1984	1985	1986	1987	1988	1989	1990	1991	1992	1993	95-97E
Sales per sh	..	..	..	..	13.70	15.81	22.78	29.02	34.63	28.04	23.70	23.65	32.85
"Cash Flow" per sh	..	..	..	..	.70	.92	1.37	1.73	1.12	1.80	1.60	2.10	3.15
Earnings per sh A	..	..	..	..	.36	.68	.87	1.14	.25	1.21	1.60	1.65	2.65
Div'ds Decl'd per sh	..	..	..	..	..	..	..	..	..	..	.10	.14	.25
Cap'l Spending per sh	..	..	..	..	.40	.83	.48	.81	.68	.58	.40	.40	.75
Book Value per sh C	..	..	..	..	1.75	3.49	4.45	6.95	7.28	9.26	12.30	11.70	14.30
Common Shs Outst'g D	..	..	..	..	6.40	10.34	11.58	13.25	13.32	19.57	28.50	22.50	35.00
Avg Ann'l P/E Ratio	..	..	..	..	9.7	7.8	7.8	7.7	34.5	8.5	*Bold figures are Value Line estimates*		13.0
Relative P/E Ratio	..	..	..	..	.66	.52	.65	.58	2.56	.54			1.00
Avg Ann'l Div'd Yield	..	..	..	..	..	..	..	..	..	..			1.5%
Sales ($mill)	..	..	..	..	87.7	163.5	263.8	384.5	461.2	548.7	675	775	1150
Operating Margin	..	..	..	..	8.9%	9.3%	10.3%	12.3%	7.3%	11.8%	13.0%	13.5%	15.0%
Depreciation ($mill)	..	..	..	..	2.1	2.6	4.6	6.9	11.5	11.4	12.0	13.0	20.0
Net Profit ($mill)	..	..	..	..	2.4	6.9	11.2	16.0	3.4	23.7	40.0	55.0	90.0
Income Tax Rate	..	..	..	..	32.3%	26.1%	25.3%	36.8%	NMF	30.6%	33.0%	33.0%	33.0%
Net Profit Margin	..	..	..	..	2.7%	4.2%	4.3%	4.2%	.7%	4.3%	5.9%	7.1%	7.8%
Working Cap'l ($mill)	..	..	..	..	16.1	24.9	37.0	88.3	77.4	125.3	175	200	300
Long-Term Debt ($mill)	..	..	..	..	20.1	17.0	19.4	117.8	117.0	91.0	Nil	Nil	Nil
Net Worth ($mill)	..	..	..	..	11.2	36.1	51.5	92.0	96.9	181.2	350	380	500
% Earned Total Cap'l	..	..	..	..	9.0%	14.5%	17.4%	9.5%	4.5%	9.3%	11.5%	14.5%	18.0%
% Earned Net Worth	..	..	..	..	21.2%	19.1%	21.8%	17.4%	3.5%	13.1%	11.5%	14.5%	18.0%
% Retained to Comm Eq	..	..	..	..	21.2%	19.1%	21.8%	17.4%	3.5%	13.1%	11.0%	13.5%	17.0%
% All Div'ds to Net Prof	..	..	..	..	..	..	..	..	..	..	6%	6%	9%

BUSINESS: Tyco Toys is a major manufacturer and distr. of toys in the USA, Canada, Europe, and the Far East. Tyco is a leading producer of "H0 Scale" elec. trains and racing cars, radio-controlled toys, and dolls. Categories: Dolls (23% of '91 sales), Activity (20%), Radio Control (15%), elec. racing cars/trains (7%), direct import (7%), and other (28%). B'ght Viewmaster Ideal 7/89, Nasta Int'l.

10/90, Playtime Products 10/90, and Helm Toys, 12/91. For sales '91: 14%. Est'd plant age: 4 yrs. Has about 1,600 employees, 7,500 sh'holders. Insiders own 10%; George Soros, 5.0%; Gary Weber, 4.0%; CGM, 5.4%; Kemper, 5.4%; First Chicago, 5.1%; FMR, 6.7%. Pres. and C.E.O.: Richard E. Grey. Inc.: Del. Add.: 6000 Midlantic Dr., Mt. Laurel, N J 08054. Tel: 609-234-7400.

Chart 1-1. Tyco Toys stock chart. (Copyright © 1992 by Value Line Publishing, Inc., used by permission. For subscription information to the Value Line Investment Survey, please call (800) 634-3583.)

12

Using projected earnings of $2.65 per share for 1992 and $3.10 per share for 1993 and a P/E of 15 to 16, analysts estimated a 1992–1993 trading range between $40 and $50 for Tyco's stock.

Charles Royce

Charles Royce runs the New York City–based Quest Advisory Corporation which manages some $1.5 billion in assets including three mutual funds. The largest by far, Royce's Pennsylvania Mutual Fund, utilizes a value concept for understanding the worth of a business.

"Ours is an updated version of similar value work popularized by Graham and Dodd in the 1930s. However, we're much more concerned about quality. The price we pay must be significantly under our value appraisal of private worth," says Royce.

The strategy pays off. Under Royce's stewardship, Pennsylvania Mutual Fund earned a place on Forbes Honor Roll three times. If you had invested $10,000 in the fund on December 21, 1976, your portfolio would have been worth $115,899 on December 31, 1991, compared with $73,757 for the S&P 500 and only $34,295 for three-month Treasury bills.

Likewise, if you had taken a dollar cost averaging approach and invested $2000 annually in the Pennsylvania Mutual Fund via a tax-sheltered IRA (individual retirement account) or similar investment vehicle from December 31, 1976, to December 31, 1991, your retirement investment would have grown to $123,827, versus $120,150 for the S&P 500 and more than double the $60,053 value for three-month Treasury bills.

In 1991, Royce's Pennsylvania Mutual Fund earned 32 percent, beating the overall market. What's more, over the past fifteen years, Royce has had only one down year, compared with three for the S&P 500. Over the past 10 years through March 31, 1992, Pennsylvania Mutual Fund returned 18.6 percent annually, ranking it number one of the 22 small-company funds with 10-year records tracked by Lipper Analytical Services, Inc., and beating the 14.4 percent earned by the Russell 2000 index of small-company stocks and the 18.1 percent return for the S&P 500.

Looking into the 1990s, Royce sees some shift back to value investing from growth investing. His rationale includes the lofty P/E ratios many growth stocks currently sport, a stable interest rate environment, and the economy's predicted emergence from recession.

Like Graham, Royce specializes in seeking out value in the form of cheap assets and strong balance sheets. According to Morningstar Fund Rating Service, Pennsylvania Mutual Fund's average price-to-book and debt-to-capitalization ratios are 2.1 percent and 17.8 percent, respectively. Both fall roughly about a half of their market counterpart ratios as measured for the S&P 500.

"We look for good businesses with good earnings and a bright future. ....all at dirt-cheap prices," says Royce.

Looking for value leads Royce to industries others have long forsaken such as oil and gas industry–related stocks and the world of real estate title insurance. In early 1992, Royce started accumulating shares in the Tulsa, Oklahoma, oil and natural gas exploration and production firm of Helmerich & Payne, Inc.

"At just over $20 per share, Helmerich & Payne shares aren't trading much over book value. The firm maintains an enviable balance sheet with less than $5 million in long-term debt, good cashflow from operations, and very dependable earning power. By 1995, I expect Helmerich & Payne to be earning $2–$3 per share versus the 88 cents per share earned in 1991," says Royce.

Helmerich & Payne's unleveraged balance sheet will provide the staying power while waiting for the natural gas exploration business to turn around. The firm's stock price dropped to $18 per share in December 1991, its lowest level since 1987, before rebounding to the low $20 per share in early 1992. (See Chart 1-2.)

"Old Republic International sports excellent management that employs a careful discipline in the property and casualty business," says Royce. By the end of December 1991, Royce had accumulated nearly 150,000 shares in Chicago-based Old Republic International Corporation at an average price under $10 per share. Trading at around $20 per share in June 1992 (adjusted for a 2-for-1 stock split in 1992), Old Republic delivered a paper profit in excess of $1.5 million—a doubling of Royce's investment. (See Chart 1-3.)

Old Republic's net income jumped over 22 percent to $4.95 per share in 1991. With roots stretching back to 1887, Old Republic has proved it can maneuver through good times and bad. The firm's strong balance sheet and conservative industry stance hold it in good stead. Its stock garners an A− rating (above average) from Standard & Poor's. For the 10-year period ended December 31, 1991, net income increased in excess of 200 percent, cash dividends grew by 62 percent, and book value per share more than tripled.

With book value keeping pace with its stock market price, Old Republic International provides a degree of downside protection not found in most stocks.

The firm's well-diversified operations by lines of insurance business, customer industry, and geography also help protect against any one segment's downturn spelling disaster for the company as a whole. Its

HELMERICH NYSE-HP

RECENT PRICE	24
P/E RATIO	48.0 (Trailing: 49.0 / Median: 26.0)
RELATIVE P/E RATIO	2.98
DIV'D YLD	1.9%
VALUE LINE	1859

TIMELINESS 3 Average (Relative Price Perform- ance Next 12 Mos.)
SAFETY 3 Average (Scale: 1 Highest to 5 Lowest)
BETA .95 (1.00 = Market)

High: 52.8 38.1 28.5 25.9 24.9 24.5 36.4 34.5 37.8 29.3 24.5
Low: 29.5 33.6 16.1 18.0 18.5 16.9 17.5 20.4 18.0 18.0 19.1

1995-97 PROJECTIONS

	Price	Gain	Ann'l Total Return
High	65	(+170%)	29%
Low	45	(+90%)	18%

Target Price Range 1995 1996 1997
Price scale: 80 50 40 32 24 20 16 12 10 8 6 4

2-for-1 split
3-for-2 split
12.0 x "Cash Flow" p sh
Relative Price Strength
Shaded areas indicate recessions

Percent shares traded: 9.0 / 6.0 / 3.0

Options: NYSE

© VALUE LINE PUB., INC. 95-97

	1976	1977	1978	1979	1980	1981	1982	1983	1984	1985	1986	1987	1988	1989	1990	1991	1992	1993	95-97
Revenues per sh [A]	2.90	3.70	5.02	5.81	7.78	11.29	13.44	8.27	7.66	7.63	6.63	6.36	6.64	7.08	9.87	8.74	9.60	10.20	13.25
"Cash Flow" per sh	.95	1.16	1.52	1.89	2.65	4.01	4.56	3.51	2.38	2.34	1.88	2.32	2.39	2.66	3.69	2.52	2.40	2.65	4.90
Earnings per sh [B]	.67	.80	1.07	1.32	1.86	2.95	2.98	1.90	.85	.74	.36	.39	.83	.94	1.97	.88	.50	.90	2.75
Div'ds Decl'd per sh [C]	.06	.07	.09	.17	.19	.24	.29	.33	.34	.35	.36	.39	.41	.42	.44	.46	.46	.48	.55
Cap'l Spending per sh	.81	.97	1.20	1.55	2.71	4.96	4.32	1.87	2.25	2.09	1.47	1.99	2.09	2.33	1.69	4.05	3.25	2.50	2.65
Book Value per sh [D]	4.25	5.37	6.35	7.49	9.28	12.04	14.54	16.12	16.63	17.02	16.88	17.40	17.83	18.34	19.83	20.06	20.40	21.40	25.50
Common Shs Outst'g [D]	25.12	25.12	25.17	25.22	25.48	25.48	25.15	25.15	25.15	25.15	24.19	24.19	24.17	24.17	24.18	24.49	24.50	24.50	24.50
Avg Ann'l P/E Ratio	8.8	10.2	9.4	19.2	14.7	15.1	8.5	11.0	25.7	27.5	NMF	29.1	25.8	26.5	16.5	28.6	37.0	40.0	20.0
Relative P/E Ratio	1.13	1.34	1.28	2.78	1.95	1.83	.93	.93	2.39	2.23	NMF	1.95	2.14	2.01	1.23	1.84	2.40	2.65	1.55
Avg Ann'l Div'd Yield	1.0%	.8%	.9%	.7%	.7%	.5%	1.1%	1.6%	1.6%	1.7%	1.9%	1.5%	1.9%	1.7%	1.4%	1.8%	2.5%	2.5%	1.0%
Revenues ($mill) [A]							338.2	208.1	192.6	192.0	160.4	153.9	160.6	171.1	238.5	214.0	235	250	325
Operating Margin							54.2%	49.8%	50.9%	47.5%	49.2%	51.4%	47.6%	48.1%	53.8%	44.2%	37.0%	40.0%	50.0%
Depreciation ($mill)							38.9	40.3	38.5	40.4	38.5	34.2	37.6	41.7	41.6	40.4	47.0	48.0	55.0
Net Profit ($mill)							75.7	47.8	21.4	18.5	7.0	22.0	20.2	22.7	41.6	21.2	12.0	22.0	65.0
Income Tax Rate							33.8%	29.9%	29.9%	23.5%	4.4%	31.5%	23.8%	29.9%	31.5%	35.0%	40.0%	40.0%	40.0%
Net Profit Margin							22.4%	23.0%	11.1%	9.6%	NMF	14.3%	12.5%	13.3%	19.9%	9.9%	5.0%	8.8%	20.0%
Working Cap'l ($mill)							59.1	87.6	84.8	118.4	108.3	135.2	135.3	114.3	146.8	108.2	75.0	70.0	140
Long-Term Debt ($mill)							105.6	93.3	87.1	85.5	79.3	74.7	70.7	49.1	5.7	5.7	5.0	5.0	Nil
Net Worth ($mill)							365.7	405.3	418.2	427.9	408.2	420.8	430.8	443.4	479.5	491.1	490	505	625
% Earned Total Cap'l							17.1%	10.4%	5.0%	4.3%	NMF	5.1%	4.6%	5.2%	9.9%	4.3%	2.5%	4.5%	11.0%
% Earned Net Worth							20.7%	11.8%	5.1%	4.3%	NMF	5.2%	4.7%	5.1%	9.9%	4.3%	2.5%	4.5%	12.5%
% Retained to Comm Eq							18.7%	9.8%	3.1%	2.3%	NMF	3.0%	2.4%	2.8%	7.7%	2.0%	Nil	2.0%	8.5%
% All Div'ds to Net Prof							10%	17%	40%	48%	NMF	43%	48%	45%	23%	53%	93%	51%	20%

Bold figures are Value Line estimates

BUSINESS: Helmerich & Payne, Inc. explores for and produces oil and natural gas; it also provides drilling services. Proved developed reserves at September 30, 1991: oil, 7.1 million barrels; gas, 295 billion cubic feet. Also produces chemical and natural gas odorants. Develops and operates commercial real estate in Tulsa. Owns 1.6 million shares of Atwood Oceanics stock; .74 million shares of Schlumberger; .9 million shares of Banks of Mid-America. Employs about 1,270. Wage costs, est'd 23% of sales. '91 deprec. rate: 5.2%. Has 4,737 shareholders. Helmerich family owns about 15% of common. Chairman: W.H. Helmerich, III. President & Chief Operating Officer: H. Helmerich. Incorporated: Delaware. Address: Utica at 21st Street, Tulsa, Oklahoma 74114. Telephone: 918-742-5531.

Chart 1-2. Helmerich & Payne stock chart. *(Copyright © 1992 by Value Line Publishing, Inc., used by permission. For subscription information to the Value Line Investment Survey, please call (800) 634-3583.)*

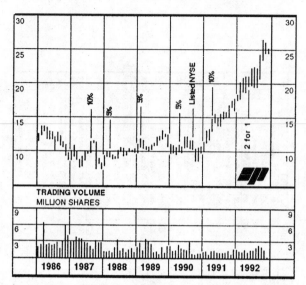

Chart 1-3. Old Republic International stock chart. (*Reprinted by permission of Standard & Poor's Corporation.*)

ranking as one of the nation's leading providers of fee-based risk management services also lends itself to earnings and financial stability.

On the operations side, Old Republic International's expense ratio for its largest insurance operations comes in a full 4 percentage points below the industry average around 28 percent. This cost advantage allows wider margins than those enjoyed by competitors and the opportunity to more selectively choose its clients.

John Templeton

John M. Templeton, who presides over the Bahamas-based investment management firm of Templeton, Galbraith & Hansberger Ltd., thrives on searching out hidden values. Altogether, the Templeton team manages 60-plus funds in both the open- and closed-end arenas. Including private accounts, Templeton manages approximately $20 billion for almost 800,000 investors worldwide.

In the value-seeking game, patience pays off. Templeton likes to say that you typically won't find his funds on top of many one-year performance standings, but his long-term investment perspective is another story. While other investment managers churn their portfolios on a quarterly basis, Templeton's average holding period approaches four to five years, plenty of time to let the bargains prosper.

The Templeton flagship fund, Templeton Growth Fund, outranks every other fund in performance over its nearly 40 years of existence. A $10,000 investment at the fund's inception on November 29, 1954, would have grown to the astonishing figure of $1.53 million on December 31, 1991 (assuming dividends and capital gains were reinvested in additional shares), versus $500,420 for the S&P 500.

A full-fledged value seeker, Templeton searches out value when others are bailing out of investments. To set the theme, a brochure for Templeton, Galbraith & Hansberger Ltd. quotes Robert Frost:

> Two roads diverged in a wood, and I—
>
> I took the one less traveled by,
>
> And that has made all the difference.

"We don't try to play the current market; we're long-term investors. Bull and bear markets will come and go so we work hard to uncover hidden value that will pay off in the long run. We make it a point to purchase when others are selling despondently and sell when others are greedily buying. When we see the overpricing or the long-term value in a situation, we are only too glad to accommodate those on the other side of the transaction," says Templeton.

At Templeton funds, more than 100 investment yardsticks are put into motion evaluating undervalued situations. Among the more common rank price-earnings ratios, price–future earnings ratios, price-to-replacement value, price–to–cash dividend ratios, and price–to–reported asset value ratios.

Among a myriad of factors that the Templeton team keeps in mind when searching for investment candidates are:

1. The price-earnings ratio.
2. Present and anticipated growth rate in earnings per share.
3. The "perfect blend" consisting of the highest possible growth rate for the lowest possible P/E.
4. Rising pretax profit margins.
5. Consistency of earning rates. Consistent earnings growth is a plus; however, too high growth rates often signal trouble ahead.
6. The validity of the company's long-range planning.
7. The level of effectiveness of the company's competitors.

8. Major company challenges other than competition.

9. The importance of maintaining a degree of flexibility. Everyone makes investment mistakes; know when to acknowledge them and cut your losses.

10. The importance of keeping a diversified portfolio to minimize losses.

"It's crucial to remember that no investment yardstick is good forever. Don't get too comfortable with any particular investment tool. Every single investment selection formula will become obsolete over time, especially if it becomes too popular. Therefore, you need to continually seek to improve your investment analysis techniques so you don't lose the ability to derive superior returns," warns Templeton.

With that caveat in mind, Templeton does offer up two investment rules that promise not to become obsolete: The first, "the good news–bad news rule," advises the investor to be on the lookout for short-term factors temporarily affecting a firm's performance or the investor's perception of the company. The second, "the hard work rule," stresses that investing is hard work and shortcuts produce mediocre investment results.

Templeton looks the world over for bargains, but that doesn't mean he forsakes unique opportunities in the United States.

"The United States represents a very stable market with still hundreds of undervalued situations. In fact, over 40 percent of our assets are invested in U.S. securities even though U.S. stocks comprise only some 35 percent of the world's common stocks," says Templeton.

Knowing when to get out of a stock is equally as important as knowing which stock to purchase and when to purchase it. For example, the Mexican Bolsa (stock market) surged 43 percent in 1990, went up another 126 percent in 1991, and continued its winning ways into 1992.

"While many people were jumping on the bandwagon in 1992, we were starting to sell many of our Mexican holdings. Cifra is an exception; although it's worth more than 40 times what we paid for it, we haven't sold yet. It still has strong growth potential. We purchase when the outlook looks worst, the time of maximum pessimism. When we bought Cifra in 1982, the Mexican economy looked a shambles. That's the time to find bargains," says Templeton.

In the United States, Templeton believes value can be found among the rubble of the insurance industry with such companies as CIGNA, Aetna, and Kemper. Another place for uncovering value is in aluminum companies worldwide. According to Templeton, the current surplus of aluminum caused by dumping by the former Soviet Union will turn into a shortage in the future since few new plants have come on line recently.

"There'll always be bull markets followed by bear markets followed by bull markets. The odds are better than even that you will see the Dow at 6000 by the end of the decade," says Templeton.

One way to begin searching for value is to study the holdings of successful value funds. In addition to the Templeton family of funds, take a look at other top performers such as Janus Venture, Nicolas II, and Sit New Beginning.

2

Cashing in on Corporate Cashflow

Given two equally promising companies with similar products, markets, management talent, raw materials, and people resources, the one with more cashflow will, more often than not, outperform its less fortunate twin. In the investment world, as in your own personal finances, cash is king.

Without adequate cash, companies cannot capitalize on market opportunities that present themselves. Financially strong firms need adequate cash reserves and cashflow to make good on dividend payouts, to pay for required goods and services, to invest in capital improvements and new technology, and to cover interest payments on both short- and long-term debt obligations.

No matter how attractive a piece of real estate may be in terms of location, unless it delivers enough cashflow to offset maintenance expenses, operating costs, and principal and interest obligations, in all likelihood the property will have to be sold.

Likewise, unless a company has sufficient cashflow to capitalize on unique opportunities in its industry, it will also lose out to competitors with better cash positions. Cash also provides companies with a safety cushion when times get tough. Cash-rich companies can better weather economic storms than their higher-leveraged counterparts.

While leveraged firms have to pay out interest expenses, cash-rich firms can actually improve their bottom lines with their interest income.

To be sure, bulging cash coffers help soften the blows of an economic slump, but more importantly, the cash hoard gives management the critical resources to make strategic acquisitions, expand production, invest in crucial research and development, and upgrade facilities to meet the demands of a recovering economy.

On the other hand, highly leveraged companies may be forced to shed assets to raise cash to meet ongoing commitments. Cash-rich firms can pick up these assets and facilities at bargain-basement prices and move to gain market share as cash-strapped firms retrench.

In addition, on the financial front, the stock market usually takes a dim view of companies slashing their dividends. The ability to pay or even increase cash dividends during economic contractions protects both the company's stock price and its overall return to investors.

Cash also provides the ability to repurchase company shares, helping to support the stock price and improve earnings per share comparisons.

Investing in companies with a secure cash position gives the investor more peace of mind knowing that his or her firm can get through the tough times. With this comfort factor in place, you are more unlikely to make a rash investment decision and bail out of a stock position too early and forfeit potential gains.

Cashflow Analysis

The Federal Accounting Standards Board (FASB) signaled the high degree of importance it attaches to company cashflow information in evaluating the future prospects of a company when it released its FASB Statement No. 95, "Statement of Cash Flows," requiring public companies to issue annual cashflow statements for fiscal years after July 15, 1988, in addition to the usual financial reports such as income statements and balance sheets.

Today, cashflow information and changes in cashflow position can easily be derived from company annual reports. FASB No. 95 also requires that specific cashflow information about investing and financing activities not resulting in cash receipts or payments be provided separately so investors can take that information into account during their investment analysis.

Thanks to the FASB, cashflow analysis and comparison of cashflow information between different investment alternatives has been made a lot easier.

The flurry of leveraged buyouts (LBOs) and the subsequent failure of a lot of these buyouts during the early and mid-eighties clearly illustrate the importance of cashflow. While many of the LBO deals looked extremely enticing on paper, the failure of the firms to generate adequate cashflow to service their high debt levels during the economic downturn toward the end of the decade caused the castle of cards to tumble and thousands of investors to lose millions of dollars.

As the sad case of failed LBOs illustrates, cashflow represents the pulse, the lifeblood, of the firm. Without adequate cashflow, opportunities to expand revenues and earnings and even the firm's ability to exist remain limited.

Besides helping to ferret out companies with healthy cashflows and good future prospects, cashflow analysis can help point out companies headed for trouble down the road. Too often, traditional accounting methods and information provide a distorted picture of a company's financial position. Cashflow helps provide a more accurate barometer of a company's true financial health. It also helps investors zero in on attractive investment opportunities that may not be readily apparent from tracking a company's earnings pattern.

Company earnings numbers are static information and don't take into account inflationary forces present in the real world. Even though a firm may be generating increasing earnings, if inflation continues to outpace those gains, the company is actually worse off at the end of the year despite a rise in earnings. A company paying dividends out of inflated earnings instead of healthy cashflow may be undermining its ability to fund future operations, crucial to the continued success of the business.

That's why so many professional investment managers, business consulting firms, and savvy investors have long utilized cashflow analysis as a key determinant in estimating the economic value of an investment and its future prospects.

It's no accident that this book on solid investment strategies follows value investing with a strategy rooted in cashflow analysis. A search for companies with comfortable cash positions, impressive cashflow streams, and improving cashflow scenarios increases the odds of making the right investment choices as well as avoiding those disastrous investment picks that can wipe out months of hard-earned investment gains. It's another valuable tool to use in fine tuning your investment strategies and returns.

David Dreman, chairman and chief investment officer of Dreman Value Management, L.P. and well-known author of *The New Contrarian Investment Strategy*, researched the impact of cashflow on the future price of stocks.

Using the cashflow data of 750 of the largest public companies from 1963 to 1985, he segregated the companies into five equal rankings each year according to their ratio of cashflow to market price and then measured their annual returns. Dreman found that over the entire 22-year period the stocks with the lowest price-to-cashflow ratio earned a 20.1 percent total annual return, versus only a 10.7 percent return for those stocks with the highest price-to-cashflow ratio. Obviously, healthy cashflow influences a company's performance and the future level of its stock price.

Just What Is Cashflow?

In order to be able to use cashflow information to improve investment returns, it's important to know just what cashflow is and how it relates to other key financial factors.

With that in mind, a good grasp of the following cashflow analysis definitions will give you a good start down the path to successful cashflow investing.

- *Cashflow.* Cashflow is the flow of funds in and out of an operating business. It is normally calculated as net income plus depreciation and other noncash items.

- *Cashflow-debt ratio.* This represents relationship of free cashflow to total long-term indebtedness. This ratio is helpful in tracking a firm's ability to meet scheduled debt and interest payment requirements.

- *Cashflow-interest ratio.* This ratio determines how many times free cashflow will cover fixed interest payments on long-term debt.

- *Cashflow per share.* Cashflow per share represents the amount earned before deduction for depreciation and other charges not involving the outlay of cash.

- *Cash ratio.* This ratio is used to measure liquidity. It is calculated as the sum of cash and marketable securities divided by current liabilities. It indicates how well a company can meet current liabilities.

- *Common and preferred cashflow coverage ratios.* These ratios determine how many times annual free cashflow will cover common and preferred cash dividend payments.

- *Economic value.* The economic value of a stock represents the anticipated free cashflow the company will generate over a period of time, discounted by the weighted cost of a company's capital.

- *Free cashflow.* Free cashflow is determined by calculating operating earnings after taxes and then adding depreciation and other noncash expenses, less capital expenditures and increases in working capital.

- *Free cashflow–earnings ratio.* This ratio shows the percentage of earnings actually available in cash. It is the percentage of free cash available to company management for investments, acquisitions, plant construction, dividends, etc. As a general rule, this ratio should be at a minimum 0.5 to 1. In other words, at least 50 percent of the earnings are in the form of free cash.

- *Quick ratio.* The quick ratio, also called acid-test ratio, is used to measure corporate liquidity. It is regarded as an improvement over the current ratio, which includes the usually not very liquid inventory. The quick ratio formula is stated as current assets less inventory divided by current liabilities. An even more liquid form of the quick or acid-test ratio divides cash, marketable securities, and accounts receivable by current liabilities. Typically, a quick ratio of 1 to 1 is satisfactory. However, an interruption or slowdown of cash receipts could spell trouble ahead. Conversely, a company with a high quick ratio may not be using its capital effectively.

Getting Information on Cashflow

Corporate cashflow information can be easily gathered from a variety of sources. First of all, in accordance with FASB No. 95, all public companies are required to provide investors with this information in their annual and quarterly financial reports. Look for the "Statement of Cashflows" (previously called the "Changes in Financial Position Statement"). It usually follows the "Balance Sheet" and "Income Statement" presentations.

The "Statement of Cashflows," or "Consolidated Statement of Cashflows" in the case of multiple business units, summarizes the company's sources and use of funds over the specified time frame. It provides clues to how well company management is using cash, where the flow is coming from (operations or borrowings), and whether cash resources are building up or being rapidly depleted.

When you evaluate a firm's statement of cashflows, ask yourself the following questions:

- Has the firm financed asset additions and replacements with internally generated cash, or is it depending on costly outside financing?
- How have business expansions been financed?
- How have strategic acquisitions been financed?
- Will cashflow adequately cover debt repayment and interest expenses?
- Will cashflow keep the cash dividend intact and growing?
- How does the firm's level of outside financing compare with industry norms?

The answers to these questions will help you determine management's risk posture; the company's ability to fund future capital equipment programs, facility expansion, and acquisitions; its capability to maintain and increase cash dividends; and its efficient use of corporate resources.

All in all, companies with large cash reserves and healthy cashflows offer the best of both worlds. They provide significant downside protection in recessionary economies since they can more easily weather tough times. On the upside, they possess the liquid resources to capitalize on market opportunities and gain major competitive advantages.

Putting Cashflow to Work

Ample cash can signal a conservative management team preparing for the oncoming recession. It can attract the attention of value seekers who make a bid for the company, driving up its stock price to the benefit of current shareholders. It can result in cash dividend increases that outpace the market, thereby increasing your investment income and total return.

The big risk in investing in companies flush with cash is that management fails to put this valuable corporate resource to work. Cash sitting in low-interest-bearing investments does little to enhance shareholder value. Even more detrimental to long-term value growth, ill-advised diversification or poorly planned ventures can quickly squander this hard-earned resource.

Free Cashflow

Cash resources and cashflow figure prominently in investment analysis, but equally important is how efficiently and effectively management puts its cash to work.

"Cashflow is extremely important to any stock investment analysis because the company's worth is reflected in the present value of its pre-cashflow. Previously, many analysts and investors made the assumption that the firm's worth was reflected in the present value of its earnings, but we're more sophisticated today," says Kenneth S. Hackel, president and founder of the investment management firm of Systematic Financial Management, Inc., in Fort Lee, New Jersey, and author of *Cash Flow and Security Analysis* (Business One-Irwin, 1992).

According to Hackel, the preponderance of permissible accounting standards makes earnings comparisons nearly useless. Cashflow analysis eliminates the distortions caused by accounting "standards." His firm's investment philosophy is simple: "selecting investments in companies with the ability to generate consistently positive and growing operating cashflow and free cashflow while easily satisfying their debt obligations."

"We look for out-of-favor stocks with rock-solid balance sheets and good cashflows, and then exercise patience. We search for stocks selling at extremely low multiples of their free cashflows," says Hackel.

While Hackel and team set a minimum price appreciation target for each investment, subsequent events such as inconsistent free cashflow or a substantial increase in the ratio of debt to free cashflow could trigger a sale.

The strategy has worked well. An investment of $100,000 on January 1, 1981, in a composite of Systematic Financial Management's accounts would have grown to $741,000 by the end of 1991. In comparison, the same $100,000 investment tracking the S&P 500 would have increased to $480,000. Over the 11-year time frame, Systematic Financial Management earned an average compound return of 20.0 percent, versus only 15.3 percent for the S&P 500.

Changes in the relation of free cashflow to market value can signal better or worse times ahead. For example, back in the late seventies, US Air Group, Inc., sported a positive correlation between the amount of free cashflow and market valuation.

By 1986, free cashflow had turned negative, and its declining slope crossed the rising market valuation slope as investors bid up US Air's stock price to new highs. The bubble burst in 1989 with the first of several losing years. The air carrier's stock plunged from a high of nearly $55 per share to $7 per share in 1991.

Using free cashflow as another valuable investment tool, a savvy investor could have uncovered US Air's undervalued situation in the late seventies, established a stake in the company, and rode the stock price up from below $6 per share to the $50 range for a healthy stock gain. Likewise, the convergence of the free cashflow and market valuation trend lines could have provided an early warning to the investor to dispose of his or her stock holdings in the air carrier before the stock plummeted in 1989.

Discounted Cashflow

Most cashflow analysts use a discounted cashflow model to estimate the present value of future cashflows, a company's worth, and the price they should reasonably expect to pay for the company's stock.

When your banker lends you money for that kitchen remodeling project, he or she expects to be paid back the money borrowed plus interest. Within the interest rate the bank charges you is a factor to cover the bank's cost of capital and a profit. Similarly, in order to properly value a company, you need to know the projected cashflows over a period of years and what those cashflows are worth in today's dollars, since you will be purchasing the company's stock with today's dollars.

That's where the discounted cashflow model comes in. It converts those future cash streams into a value we can relate to today. To accomplish this, it uses an appropriate discount rate to cover the firm's cost of capital. While analysts may differ in the rate they use for cost of capital (internal cost of capital versus outside cost of capital versus average cost of capital, etc.), the discounted cashflow principle remains the same.

The individual investor can also discount the cashflow from dividends expected to be received from a stock in order to value its share price. Whether you're using dividends or corporate cashflows to properly value a prospective investment, the basic discounted cashflow formula is

$$V = \frac{CF1}{(1 + r)} + \frac{CF2}{(1 + r)} + \frac{CF3}{(1 + r)} + \frac{CF4}{(1 + r)} + \frac{CF5}{(1 + r)}$$

where V = value

CF = period cashflow

r = discount rate/cost of capital

Michael Mauboussin and Discounted Cashflow Analysis   "You need to focus on three factors when analyzing a business or stock. First of all, what will the cashflows be? Second, when are they expected to be received? Third, how certain are they? This analysis will enable you to estimate the economic value of a company by discounting the relevant cashflows at the cost of capital," says Michael Mauboussin, a food industry analyst specializing in discounted cashflows analysis with First Boston in New York City (previously with County NatWest USA).

Mauboussin concentrates on identifying *value drivers* in a business, those variables that determine free cashflow such as sales growth, operating margins, and fixed and working capital requirements. He uses a weighted-average cost of capital in his discounted cashflow projections and also employs an estimate of how long it will take competitive forces to drive returns down to their cost of capital.

Back in November 1991, Mauboussin changed his recommendation on Kellogg Company, the world's largest manufacturer of ready-to-eat cereals, from a hold to a buy based on his estimates of the firm's value drivers and discounted cashflow model.

Kellogg stood to benefit from its industry-dominant position, a growing global presence, its underleveraged financial stance, increased manufacturing efficiencies, and the generation of substantial surplus cashflow.

"We believed the market had yet to fully value Kellogg's long-term potential, and our discounted cashflow analysis reflected a value around $120 per share (before the late 1991 2-for-1 stock split). [See Chap. 5, "Stock-Split Specials."] That translated into a nearly 14 percent value premium in relation to market price," says Mauboussin.

Factors that aided Mauboussin in his positive assessment of Kellogg included:

Sales per employee continue on a steady upward slope.

Gross margins rose in 1991.

A capital investment of $3 billion over the past 10 years positions Kellogg with sufficient capacity for the next 5 to 7 years.

Demographics point to rising per capita cereal consumption with the aging of the baby boomers.

A strong international presence promises to fuel growth in the decade ahead.

On the financial front, Kellogg's burgeoning cash generation could move the firm to step up its share repurchase program. Further, financial leverage could lower the firm's cost of capital as lower-cost debt replaces equity in the capital structure.

In his analysis, Mauboussin used Kellogg's weighted-average cost of capital of 11.8 percent, sales growth of 11 percent annually, and operating margins in the 18 to 20 percent range. (See Charts 2-1 and 2-2.) At the time of Mauboussin's research, Kellogg's stock traded at $105¼, compared with the implied value of $119.55 per share.

He projected a 12- to 18-month price target range of $130 to $140 per share. Since then the stock has split 2 for 1, and the trading range has been converted to $65 to $70 per share after the stock split.

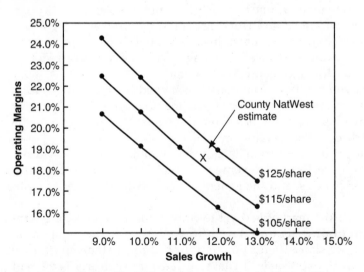

Chart 2-1. Kellogg Key Values Drivers and Implied Value. (*Source: County NatWest estimates*)

Year	Cash flow	Pres. value cash flow	Cum PV cash flow	Pres. value residual value	Cum PV CF+ PV residual	Increase in value
1991E	$595.0	532.7	532.7	5,264.4	5,797.1	950.6
1992E	$629.7	504.7	1,037.4	5,370.6	6,407.9	610.9
1993E	$749.7	537.9	1,575.3	5,547.0	7,122.3	714.3
1994E	$846.7	543.9	2,119.2	5,593.8	7,713.1	590.8
1995E	$973.9	560.1	2,679.3	5,697.2	8,376.5	663.5
1996E	$1,112.9	573.0	3,252.3	5,771.9	9,024.2	647.7
1997E	$1,263.8	582.5	3,834.8	5,818.0	9,652.8	628.7
1998E	$1,410.9	582.2	4,417.0	5,864.0	10,281.0	628.2
1999E	$1,604.7	592.8	5,009.8	5,909.8	10,919.6	638.6
2000E	$1,780.4	588.8	5,598.6	9,322.3	14,920.9	4,001.3
						10,074.4

Corporate Value	14,920.9
Less: Market Value of Debt	575.00
Shareholder Value	14,345.9
Shareholder Value per Share	$119.55
Current Stock Price	$105.25
Premium/Discount to Market Price	13.6%

Note: Weighted average cost of capital=11.8%. In $ Millions.

Chart 2-2. Kellogg: cash flows and shareholder value. (Source: County NatWest estimates.)

In the seven months following Mauboussin's discounted cashflow projections and valuation of Kellogg, the firm's stock price rose beyond the $60 per share valuation (adjusted for the 2-for-1 stock split) to reach $67 per share, near the high end of the 12- to-18-month projection. (See Chart 2-3.)

In January 1992, Mauboussin raised his buy recommendation on the H. J. Heinz Company to accumulate. Asset restructuring in the form of the swap of cyclical, nonstrategic corn milling operations for a fast-growing, well-positioned food service business (JL Foods) promised enhanced cashflow prospects, reduced cyclicality, and enlarged debt capacity.

Other pluses: an accelerated marketing program, cost-cutting efforts, and a stepped-up share repurchase program.

"I felt the market had yet to recognize the merits of Heinz's unprecedented operating and financial maneuvers," says Mauboussin.

KELLOGG CO. NYSE-K

RECENT PRICE	57	P/E RATIO	21.0	(Trailing: 22.4 Median: 15.0)	RELATIVE P/E RATIO	1.34	DIV'D YLD	2.0%	VALUE LINE	1478

TIMELINESS 2 Above Average (Relative Price Perform-ance Next 12 Mos.)

SAFETY 1 Highest (Scale: 1 Highest to 5 Lowest)

BETA .95 (1.00 = Market)

| | High: | 6.9 | 7.8 | 8.3 | 10.7 | 18.0 | 29.4 | 34.4 | 34.3 | 40.8 | 38.8 | 67.0 | 67.0 |
| | Low: | 4.3 | 5.4 | 6.3 | 6.8 | 9.6 | 15.8 | 18.9 | 24.5 | 28.9 | 29.4 | 35.0 | 54.4 |

1995-97 PROJECTIONS

	Price	Gain	Ann'l Total Return
High	75	(+30%)	10%
Low	65	(+15%)	6%

Insider Decisions

	M	J	J	A	S	O	N	D	J
to Buy	0	0	0	0	4	1	0	1	0
Options	0	1	0	1	0	1	0	0	0
to Sell	1	0	0	1	2	2	0	1	0

Institutional Decisions

	2Q31	3Q31	4Q31
to Buy	104	97	123
to Sell	90	101	116
Hld's(000)	173796	173194	174261

| | Percent shares traded | 6.0 / 4.0 / 2.0 | |

Options: ASE

Relative Price Strength

2-for-1 split

Shaded areas indicate recessions

Target Price Range 1995 1996 1997

	1976	1977	1978	1979	1980	1981	1982	1983	1984	1985	1986	1987	1988	1989	1990	1991	1992	1993	© VALUE LINE PUB., INC.	95-97
4.54	5.02	5.53	6.04	7.04	7.59	7.74	7.76	10.57	11.88	13.52	15.37	17.69	19.08	21.47	24.06	26.25	29.65	Sales per sh	41.30
.51	.56	.59	.66	.75	.83	.91	.94	1.29	1.44	1.71	2.06	2.52	2.42	2.91	3.45	3.65	4.40	"Cash Flow" per sh	6.25
.43	.45	.48	.53	.61	.67	.73	.75	.85	1.14	1.34	1.60	1.95	1.73	2.08	2.51	2.90	3.20	Earnings per sh ^A	4.65
.25	.28	.30	.32	.34	.36	.38	.41	.45	.51	.51	.65	.76	.86	.96	1.08	1.25	1.45	Div'ds Decl'd per sh ^B■	2.00
.30	.25	.30	.27	.40	.48	.40	.51	.93	1.00	1.33	1.94	2.19	2.09	1.33	1.39	2.00	2.35	Cap'l Spending per sh	3.50
1.60	1.77	1.95	2.16	2.65	2.55	2.89	3.20	1.98	2.77	3.64	4.91	6.03	6.71	7.88	8.98	10.00	11.45	Book Value per sh ^C	18.65
304.88	305.56	305.64	305.72	305.73	305.73	305.79	305.97	246.26	246.74	247.12	246.82	245.96	243.75	241.32	240.46	240.00	240.00	Common Shs Outst'g ^D	230.00
14.2	13.6	11.4	9.3	7.8	8.0	8.7	9.3	9.7	12.2	17.5	18.6	14.4	20.0	16.0	19.5	Bold figures are Value Line estimates		Avg Ann'l P/E Ratio	15.0
1.82	1.78	1.55	1.30	1.04	.97	.96	.79	.90	.99	1.19	1.24	1.20	1.51	1.19	1.24			Relative P/E Ratio	1.15
4.1%	4.6%	5.6%	6.6%	7.1%	6.7%	6.1%	5.8%	5.2%	3.2%	2.2%	2.2%	2.7%	2.5%	2.9%	2.2%			Avg Ann'l Div'd Yield	2.5%
						2367.1	2381.1	2602.4	2930.1	3340.7	3793.0	4348.8	4651.7	5181.4	5786.6	6300	7000	Sales ($mill)	9500
						19.1%	20.0%	20.3%	21.6%	22.2%	21.2%	21.5%	19.4%	21.0%	21.6%	22.0%	22.5%	Operating Margin	23.0%
						55.9	62.8	63.9	75.4	92.7	113.1	139.7	167.6	200.2	222.8	250	275	Depreciation ($mill)	365
						222.1	225.4	254.2	281.1	330.4	395.9	480.4	422.1	502.8	606.0	670	765	Net Profit ($mill)	1070
						45.2%	47.2%	46.6%	46.7%	45.6%	40.5%	38.0%	36.7%	38.3%	38.4%	38.5%	38.5%	Income Tax Rate	38.5%
						9.4%	9.5%	9.8%	9.6%	9.9%	10.4%	11.0%	9.1%	9.7%	10.5%	10.6%	10.9%	Net Profit Margin	11.5%
						256.5	302.4	87.4	173.8	43.2	d51.5	d120.3	d131.1	668.2	d151.4	d120	90	Working Cap'l ($mill)	465
						11.8	18.6	364.1	392.6	264.1	264.1	272.1	371.4	295.6	15.2	15.0	215	Long-Term Debt ($mill)	500
						884.7	977.9	487.2	683.0	898.4	1211.4	1483.2	1634.4	1901.8	2159.8	2405	2700	Net Worth ($mill)	3685
						25.1%	22.7%	30.0%	28.0%	29.9%	27.4%	28.1%	22.1%	23.5%	27.9%	29.0%	27.5%	% Earned Total Cap'l	25.5%
						25.1%	23.0%	52.2%	41.2%	36.8%	32.7%	32.4%	25.8%	26.4%	28.1%	28.0%	28.0%	% Earned Net Worth	27.5%
						11.9%	10.4%	28.8%	24.9%	22.8%	19.5%	19.8%	13.0%	14.2%	16.1%	15.5%	15.5%	% Retained to Comm Eq	15.5%
						52%	55%	26.8%	39%	38%	40%	39%	50%	46%	43%	45%	45%	% All Div'ds to Net Prof	43%

BUSINESS: Kellogg Company, the world's largest manufacturer of ready-to-eat cereals (38% of U.S. market, 52% of non-U.S. market), also produces frozen foods, dessert items, and other convenience foods. Brand names include: Kellogg's, Frosted Flakes, Rice Krispies, Frosted Mini-Wheats, Special K, Froot Loops, Nutri-Grain, Apple Jacks, All-Bran, Pop-Tarts, Eggo, Mrs. Smith's. Foreign oper- ations accounted for 41% of sales, 36% of net income in 1991. Labor costs: 18% of sales; advertising, 12%; '91 depreciation rate: 5.7%. Estimated plant age: 6 years. Has 17,000 employees, 23,100 stockholders. W.K. Kellogg Foundation controls 34% of common. Chrmn., CEO, & Pres: Arnold G. Langbo. Inc.: Delaware. Address: Battle Creek, MI 49016. Tel.: 616-961-6122.

Chart 2-3. Kellogg stock chart. (Copyright© 1992 by Value Line Publishing, Inc., used by permission. For subscription information to the Value Line Investment Survey, please call (800) 634-3583.)

30

Year	Cash flow	Pres. value cash flow	Cum PV cash flow	Pres. value residual value	Cum PV CF+ PV residual	Increase in value
1993E	$497.6	449.5	449.5	6,699.8	7,149.3	1,676.4
1994E	$556.3	454.0	903.5	6,783.9	7,687.4	538.1
1995E	$672.6	495.8	1,399.3	6,794.4	8,193.7	506.3
1996E	$774.8	515.9	1,915.3	6,801.8	8,717.1	523.4
1997E	$909.6	547.2	2,462.4	6,837.6	9,300.1	583.0
1998E	$1,031.9	560.7	3,023.1	6,836.2	9,859.3	559.3
1999E	$1,183.6	581.0	3,604.1	6,799.2	10,403.4	544.0
2000E	$1,348.3	597.9	4,202.0	6,761.8	10,963.8	560.4
2001E	$1,506.2	603.3	4,805.3	6,657.9	11,463.2	499.5
2002E	$1,677.5	607.0	5,412.3	6,555.7	11,968.0	504.7
2003E	$1,861.0	608.3	6,020.6	6,455.0	12,476.6	507.6
2004E	$2,057.9	607.6	6,628.2	6,355.9	12,984.1	508.5
2005E	$2,269.2	605.3	7,233.5	6,972.5	14,206.0	1,221.9
						8,733.1

Marketable Securities	400.0
CORPORATE VALUE	14,606.0
Less: Market Value of Debt	1,800.0
SHAREHOLDER VALUE	12,806.0
Shareholder Value per Share	$48.14
Current Stock Price	$41.00
Premium/Discount to market price	17.4%

Chart 2-4. H. J. Heinz: Cash flows and shareholder value. (*Source: County NatWest estimates*)

This time, the discounted cashflow model produced a value of $48.14 per share, compared with the then current market price of $41 per share. That represented a 17.4 percent value premium over the stock market price. (See Chart 2-4.)

Heinz's boost in operating margins and low cost of capital (in relation to industry averages) proved to be the major value drivers. In addition, aggressive share repurchases promised to raise shareholder value.

While the heavier marketing emphasis and restructuring efforts may have worked to increase future value, they did drop operating earnings for fiscal 1992 ended April 30, 1992, to $1.89 per share from $2.13 per share earned in the prior fiscal year.

In this case, the market took the bad earnings news to heart and continued to overlook the apparent undervaluation situation as suggested by the discounted cashflow analysis. By mid-1992, Heinz's stock price dropped below $37 per share, widening the difference between Heinz's estimated underlying value and the stock market price. (See Chart 2-5.)

HEINZ (H.J.) NYSE-HNZ

| | | RECENT PRICE | 36 | P/E RATIO | 16.7 | (Trailing: 18.8 Median: 13.0) | RELATIVE P/E RATIO | 1.02 | DIVD YLD | 3.0% | VALUE LINE | 1472 |

TIMELINESS 3 Average (Relative Price Perform-ance Next 12 Mos.)

SAFETY 1 Highest
(Scale: 1 Highest to 5 Lowest)

BETA 1.00 (1.00 = Market)

1995-97 PROJECTIONS

	Price	Gain	Ann'l Total Return
High	65	(+80%)	18%
Low	50	(+40%)	11%

Target Price Range 1995 | 1996 | 1997

Options: CBOE

Shaded areas indicate recessions

Relative Price Strength

BUSINESS: H.J. Heinz Company manufactures soups, ketchup, baked beans, pickles, vinegar, baby foods, *9 Lives* cat food, *Ore-Ida* frozen potatoes, various condiments, *Star-Kist* tuna. Operates *Weight Watchers* programs; sells *Weight Watchers* and *Alba* low-calorie products. Sold Hubinger (corn processing), 6/91; bought JLFoods (foodservice supplies), 8/91. In '90 foreign operations pro-vided 42% of revenues, 47% of net income. Marketing costs were 8.3% of sales. Has 49,100 shareholders, 34,100 employees. '90 depreciation rate: 7.1%. Est'd plant age: 6 years. Insiders control 10% of common stock; Heinz family & trusts, about 20%. Chairman, President, & C.E.O.: A.J.F. O'Reilly. Incorporated: PA. Address: P.O. Box 57, Pittsburgh, PA 15230. Telephone: 412-456-6014.

Chart 2-5. Heinz stock chart. (Copyright© 1992 by Value Line Publishing, Inc., used by permission. For subscription information to the Value Line Investment Survey, please call (800) 634-3583.)

Robert L. Renck, Jr. and the Surplus Cash Flow Method. R. L. Renck & Co., Inc., a New York City institutional research firm and money manager, uses a Surplus Cash Flow* (pretax income plus depreciation minus capital expenditures) valuation methodology to ferret out valuation extremes (both undervalued and overvalued companies) for both long and short positions.

"We use the Surplus Cash Flow methods to screen for valuation extremes and then apply fundamental analysis with particular attention to balance sheet and other value analysis," says Robert L. Renck, Jr., managing director.

According to Renck, the appropriate yardstick of price to Surplus Cash Flow is a function of interest rates. As interest rates change, so does the multiplication factor. For example, in 1984 Renck estimated market value for companies at 9 to 10 times Surplus Cash Flow. In order to achieve a 50 percent upside potential, Renck would then invest in companies selling at less than 6 times Surplus Cash Flow.

With the substantial decline of interest rates since 1984, Renck adjusted the factor upward to 11 times Surplus Cash Flow. Now, assuming the company's fundamentals are in order, Renck considers firms selling at less than 7.5 times Surplus Cash Flow as candidates that can deliver 50 percent upside potential to an investor.

While Renck concentrates on Surplus Cash Flow as its primary investment tool, it also employs a variety of computer screening criteria to uncover uncommon values and uncommon risks as follows:

Uncommon Value Criteria

- A price to book value of less than 1.5 times
- A yield greater than the market
- A price-to-earnings ratio less than the market
- Debt to total capital of less than 33.0 percent
- A price–to–Surplus Cash Flow multiple of less than 7.5 times

Uncommon Risks Criteria

- A price to book value greater than 1.5 times
- A yield less than the market
- A price-to-earnings ratio 30 percent greater than the market
- Debt to capital of over 50 percent
- A price–to–Surplus Cash Flow multiple greater than 12.5 percent

*Surplus Cash Flow is a registered trademark of SCF Partners, L.P.

A look at the change in the percentage of companies in different categories of price to Surplus Cash Flow over time reflects changes in the level of the stock market. For example, at the end of 1984 when the Dow Jones Industrial Average closed at 1211.57, down over 47 points from the previous year, 28 percent of the stocks in Renck's universe of 1100-plus firms had price–to–surplus cash multiples of less than 6 times. By August 1987, that dropped to 4 percent as the market surged to new highs. Then came the October 1987 crash. With it, the percentage of stocks in the low-multiple category surged to 21 percent, signaling possible undervaluations.

On the other extreme, companies with price–to–Surplus Cash Flow multiples greater than 12 times stood at 35 percent at the end of 1984. It rose to 59 percent by August 1987 and then declined to 37 percent in the wake of the October 1987 crash.

By the end of August 1991, the percentages in the low-multiple and high-multiple categories were once again sending possible warning shots across the bow with 7 percent and 55 percent, respectively, as shown in Table 2-1.

Table 2-1. Percentage of Companies by Price to Surplus Cash Flow

Price/SCF*	12/30/84	8/28/87	10/30/87	8/27/91
< 6 ×	28	4	21	7
6 × to 9 ×	26	18	26	19
9 × to 12 ×	11	19	16	19
> 12 × or < 0 ×	35	59	37	55

SOURCE: SCF Partners, L.P., An Affiliate of R. L. Renck & Co., Inc.

*SCF is a registered trademark of SCF Partners, L.P.

Potential Future Winners

Table 2-2 presents a diversified list of companies with the ability to generate significant free cashflow over the next half decade. Review the list and check out each firm's fundamentals, growth prospects, industry competition, etc., to determine if the market has fairly priced its shares. If not, take advantage of the market's inefficiency to improve your portfolio's return on investment.

Table 2-2. Companies with the Potential to Generate Free Cashflow*

Company	Business	1992 SCF/share
Apple Computer	Computers	$6.56
National Presto	Small appliances	$6.25
Philip Morris	Tobacco, consumer	$10.18
Ralston Purina	Pet food	$5.64
Texas Instruments	Electronics	$3.93

*Table data compiled September 1991.

3

Small-Cap Gems

Ferreting Out Solid, Small-Cap Stocks

Big Stocks versus Small Caps

Any investor can safely invest in the Blue Chips of the world and sit back and collect dividends and enjoy fairly stable capital gains over the years. But the more venturesome seek out extraordinary gains by ferreting out the solid, small-cap companies that hold out promise to become the IBMs, Telemexes, and Xeroxes of tomorrow.

For decades, debate over the wisdom of investing in big stocks versus small caps has raged on. Taking a long-term perspective, small companies have outperformed large companies by a wide margin. According to a study by Roger F. Ibbotson and Rex A. Sinquefield, $1 invested in the small-company stocks in 1925 would have grown to $1847.63 by the end of 1991 versus only $675.59 for each $1 invested in common stocks in general and only $21.94 for each $1 invested in long-term government bonds. That's nearly three times more wealth created by investing in small-cap companies over the 66-year period. (See Chart 3-1.)

More recently, small-cap stocks began a period of outperformance which promises to continue. Since October 31, 1990, the NASDAQ Composite of over-the-counter stocks has increased 91.7 percent, versus an average increase of 36.5 percent for the Dow Jones Industrial Average, the S&P 500 Index, and the S&P Industrial Index.

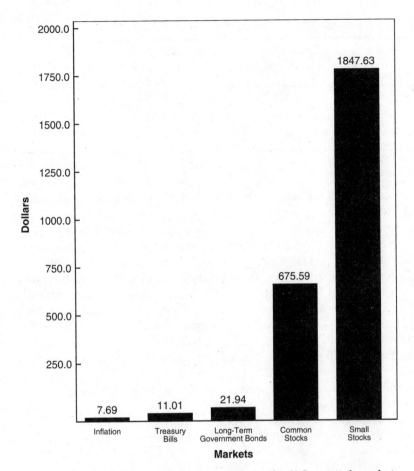

Chart 3-1. Wealth indices of investments in the U.S. capital markets 1925–1991. Year-end 1925=$1.00. (*From Ibbotson, Roger G. and Rex A. Sinquefield*, Stocks, Bonds, Bills, and Inflation (SBBI), *1982, updated in* Stocks, Bonds, Bills *and Inflation* 1991 Yearbook ™, *Ibbotson Associates, Chicago. All rights reserved.)*

Of course, the road hasn't exactly always been a smooth one. For instance, the October 1987 crash crushed many small-company stocks as investors fled to more liquid, stable investments. In fact, after 2½ decades of small-cap stocks outperforming the big stocks, the last half of the eighties saw the opposite occur. However, as we enter the nineties, the small caps appear to be coming to life once again.

The recent rejuvenation of small-cap stocks has historical precedence. Market research indicates that small-cap stocks have soared by more than 40 percent in the 12-month periods following every recession over

Table 3-1. Small-Cap Underperformance Followed by Rally*

Year ending under performance	3-year period		5-year period		10-year period	
	S&P 500	Small caps	S&P 500	Small caps	S&P 500	Small caps
1931	39%	185%	176%	559%	87%	219%
1973	25%	93%	24%	198%	174%	1118%
1990	?	?	?	?	?	?

*Total cumulative returns.

the past 40 years. And once the bull market in small-cap stocks begins, it often extends for five years or more.

A 1988 study by David L. Babson & Company indicated sharp price rallies by small-cap stocks for the 3-, 5-, and 10-year time frames after periods of small-cap stock underperformance. For example, as shown in Table 3-1, small-cap underperformance ended in 1931 followed by a 185 percent gain versus 39 percent, 559 percent gain versus 176 percent, and 219 percent gain versus 87 percent for small-cap stocks (smallest quintile of the New York Stock Exchange) versus the S&P 500 for the 3-, 5-, and 10-year periods, respectively. The same held true for the 3-, 5-, and 10-year periods following the small-cap underperformance that ended in 1973.

Can the nineties repeat the strong small-cap performance numbers? Time will tell.

The same Babson study also reported that, as shown in Table 3-2, small-cap stocks outperformed the S&P 500 for the 3-, 5-, and 10-year periods following major market declines that ended in 1932, 1937, 1941, and 1974.

A number of factors combined to end the small caps' domination in the eighties. Among the most prominent theories put forth include the

Table 3-2. Small-Cap Performance after Market Declines*

Year ending market decline	3-year period		5-year period		10-year period	
	S&P 500	Small caps	S&P 500	Small caps	S&P 500	Small caps
1932	124%	323%	95%	193%	144%	386%
1937	18%	26%	25%	66%	151%	645%
1941	81%	319%	128%	542%	393%	1036%
1974	58%	202%	99%	434%	296%	1320%

*Total cumulative returns.

high percentage of the stock market that has become institutionalized. For example, the average S&P 500 stock currently claims more than 60 percent institutional ownership. In addition, institutional assets in big-cap index funds have grown from $10 billion in 1980 to over $170 billion at the start of the nineties.

Overall, U.S. institutions owned $1.6 trillion in equities, or 39 percent of total outstanding stock, in the United States at the end of September 1991, up from $8.7 billion, or 6.1 percent, at the end of 1951.

Another major factor is that growing foreign investor interest in U.S. stocks rests primarily in stable, large-cap issues. During the eighties, foreign investors were net purchasers of U.S. stocks in the amount of nearly $220 billion. According to U.S. Federal Reserve statistics, foreign investors owned 5.9 percent of U.S. equities at the end of September 1991.

Finally, the eighties produced one of the longest bull markets on record, with returns from equities substantially above historic averages.

Looking ahead, large stocks will be hard-pressed to keep up the levels of returns in recent years, making a shift to smaller-cap stocks more attractive. In addition, individual investors are entering the investment arena in unprecedented numbers and at younger ages. According to the *1991 Fact Book* put out by the New York Stock Exchange, Inc., more than 51 million individuals owned stock in the United States in 1990, up 33 percent from the 30 million stock-owning individuals in 1980. The average age of U.S. shareholders has dropped to age 43 in 1990 from age 53 in 1975.

This bodes well for small-cap investments. With more years until retirement age, younger investors can afford to try to improve investment returns by investing in less-known smaller-cap stocks.

This doesn't mean you should plunge headlong into small-cap stocks. Remember, unless you stick to mutual funds, you purchase individual stocks, not the broad small-cap segment. Like your other investment strategies, this means you must do a bit of work to search out and find those small-cap companies with the best prospects to deliver superior performance and investment returns.

Picking Small Caps

While every small-cap investment manager uses his or her own special analysis techniques, here are some basic criteria to help uncover unique investment opportunities in the small-cap segment.

- Search for companies with attractive market niches that larger competitors cannot economically enter. The advantage of these companies may stem from technological breakthroughs, marketing strategies, raw material sources, geography, etc.

- Look for companies that have minimum or no debt to help weather setbacks and economic downturns.
- Choose companies with adequate cash plus ample capital and lines of credit to provide operating flexibility and the resources for growth.
- Search for companies that have a track record of high return on equity.
- Make sure the companies you choose have revenues and earnings growth projected to exceed 15 percent annually for the next five years.

There are plenty of information sources you can consult. A number of brokerage houses regularly publish reports on small-cap and emerging growth companies. For example, Dain Bosworth Inc. launched its *Northern Exposure* publication in late 1991 to focus on emerging growth companies in the territory from Wisconsin to the West Coast and as far south as Missouri and Nevada. Likewise, Piper, Jaffray & Hopwood, Inc., covers small-cap stocks in its monthly *Midwest Spectrum*. Ask your broker for copies of reports on attractive small-cap companies.

In addition, business publications, such as *Business Week, Forbes,* and *Inc.,* publish honor rolls of the 100 or 200 best small or growth companies in the nation. These publications make great starting points to initiate your research.

Some Small-Cap Gems

In March 1990, my article "Small Stocks with Big Ideas" appeared in *Changing Times* (now *Kiplinger's Personal Finance Magazine*). The article featured a number of small-cap companies that either operated in niche businesses avoided by large potential competitors or delivered products or services that commanded premium prices.

Cardinal Distribution

One of those stocks, Cardinal Distribution, Inc., I covered in earlier stories for *Investor's Daily* (now *Investor's Business Daily*) on August 5, 1989, and *OTC Review* (now called *Equities*) in October 1987.

Cardinal Distribution, headquartered in Dublin, Ohio, serves the drug distribution segment based on high value-added support services to customers. The prescription works. From fiscal 1985 to fiscal 1991, the firm's revenues more than tripled to nearly $1.5 billion from $429 million. Earnings followed suit, jumping to $1.20 per share from $0.36 cents per share. The results came on the heels of a balanced attack of strategic acquisitions and internal growth.

Savvy investors took notice, bidding up the stock to almost continuous new highs, seasoned with numerous stock splits (see Chap. 5, "Stock-Split Specials") along the route. Cardinal's stock, among many others, faltered with the October 1987 crash. It dropped from a high of $10⅜ per share to less that $5 per share before once again resuming its upward trek to hit highs of $9½ per share in 1988, $15¾ in 1989, $23¼ in 1990, and $38¾ in 1991 (adjusted for stock splits).

A $6000 investment for 1000 shares of Cardinal Distribution common stock in early 1985 would have grown to $38,750 at its stock price peak in 1991, increasing the original stake more than sixfold.

In mid-1992, Cardinal traded around the $28 per share range before the company announced an agreement to acquire Durr-Fillauer Medical Inc.'s wholesale drug unit. The $181 million acquisition would boost Cardinal's annual revenues nearly 100 percent to around $3 billion plus make it the nation's third largest drug distributor. Not bad for a one-time small-cap operator. The market reacted with an immediate $1¾ per share jump in Cardinal's stock price the day of the announcement.

Structural Dynamics Research Corporation: A *GLR* Pick

Structural Dynamics Research Corporation (SDRC), another stock featured in the *Changing Times* article, also has made giant strides in revenues, earnings, and stock price gains.

While I would love to claim the credit for recommending Structural Dynamics, in all honesty, the stock first came to my attention via Elliott Schlang, who initiated coverage of SDRC in the *Great Lakes Review* (*GLR*) on February 14, 1990, while at Prescott, Ball & Turben, Inc., in Cleveland, Ohio. Schlang, now a senior vice president with Kidder-Peabody & Company in Cleveland, publishes the *Midwest Review*.

The *GLR* first recommended SDRC at $8 per share. The stock closed out 1991 at $29 per share on a 30 percent earnings increase to 60 cents per share from 48 cents per share a year earlier. SDRC is a leading international supplier of mechanical design automation software and engineering services. (See Chap. 8, "Defensive Stocks," for a more detailed discussion of SDRC.)

Schlang and the *GLR* achieved an enviable track record. From inception on March 17, 1981 through December 31, 1991, the 73 *GLR* recommendations increased an average 138 percent versus only 54 percent for the Dow Jones Industrial Average, 51 percent for the S&P 500, and 44 percent for the NASDAQ Composite. As you can see, selective investment does pay off.

Other *GLR* Picks

Some of the more spectacular *GLR* recommendations as of January 31, 1992, with open positions include Hillenbrand Industries, Inc., a casket manufacturer, with a 711 percent gain since March 31, 1981; A. Schulman, Inc., a plastics supplier, with a 675 percent gain since August 1, 1985; and MEDSTAT Systems, a medical benefits software company, with a 264 percent gain since June 18, 1990.

The *GLR* investment rationale combines a focus on emerging growth companies, concentrating especially on their operational advantages over their larger competitors, with stringent investment guidelines governing when a stock will be admitted to or deleted from the 30 or so stocks covered in the *GLR*.

To illustrate, companies with revenues over $500 million often graduate from the *GLR* listings and move on to the mainstream research department. Major criteria to find winners include a consistent pattern of earnings growth well in excess of inflation, a high return on equity and sales, a self-funding balance sheet, a price-earnings ratio at a fraction of the growth rate, and flexible labor policies.

Low foreign exposure, which reduces currency and political risks, and limited institutional ownership, which boosts the appreciation potential as the stock gets discovered by more and more institutions, add to the stock's appeal. In addition, a heavy flavor of insider ownership gives clues on the degree of commitment of management.

"There's no substitute for the entrepreneurial drive. It makes a whole world of difference when management's financial future is tied to the performance of their company's stock," says Schlang.

Schlang's overall philosophy transferred with him to Kidder-Peabody. "In the long run, short-term market fluctuations are relatively unimportant. I concentrate on searching for the best-quality companies at the right prices," says Schlang.

That includes purchasing companies at ½ to 1 times the firm's projected growth rate and looking for selling opportunities when its price-earnings ratio equals 1½ times the projected growth rate, depending on the interest rate environment.

To illustrate, a company must be trading at a maximum of 24 times earnings if its projected growth rate amounts to 24 percent. Likewise, the stock will be monitored for sale when the price-earnings ratio surpasses 36.

Under Schlang's guidance, the *GLR* attracted a large following, with some 40,000 retail customers and more than 1000 institutions tracking *GLR* recommendations. He hopes to repeat, under the *Midwest Review* umbrella, his earlier success.

Like any good investor, Schlang preaches diversification to limit the losses on any one sour pick. Even with the *GLR*'s impressive earnings gains, some 17 percent wrong picks crept into the portfolio over the years.

One of the more recent *GLR* recommendations, Medex, Inc., joined the ranks of the elite on November 21, 1992, at a recommended purchase price of $28 per share. In early 1992, the Hilliard, Ohio, specialist in precision fluid and drug infusion products saw its stock surge to $39½ per share before falling back to the $30 per share level in mid-1992 due to rotation out of health stocks and into cyclicals.

Medex's revenues, up every year for 16 years, have compounded an average of 29 percent per year since fiscal 1987. Net income and earnings per share also enjoy a 16-consecutive-year string of improving results, with annual average rates of 24 percent and 19 percent, respectively. Another plus, cash dividends have compounded at a 23 percent clip since 1987.

Recent strategic acquisitions position the company well in the neonatal and pediatric intensive care and home markets. Medex stands to benefit from our nation's aging population and the breadth of its product line. *GLR* anticipates an annual growth rate of 20 to 25 percent over the next five years.

Comparing the Small-Cap Picks

Of the 10 companies highlighted in the March 1990 *Changing Times* article, 8 rose while only 2 declined. If 500 shares of each stock had been purchased on that date, that portfolio would have grown from $72,944 to $117,065 by December 31, 1991. That's more than a 60 percent increase in value in less than two years. (See Table 3-3.)

Healthdyne. As you can see from Table 3.3, the stock with the largest gain during that period was Healthdyne, with a stock price increase of 173 percent. Again, I must give credit elsewhere for that pick. That recommendation came courtesy of Binkley C. Shorts, at the time manager of the OTC Securities Fund, a longtime small-cap investor. Shorts expressed his fondness for Healthdyne's future prospects despite the firm's inability to remain consistently profitable since going public back in 1981.

The second largest provider of home infusion therapy turned the cor-

Table 3-3. *Changing Times* March 1990 Recommendations Performance Chart

Stock issue	Recommended Price*	Price, 12/31/91*	Percent gain (loss)
Cardinal Distribution	$16.00	$30.50	91%
Fiserv	15.18	37.75	149
Healthdyne	9.50	26.00	173
Hunt Manufacturing	20.00	14.75	(26)
LDI	14.28	14.50	2
Modern Controls	8.66	18.25	111
Pall Corp.	22.88	27.13	18
Structural Dynamics	14.88	29.00	95
S-K-I Ltd.	12.50	10.00	(20)
X-Rite	12.00	26.25	119

*Adjusted for stock splits.

ner and showed a 6 cent per share profit in 1989 after three years of losses. Shorts noted the 30 percent growth rate for home infusion expenditures and improving results at the company's three operating segments.

Things panned out as Shorts projected. By 1991, all three business segments turned a profit, boosting earnings to the 70 cents per share level in 1991 from 33 cents per share in 1990.

Looking to the future, more and more health services will be shifted away from the hospital environment, benefiting companies like Healthdyne. On top of that, as Healthdyne's services for the care of pregnant women and their babies prove to be the low-cost route to prevent more serious and costly illnesses, demand promises to surge.

Fiserv. Shorts also came through with another big winner: Fiserv Inc., which provides specialized data processing for financial institutions. Fiserv gained nearly 150 percent on steadily increasing revenues and earnings per share growth above 20 percent annually. Paced by internal growth and key acquisitions, Fiserv boosted earnings to $1.25 per share in 1991 from $1.07 per share in 1990.

Earnings may temporarily slow a bit with the loss of clients taken over by the Resolution Trust Company, but internal expansion and integration of the Citicorp Information Resources acquisition should more than offset the negative effect in the long term. In addition, consolidation of operations in the firm's new $13 million headquarters in Milwaukee, Wisconsin, will provide operating efficiencies that flow to the bottom line.

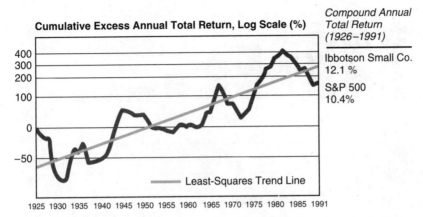

Chart 3-2. Small company returns versus S&D 500 long-term superiority, cyclical pattern. (*Source: Ibbotson Associates, Wellington Management Company*)

Shorts on Small Caps

As chief of the OTC Securities Fund (at the time of this writing, Wellington Management Company was negotiating to sell this fund to T. Rowe Price), Shorts and Wellington Management Company specialized in investing in small companies that could produce superior results over the long term. (See Chart 3-2.)

"The over-the-counter small-cap market is far less efficient than the formal exchanges, an attribute which allows the investor to capitalize from thorough, independent research via enhanced returns. It's important to stake out your claim before institutional investment, because that's when pricing inefficiencies are most likely to occur," says Shorts. (See Chart 3-3.)

Like Schlang, Shorts toots the diversification horn. It makes sense; small companies are just plain riskier to own than large companies, and so it pays to diversify to spread the risk. In the $300 million OTC Securities Fund portfolio, Shorts typically held some 225 companies.

"The small-cap phenomenon runs in cycles, with small caps outperforming larger stocks in approximately five-year cycles and then underperforming large firms for periods averaging five years. The 1991 small-cap performance was great. It's too early to tell, but the nineties may be the start of another period where small caps outshine their larger counterparts," says Shorts.

He warns against investing in companies in which bigger firms with economies of scale can put the smaller companies at a severe competitive disadvantage. Also stay clear of companies with short product life

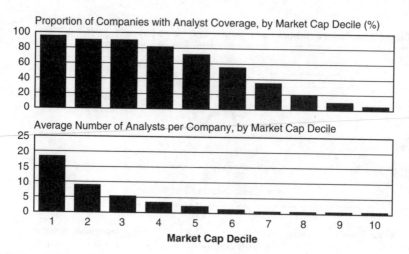

Chart 3-3. Small company sector is less efficient: analyst coverage of large and small companies. (*Source: IRES, Wellington Management Company*)

cycles and high-tech products. The rationale for this caveat is that these types of firms must continually reinvent themselves, increasing the odds they might stumble.

"Don't let an earnings drop scare you away; they often create buying opportunities when the institutions start fleeing. You have to be tolerant; during growing phases earnings will come in spurts. But make sure you are buying value with a long-term perspective. Ask yourself if it's a business you can embrace that fulfills a need. Then take a good, hard look at the numbers. Growth and earnings will show if they're present," says Shorts.

Knowing when to sell is as important as, if not more important than, knowing when to buy. Shorts culls his holdings of companies acquired by other firms, companies that mature, and positions that grow too large in relation to the rest of the portfolio.

"Small companies are the bone marrow of the U.S. economy. They are the exciting firms that are creating innovation and change. Sure they are riskier, but they also deliver greater potential for real home runs," says Shorts.

Surgical Care Affiliates. A real coup, Shorts added Surgical Care Affiliates, Inc., to his portfolios in 1987 at $1.50 per share (adjusted for stock splits). He sold the bulk of the stock as it spurted up to a high of above $43 per share in 1991.

"Surgical Care stood to benefit from growing health-care expenditures, its ability to contain health-care costs, and its reputation as the best by far of the outpatient surgical care firms," says Shorts.

From earnings of 11 cents per share in 1988 on $53 million in revenues, Surgical Care grew to earn 57 cents per share on revenues of $170 million. The firm's solid performance earned it a sixteenth place in *Fortune*'s "Best Stocks of 1990" and a sixty-third ranking on *Business Week*'s 1991 100 Best Small Corporations list.

The hearty results continue. In mid-1992, case volume at its surgical-care centers increased 35 percent, and new acquisitions and new center construction expanded market share. In May 1992, the board of directors provided another boost to shareholders, hiking the cash dividend by 48 percent to 4 cents per share quarterly.

Street estimates put earnings gains in excess of 20 percent for the next several years.

Identifying economic trends plays a big role in Shorts's investment strategy. For example, recognizing the significance of health-care cost containment put Shorts on the trail of Surgical Care Affiliates, Critical Care America, and Health Care Compare, all companies that successfully rose from the ranks of small-cap companies to the mid-cap range and treated their shareholders to tremendous profits in the process.

Costco and Consolidated Stores.   For the nineties, Shorts sees consumers trying to stretch their dollars farther, making value retailers such as Costco Wholesale Corporation and Consolidated Stores Corporation attractive investments.

"The growing attraction of the warehouse concept to cost-conscious consumers will continue to fuel Costco's growth," says Shorts.

Since going public in 1986, Costco has worked right through the recession, adding stores at a brisk pace. From revenues under $400 million in fiscal 1986, the wholesale cash-and-carry chain bolstered revenues to the $5.3 billion level by the end of fiscal 1991.

Helping consumers get more bang for their buck kept the earnings picture bright at Costco despite the lackluster earnings and deficits being experienced by others in the retail segment. From a deficit of $0.26 cents per share in fiscal 1985, Costco posted a string of solid earnings, hitting a record of $1.11 per share in fiscal 1991. Another 30 percent earnings gain is projected for fiscal 1992. However, Costco's stock took a 4-point hit, with news that comparable store sales for initial weeks in the 1992 fiscal fourth quarter grew by only 10 percent. If Shorts's prophecy proves right, the 1992 stock price downturn should be another buying opportunity for savvy investors.

Likewise, following the October 1987 crash, Costco's stock price plummeted from $6 per share to $2⅞ per share, losing more than half of its market value. Investor panic put aside a near doubling of revenues and Costco's maintenance of its healthy 11 percent-plus margins and dropped the stock to record lows—obviously a buying opportunity for the patient investor who recognized value.

From its 1987 trough, Costco's stock soared to new heights with record prices of $17⅞ per share in 1989, $24½ per share in 1990, and $59¼ per share in 1991, adjusted for stock splits.

Insiders own nearly 18 percent of Costco stock, making their stake in the company's success an important factor. Management plans to open 10 to 15 new stores annually. This, combined with an expansion of products carried and growing consumer acceptance of warehouse retailing, bodes well for future Costco prospects.

"Previous management problems at Consolidated Stores hampered the company from achieving its true potential. The installation of a new management team put Consolidated back on track," says Shorts.

Consolidated's improving fortunes are also riding on the backs of the cost-conscious consumer. The firm specializes in "closeout" merchandise purchased at substantial discounts due to overruns, discontinued product lines, bankruptcy sales, and packaging changes.

To be sure, the investor in Consolidated Stores had to have faith in new management and the company's ability to turn the firm around in the midst of one of the nation's most severe retail crises in recent history.

Earnings per share dropped from 63 cents per share in fiscal 1985 to 29 cents per share in fiscal 1987. Declining earnings and the October 1987 stock market crash sent Consolidated Store's stock price spiraling downward from a high of $23⅝ per share in 1986 to $2⅝ per share in 1987.

At the same time, long-term debt rose from less than $5 million in 1985 to nearly $55 million in 1987. Things got worse from there. Consolidated Stores lost 15 cents per share in 1989 on declining revenues, and debt rose to over $91 million. Early 1991 saw the company's stock price dip below $2 per share.

The injection of new management, enhanced customer-driven focus, and innovative merchandise and distribution systems helped turn Consolidated Stores around. The firm eked out earnings of 10 cents per share in fiscal 1990 with a return to rising revenues. Another boost to 44 cents per share in fiscal 1991 and projected earnings of 52 cents per share for fiscal 1992 illustrate the retail company is indeed back on track. Since 1989, Consolidated has pared its long-term debt load 44 percent to $50 million. The stock also recovered, surging to a record high of $16⅝ per share in early 1992.

A new store format, All for One, promises to tap a new segment by locating in high-traffic strip malls and enclosed malls. If all goes as planned, management intends to open up to 20 All for One stores annually for the immediate future.

Putnam Voyager Fund: Food Lion

Matthew Weatherbie, vice president and fund manager for the Putnam Voyager Fund in Boston, Massachusetts, uses a two-pronged investment approach blending a mix of small-cap stocks with blue-chip opportunity stocks. The results have been impressive.

According to Lipper Analytical Services, Inc., the Putnam Voyageur Fund ranked in the top 7 percent of the 42 capital appreciation funds tracked by Lipper and in the top 5 percent of the 367 equity funds in existence during the 10-year period ended January 31, 1992. (See Chart 3-4).

"We spend lots of time assessing a small-cap firm's management strength, its balance sheet, and financial ratios. We look for high earnings growth with a projected minimum of 17 percent over the next several years. In effect, we're looking for the next Walmart," says Weatherbie.

Weatherbie also takes a long-term perspective for hidden value to re-

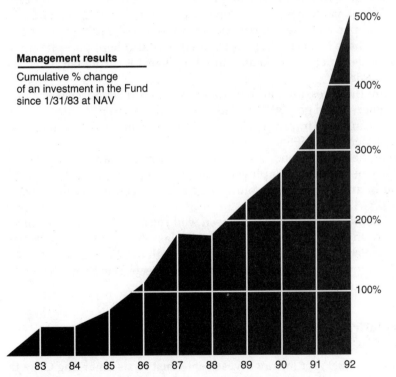

Chart 3-4. Performance of Putnam Voyager Fund.

flect in the firm's stock price. The Putnam Voyager Fund's typical holding period for its small-cap segment of its portfolio runs two years or longer.

One company that's been a long-term holding for Putnam Voyager Fund is Food Lion, Inc., the Salisbury, North Carolina, supermarket chain with over 900 supermarkets operating in 12 states. Around 125 stores were planned to be opened in 1992 with further market penetration into Texas and new expansion into Louisiana and Oklahoma.

"Food Lion is a well-managed business. It sports an innovative and dynamic management. Its `everyday low-price formula' gives it a competitive advantage in a mature industry. They do 1000 things better than their competitors and maintain a cost advantage with low overhead," says Weatherbie.

All this translates into the highest profit margins in the industry and an enviable string of 24 consecutive record-breaking years. Compounded growth for the 10-year period through 1991 saw the number of Food Lion stores increase at a 20.1 percent clip. Likewise, during that same time frame, net income rose at a compounded 26.7 percent rate and book value per share jumped a compounded 26.2 percent.

Earnings per share have nearly doubled since 1988, hitting a record 64 cents per share in 1991. Dividend growth has also kept pace, rising to nearly 15 cents per share on an annual basis in 1991 from 6.6 cents per share in 1988.

Despite the recession and consumers shifting their purchases away from higher-priced goods, Food Lion's net income as a percentage of net sales continued to improve, rising to 3.19 percent in 1991, compared with 2.95 percent in 1988.

One of the keys to Food Lion's low-cost operations and high productivity lies in the firm's employee profit-sharing plan, under which 15 percent of annual wages is contributed to the accounts of eligible employees.

Food Lion's shareholders have been well-rewarded. From a low of $9 per share in early 1989, the company's class A nonvoting stock has nearly tripled to close out 1991 at a record high of $25⅛ per share.

"The way we view Food Lion's future prospects, there's no reason to remove it from our portfolio," says Weatherbie.

Piper Jaffray's Emerging Growth Fund

In Minneapolis, Piper Jaffray Investment Trust Inc.'s Emerging Growth Fund emphasizes long-term capital appreciation by focusing on emerging growth companies in the Piper Jaffray market area.

The average total return for the Emerging Growth Fund for the year ended December 31, 1991, assuming all distributions were reinvested at net asset value (NAV), totaled 65.43 percent, compared with 51.57 percent for the Lipper Small Company Growth Funds Average.

Since the inception of the Emerging Growth Fund in April 1990, it has earned a compound total return of 46.66 percent, versus 28 percent for the Lipper Small Company Growth Funds Average and 26.84 percent for the NASDAQ Index. (See Chart 3-5).

At the end of 1991, Piper's Emerging Growth Fund had major holdings in health care and technology, around 26 percent and 19 percent of its portfolio, respectively.

"We look at earnings growth, financial strength, industry outlook, competitive advantages, market-entry barriers, where we are in the economic cycle and investment themes such as the aging population and environmental concerns. In addition, quality management is key," says Sandra K. Shrewsbury, co-manager of the Emerging Growth Fund.

On the industrial front, Shrewsbury finds favor with G&K Services, Inc., a Minneapolis-based supplier of uniforms, wiping towels, dust mops, and other industrial supplies to a wide variety of businesses.

"G&K Services represents an attractive situation with nearly 20 percent compounded annual growth in earnings, a strong financial history, and expanding markets with the fiscal 1991 acquisition of Work Wear Corporation of Canada, Ltd. (its largest single expansion and Canada's largest uniform-leasing firm). It's a well-managed company capable of generating earnings multiple expansion over the long term. We expect G&K Services' average earnings growth to be 20 percent over the next three to five years," says Shrewsbury.

The company ranks as the third largest public North American firm in the $3.5 billion industrial laundry and uniform-leasing business, serving 23 states from 21 processing plants and 26 sales and service centers. In addition, G&K operates from 22 locations in Canada.

It's a dirty business, but G&K appears to be cleaning up. Its diversified customer base helps make the company recession-resistant. Despite serving a bevy of Fortune 500 companies, no single customer accounts for more than ¼ of 1 percent of total revenues. Strong cashflow provides plenty of capital for internal growth and additional acquisitions.

Currently, the U.S. uniform-leasing business is expanding at a 7 to 8 percent clip, about twice the growth rate of the gross national product. There's plenty of room for additional growth. Only 20 percent of the 120-plus million U.S. work force wears clothing furnished by employers. Of these 24 million uniform wearers, only one-third currently wear leased uniforms. Market growth promises to come from conversion of uniform ownership to leasing plus a wider use of uniforms in the work

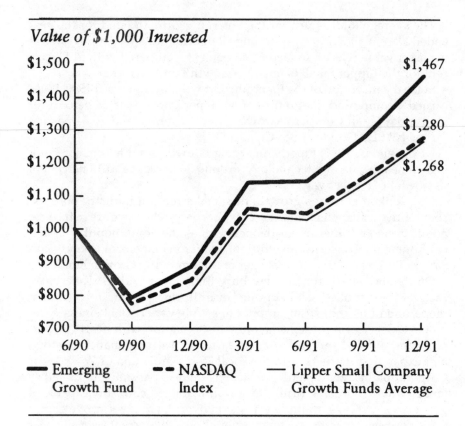

Value of $1,000 Invested

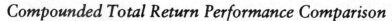

Compounded Total Return Performance Comparison

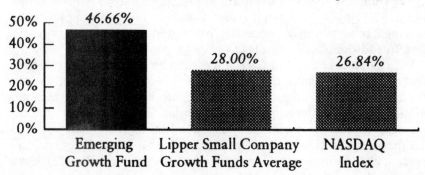

Chart 3-5. Total return performance comparison charts. Figures for both charts represent the first full quarter after inception through December 31, 1991. Calculations exclude sales charges. These charts are for illustrative purposes only.

force overall. It's estimated that if only 1 of every 10 uniformed employees switched to leasing, it would add 25 percent to the uniform-leasing market.

Within the uniform-leasing industry, for the 10-year period ended fiscal 1990, G&K revenues grew by 13 percent annually, compared with only 7 percent for the industry average. Continued market-share growth should be spurred by further consolidation of the fragmented industry. The top six uniform-leasing companies control less than 40 percent of the U.S. market.

Since fiscal 1988, revenues have grown over 87 percent to $176.2 million. Earnings, after a string of seven consecutive increases, suffered a brief dip in fiscal 1991 due to costs associated with the large Canadian acquisition and a concurrent Canadian recession. Earnings grew from 6 cents per share in fiscal 1983 to 76 cents per share in fiscal 1990 before declining to 58 cents per share in fiscal 1991.

So far in fiscal 1992, earnings are back on track. The year-long program to upgrade the acquired Canadian facilities is starting to pay dividends, with Canadian operations showing a sharp rise in earnings for the first half of fiscal 1992.

G&K's stock price is also back on track. From a high of $16½ per share in mid-1990, its price slumped to $9⅛ per share toward the end of 1990. Since then, it hit a high of $17⅝ per share in late 1991 and another high of $20 per share in early 1992 before drifting lower.

G&K has fared well in comparison to the S&P 500. Over the 10-year period ended June 29, 1991, G&K earned a compounded rate of return averaging 22.7 percent, versus 10.9 percent for the S&P 500. (See Chart 3-6).

The following companies were the top ten growth company holdings of the Emerging Growth Fund on December 31, 1991. There's plenty of food for thought here. Investigate their prospects on your own.

- *Novell.* Supplier of high-performance networking software

- *Amgen.* A leading biotechnology company

- *Minntech Corporation.* A manufacturer of medical devices and water filtration devices

- *St Jude Medical.* A leading supplier of mechanical heart valves with a 65 percent share of the worldwide market share

- *SCIMED Life Systems.* The second largest manufacturer of coronary angioplasty catheters

- *Jostens.* A leading supplier of class rings, yearbooks, awards, and school pictures as well as a supplier of educational software and custom imprinted sportswear

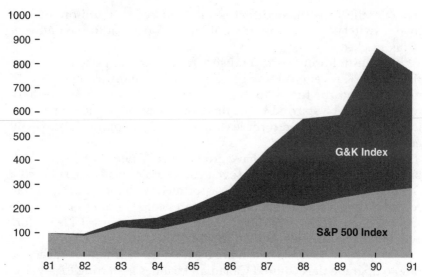

Chart 3-6. This 10-year chart compares the total return earned on an investment in G&K services, Inc., with the Standard's & Poor's 500 common stock index. Over the 10-year period ended June 29, 1991, G&K's compounded rate of return averaged 22.7 percent, compared with the 10.9 percent for the Standard & Poor's 500.

- *Cisco Systems.*   A provider of internetworking systems to connect and manage communication among local and wide-area networks
- *Buffets, Inc.*   A country buffet–style restaurant chain
- *A. G. Edwards.*   A securities brokerage and financial services holding company
- *United Healthcare.*   A diversified health-care provider

Your Turn

It's time for you to analyze overall small-cap performance in relation to its historical track record. While past performance does not guarantee future gains, those who ignore history do so at their own peril. After all, it's hard to argue with success.

Search out those small-cap firms with the potential for significant revenue, earnings, and stock price gains.

"Major investments gains are made off the beaten path. I don't know how to pick large, established companies and make good money off of them," says Schlang.

4
Strategic Industry Investments

Finding Companies in Industries Poised to Take Advantage of Special Circumstances

Choosing the right industry can be as important as investing in the right company—and perhaps even more important. The management of a number of solid, well-performing banks saw their stock prices plummet in the wake of the banking industry crisis in the late eighties and early nineties. Consumer and investor worries drove down the stock prices of good financial institutions along with those that were experiencing severe operating and loan quality difficulties.

On the other side of the coin, companies with lackluster earnings and less-than-bright future prospects often ride the crest of good fortune experienced by the industry in general and blue-chip performers within their industry grouping.

Industry Analyses: An Essential Part of Your Investment Strategy

Industry analysis forms an important part of a solid investment strategy. Understanding the industry outlook and where your prospective investment fits in the overall picture can play a big part in enhancing your investment returns. Study the industry via industry roundup discussions such as those found in *Value Line Investment Survey, The Wall Street Transcript,* Standard & Poor's *The Outlook,* and industry trade publications.

The real challenge lies in detecting those special industry circumstances and the best prospects within those industries before the rest of the pack. By beating other investors, especially the institutions, to the punch, you can earn those extraordinary investment returns you seek.

Many theorists talk about top-down investment analysis, that is, looking at the big economic picture and working downward to the micro view of which individual company to invest in. On the other extreme, bottom-up investors first focus on the individual company and then work their analysis upward toward the macro economic scenario.

I call the industry analysis focus the "middle-out" approach. You begin by focusing on the economic prospects of the industry as a whole and then move upward to look at the macro economic view and downward to unearth the best individual company prospects within that industry.

Industries That Follow a Cyclical Pattern

Some industries such as paper, automotive, natural resources, and metals exhibit a fairly consistent cyclical pattern tied to the world's and nation's economic climate. Within those industries, some firms are better positioned to weather recessionary storms, while others respond faster to a turn for the better in the economic environment. (For a more detailed discussion on cyclical investments, see Chap. 6, "Cyclical Stocks.")

Knowing how to distinguish one from the other can help prevent disaster in your portfolio or yield exciting returns as you make the right investment decisions at the right time.

Turnaround Stocks and the Defense Industry

Another special situation, turnaround stocks, can also fall either within or outside an overall industry pattern. For example, after the tearing down of the Berlin Wall, the breakdown of communism in the Eastern bloc countries, and the demise of the Soviet Union itself, U.S. defense spending took a drastic drop, with even more proposals to slash it further.

To be sure, the stocks of many companies serving the defense industry dropped precipitously. However, not all defense suppliers will be impacted to the same degree. Certainly, some defense companies will be hard-pressed to recover from defense budget cuts. Others, on the other hand, are better positioned to shift their product line to nonmilitary markets.

In addition, some firms have the resources to diversify into related commercial markets with strategic acquisitions, while other companies can even benefit from the shift away from weaponry to sophisticated, high-tech surveillance equipment. While there may not be any civilian uses for nuclear submarines, navigation technology and satellite communications systems can find a home in the space program and commercial applications.

The fact that the military supply market is undergoing a great deal of adjustment to the new world order presents a challenge to uncover those defense industry firms best positioned to take advantage of the changing situation. Look for firms with solid cash positions, commercial applications for their product lines, a successful acquisition track record, and qualified management to assess the industry scenario and make the appropriate moves.

Use the overall market panic and flight from defense-related stocks to purchase value for long-term appreciation. See Chap. 9, "Tempting Turnarounds," for in-depth coverage of this unique investment strategy.

Other Situations—With an Emphasis on Health-Care Stocks

In addition to strategic cyclical and turnaround investment opportunities, other special situations exist that can lead to higher-than-average investment returns. You need to learn how to discover these undervalued and/or unrecognized situations.

A number of mutual funds such as the Fidelity's Special Situation Fund, the Legg Mason Special Investment Trust, the Piper Jaffray Sector Performance Fund, and the Value Line Special Situation Fund specialize in this area. Keep track of new additions and deletions to their portfolios, shifts from one industry segment to another, and increases or decreases in holdings of a specific stock for clues of improving or declining investment opportunities.

The Piper Jaffray Sector Performance Fund divides its portfolio into 11 industry groupings with weightings as of December 31, 1991, ranging from a high of 34.7 percent for health care to a low of 0 percent for the transportation industry. Other major holdings included financial services companies with 14.1 percent, utilities with 11.2 percent, and technology with 9.7 percent.

Companies among the top three holdings in the Sector Performance

Fund were Health Images (an operator of magnetic resonance imaging diagnostic centers), TFC Financial (the largest thrift headquartered in Minnesota), and Integrated Health Services (a provider of subacute medical care).

For the year ended December 31, 1991, the Sector Performance Fund earned a total return of 40.7 percent, versus only 38.8 percent for the Lipper Capital Appreciation Funds Average. To be sure, the fund's heavy weighting in health-care stocks during that period helped boost its investment returns.

Taking an even more concentrated industry approach, Invesco's Financial Strategic Health Sciences (FSHS) earned a 91.8 percent return for 1991, more than three times the 30.4 percent earned by the nation's top companies as measured by the S&P 500.

In fact, over the past five years, Financial Strategic Health Sciences earned the number one ranking over all other equity funds with a 378.1 percent return, versus 238.3 percent for the Health & Biotechnology Index compiled by Lipper Analytical Services, Inc., and 104.5 percent for the S&P 500.

John Kaweske, the portfolio manager who guided FSHS to its impressive record, explains the lure of health-care investing. "Biotechnology is still in its infancy. From a dozen or so biotech products currently approved by the FDA, revenues of $2 billion were generated in 1991. By 1995 that will grow to $8 billion, including other products currently in the approval pipeline. Sales will grow to $40 billion by the turn of the century," says Kaweske.

Other health-care industry attractions include the aging world population, a growing consumer awareness of new health-care products, and increasing innovative research and development activities. Today, major pharmaceutical companies invest more than $9 billion annually in research and development. And add another $7.5 billion annually for government-sponsored National Institutes of Health funding and an additional $2 billion to $3 billion from private foundation and venture capital sources.

According to statistics from the government's Health Care Finance Administration, health expenditures accounted for nearly 13 percent of the U.S. gross national product in 1991, up from only 12 percent in 1990. Moreover, that trend is being experienced the world over.

Like any good value finder, Kaweske searches out companies serving niche markets with innovative strategies, products, and services; with superior management; and with superior returns on equity.

"We look for companies with technical innovation prospects and/or cost-containment products and services. This includes pharmaceutical, biotechnology, medical device, health-care delivery, health-care facility operators, mail-order pharmaceutical, and health-care utilization review firms," says Kaweske.

While biotechnology and health-care mutual funds and stocks rode high through the late eighties and all of 1991, the year of 1992 proved to be a different story. For example, the 108-stock Medical/Biomedics group average fell from a high of around 400 in January to 320 in late February, and through March 1992 Financial Strategic Health Sciences had declined by 11.8 percent from its 1991 close.

This clearly illustrates three key points to remember in strategic industry investing.

- Maintain a diversified portfolio to guard against any one or more sectors' poor performance from devastating your investment returns.

- Remember that no investment goes up forever. Learn when to take your profits and run.

- Keep in mind that just as investments get overvalued, they also get oversold. Therefore, look for opportunities to reestablish a position.

To illustrate, even though the health-care/biotechnology sector took its lumps in 1992, the underlying factors that made it attractive in the first place still exist. The questions that need to be answered in this or any other situation where a sector is under siege by frightened investors is how far down is enough and what are you willing to reasonably pay for the long-term value you recognize?

Healthdyne, one of the stocks in the FSHS portfolio and the small-cap stock that returned the largest gain (173 percent) from the list of recommendations in my March 1990 *Changing Times* article on small-cap investments (see Chap. 3, "Small-Cap Gems"), still holds a lot of promise.

Like many of its health-care counterparts, Healthdyne traded in mid-1992 far below its 52-week high of $30 per share, around the $22 per share range. This was despite earnings increasing more than 30 percent in 1991 to 67 cents per share and a more than 60 percent jump in earnings if you exclude the effects of nonrecurring expenses related to the exercise of stock options.

On top of that, 1992 revenues were flowing in at better than 35 percent increases over prior-year results, and earnings jumped even higher. All three operating segments contributed to the significant gains.

The future looked even brighter with new products coming on line, expanded marketing efforts, and growing market shares. The patient investor can take positions in attractive companies like Healthdyne, purchasing on weakness and then waiting for the market's eventual reawakening to the underlying value of a company in an industry sector currently out of favor.

Hooper Holmes, Inc., represented another unique health-care investment situation in mid-1992. This health-care and health information services company, based in Basking Ridge, New Jersey, recorded revenue and net income gains of 22 percent and 20 percent, respectively.

Ignoring long-term prospects, investors fleeing the health-care sector pushed down Hooper Holmes's stock price from an all-time high of $15⅞ per share in late 1991 to $13 per share in mid-1992 (adjusted for a 3-for-2 stock split in February 1992)..(See Chap. 5, "Stock-Split Specials"). While not as drastic a stock price drop as that incurred by other health-care companies, Hooper Holmes's nearly 3-point decline from its high represented a greater than 18 percent reduction in its market value.

Continuing its excellent track record in acquisitions, Hooper Holmes completed the April 1992 purchase of Professional Insurance Exams, Inc., a health information services company serving California markets. It was also negotiating with several other potential acquisition candidates to enhance its product and service lines and boost market share.

Another company on my March 1990 *Changing Times* listing of small recommendations, Modern Controls, Inc.—with a 111 percent gain— serves a variety of industries from pharmaceuticals to food processing with its technology designed to test packages and packaging materials, films, and pharmaceutical products.

In addition to serving growing industries, Modern Controls is a leading developer, manufacturer, and marketer of high-technology testing instrumentation.

For 1991, Modern Controls achieved its fifth consecutive year of increased earnings with a record 59 cents per share, up 16 percent over 1990 results. Return on shareholder's equity came in at 27 percent for both 1990 and 1991.

Companies like Modern Controls that serve niche markets with niche products have garnered a lot of attention. In 1991 alone, *CFO Magazine, Financial World, Equities Magazine, Corporate Report Minnesota,* and *Forbes* bestowed performance awards on Modern Controls. The honors included rankings in the "Strongest Companies under $275 Million," "Top Growth Companies," "The High Tech 100," "Fastest-Growing NASDAQ Companies," and Forbes' "200 Best Small Companies" for the fourth time in a row.

From oxygen permeation applications to pharmaceutical tablet-weighing technology, Modern Controls helps its customers cut costs and improve efficiency.

Its new products continue to gain added market acceptance backed

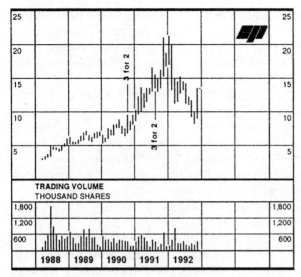

Chart 4-1 Modern Controls stock chart. (*Reprinted by permission of Standard & Poor's Corporation.*)

by a solid research and development program and customer education seminars.

Financially, the future also looks bright. Modern Controls sports a healthy cash position, with over $8 million in marketable securities, $2 million in cashflow, and no long-term debt whatsoever.

From an all-time high of $21¼ per share, Modern Controls' stock price dropped by more than a third to $14 per share in mid-1992. (See Chart 4-1.)

The value is there; it's just a matter of time before the market drives the stock up to its former heights and beyond.

Be sure to take a look at the markets the company serves. In the case of Modern Controls, two of its major markets, pharmaceuticals and food processing, are expected to grow in excess of 20 percent.

Acquisitions and the Banking Industry

In analyzing your prospective investments, you also need to consider growth potential through acquisitions. Though the banking and savings and loan industries are shrinking due to bank consolidations and takeovers by the Resolution Trust Company in the savings and loan segment, Fiserv Inc. continues its impressive revenue growth track record via acquisitions, expanded services, and additional market share.

Fiserve provides full-service data processing and information management services to banks, credit unions, savings institutions, and other financial firms.

Revenues surged more than 50 percent in 1991 to $281 million, while earnings rose 20 percent to $1.27 per share.

Acquisitions play a big role in Fiserv's growth strategy, but it doesn't seek out turnaround candidates. It concentrates on purchasing well-run companies that can immediately contribute to higher earnings and complement Fiserv's operations. That philosophy considerably cuts down the risk of making a bad acquisition and negatively impacting company performance. Strong cashflow helps finance most acquisitions without taking on a huge debt load and added risk.

Markets in 40 other countries besides the United States provide geographical diversification plus additional opportunities for growth. Since 1987, Fiserv expanded the number of clients it serves by 180 percent to 1400 clients and more than 3500 separate financial institutions.

Keeping up with the changing financial playing field ranks high. In an adept move, Fiserv garnered L. William Seidman, former Federal Deposit Insurance Corporation chairman, for its board of directors. Seidman's practical knowledge of the industry and its major players and his visible image should prove to be a major plus for years to come.

Investigate what extra efforts a company is making to gain an edge on its competitors. Also consider the risks associated with those moves. It may be as simple and risk-free as a board appointment such as Seidman's or as complicated and risk-intensive as heavy research and development efforts in new fields.

Fiserv's chairman and chief executive officer routinely stresses that his company's continuing success depends on meeting the service and technology demands of a changing industry. Unless top management has a clear picture of the industry, its competitors, and the overall economic environment, long-term revenue and earnings progress remains unlikely.

Investors may be recognizing Fiserv's potential to grow. In mid-1992, its stock traded just a tad below its all-time high of $39½ per share.

Within the mainline banking industry itself, investors need to learn to differentiate between the industry laggards with problem loans and the solid performers. In the wake of the banking crisis, industry consolidation offers unique opportunities for well-positioned superregional banks to extend their markets nationwide. More importantly, it offers strategic industry investors the opportunity to earn for substantial investment gains.

The selective bank stock purchaser should be able to outperform the market. Regional superpowers spreading their wings to penetrate other markets include such stalwarts as Norwest Corporation of Minneapolis, Minnesota, and Banc One Corporation of Columbus, Ohio.

In addition to propelling earnings by market-share gains, new financial products, and services and strategic acquisitions, aggressive super-regionals stand to benefit from the anticipated improving domestic economy.

Traditionally, banks have performed best during two cyclical points. The first occurs when the economy has hit bottom as characterized by a falling inflation rate and a dramatic loosening of interest rates by the Federal Reserve Board in an attempt to stimulate the economy.

This results in a widening of the gap between the rates financial institutions pay depositors and the rates they, in turn, charge for loans. As an added bonus, as interest rates fall, the banks' bond portfolios generate capital gains.

Next, midway through the economic recovery cycle, the banks have already put the bulk of bad-loan charge-offs behind them. Improving credit conditions then contribute to large earnings gains after loan loss reserves have been replenished.

Don't be caught up in the rush to purchase bank stocks. Plan ahead; do your homework. Investigate the quality of assets, the degree of portfolio diversification, the success of past acquisitions, the depth and breadth of management, and the economic viability of major markets when others are shedding their bank stock holdings. Build your portfolio before others see the light at the end of the tunnel.

Take Banc One, for example. The Columbus, Ohio, regional superpower looks to extend its reach. It possesses an excellent acquisition track record with previous strategic acquisitions in neighboring states plus forays into Texas and, more recently, Arizona and Colorado. These moves into previously depressed economic areas allowed Banc One to purchase market share at a discount plus participate in the economic rejuvenation of these regions. The Banc One strategy also involves taking a major presence in any markets it serves, striving to be either number one or two in market share.

According to Chairman John McCoy (the third generation of McCoys to head the Ohio firm), Banc One does not get into bidding wars. It stakes its success on its ability to serve the market, on the local talent to run the local branch operations, and on a computerized management information system that allows management to highlight improvement or problem areas that need attention.

Comparing your prospective investment's performance with other industry players helps separate the potential winners from the run-of-the-mill firm. At the end of June, Banc One's net interest margin, a key profitability indicator in the banking industry, stood nearly 200 basis points above the national banking average—obviously, a major competitive advantage.

Banc One also pays attention to cost control. Its overhead ratio comes in a solid 850 basis points below the banking industry average, another competitive advantage. Compare your potential investment's operating ratios with those of other industry firms or industry averages to determine whether or not it will lead the pack or be at a competitive disadvantage in the fight for market share and profits.

Find out what key performance statistics relate to the industries you follow and then use those numbers to help uncover the companies with a competitive edge. Brokerage houses regularly publish industry updates which provide key statistics as well as an overview of major industry trends. Keep up to date on your industry reading to enable you to uncover star performers.

Evaluating the Prospects of Insurance Industry Stocks

Moving to the life insurance industry, a shakeout in the late eighties and early nineties spawned opportunities for the investor with an eye for value and excellent future prospects.

In my interview with John Templeton in Chap. 1, "Value Investing," Sir John pointed out the life insurance sector as one of the major remaining opportunities for significant gains in the U.S. market despite weekly new highs in the Dow Jones Industrial Average.

As with bank analysis, it's important to focus on the quality of insurance company assets, product diversification, major markets, and management's reaction to changing industry conditions.

National Western Life Insurance Company of Austin, Texas, had its share of problems. From earnings of $2.19 per share in 1988, National Western's financial performance dropped to a gain of $0.18 cents per share in 1989 before hitting the dumper with a loss of $1.37 per share in 1990.

On the surface, this was not a very promising stock to invest in. The life insurance company's stock price plunged from a high around $14½ per share in mid-1989 to $5⅜ per share in December 1990.

However, management took action to get the company back on track. In 1991, National Western shed its money-losing commercial and residential mortgage operations. Lower interest rates also helped in getting the firm closer to its target interest rate spread.

A look at the asset portfolio shows that investment-grade corporate bonds accounted for 50 percent of total assets, compared with only 35 percent for the average of all life insurance companies. In addition, its holdings of higher-risk assets, such as real estate and lower-grade bonds, were well below industry averages.

A conscious effort to continually reduce its holdings of junk securities during 1991 resulted in slashing the percentage of non-investment-grade bond holdings to 1.64 percent of assets at the end of 1991 from 6.9 percent a year earlier.

While the company does have annuity products, management stated that President's Bush proposal to end their special tax benefits would only minimally affect National Western.

The firm ranked in the top 10 percent of all U.S. life insurers at the end of 1991 with $7 billion of life insurance in force and $2.6 billion in assets. Its leading products consist of universal life insurance and flexible-premium annuities. It does not market any group insurance policies.

Management's firm actions plus an improving interest rate environment paid off. National Western posted record earnings for 1991 to the tune of $7.41 per share. Its stock price followed suit, skyrocketing from the 1990 low of $5⅜ per share to hit a high of $40¼ per share in March 1992. By mid-1992, the stock price tumbled to $28 per share despite strong period-to-period earnings comparisons.

In the volatile insurance industry, keeping a pulse on the interest rate environment, proposed legislation, asset quality, and operating costs is paramount in preserving the safety of your investment. Your investment analysis doesn't stop after you have made your stock purchase. In fact, it's even more important now because your money is at stake.

Investing in Service-Oriented Companies: Mail Boxes etc.

Keeping track of economic trends will help you discover industries and companies that should outperform the rest of the market. For example, the U.S. economy is increasingly becoming more service-oriented. Look for firms in the service industry with special niches capable of providing double-digit growth for the next 5- to 10-year time frame.

A perfect example is San Diego-based Mail Boxes Etc. Cofounder A. W. (Tony) DeSio saw an unfilled service need that Mail Boxes Etc., set out to fulfill. Today, the company operates an international retail distribution system for postal, business, and communications services. Sure, their prices may be a bit higher on some products and services than others providing the same product and service, but busy people are more than willing to pay for convenience.

From less than 260 business centers in fiscal year 1986, Mail Boxes grew to nearly 1800 business centers at the end of fiscal 1992 ended April 30, 1992. This makes the firm the largest franchisor of neighborhood service centers specializing in postal, business, and communications in the nation.

Overall, Mail Boxes franchises reported in excess of $450 million in sales in fiscal year 1992. Company revenues rose 19 percent—$36 million compared with $30 million in fiscal year 1991. Net income increased 36 percent to $5.5 million, and earnings (adjusted for the 2-for-1 stock split in April 1992) jumped 28 percent to 46 cents per share in fiscal 1992 from 36 cents per share a year earlier. (See Chap. 5, "Stock-Split Specials.")

There doesn't appear to be any end in sight. Spurred by recognition of Mail Boxes' industry dominance, a new sales seminar training program, and a national business opportunity seminar series, sales of franchises hit all-time highs in the second and fourth quarters of fiscal 1992.

Moving into the international market, Mail Boxes is making great strides in the expansion of its foreign MBE Master Licenses. The company reports significant progress in the development of MBE networks in Canada, England, France, Mexico, and Spain.

Another move at service expansion has not panned out so well, as of yet. The MBE Service Corporation subsidiary continues to post losses, but the losses are narrowing. For fiscal year 1992, MBE Service cut its operating losses 50 percent.

Established in August 1990 to provide federal income tax return processing and electronic filing, MBE Service's operating results were hit with startup problems, delayed income tax form processing, and customer dissatisfaction.

Management took action and inked an agreement with H&R Block, the world's largest tax preparation firm, for the electronic processing of income tax forms through MBE centers during next year's tax season.

On the financial front, Mail Boxes sold a 9.4 percent equity stake in the company to United Parcel Service (UPS) of America, Inc., in September 1990 for $10.1 million. In addition, UPS also paid another $1.2 million for warrants entitling it to increase its equity position to approximately 17 percent over a three-year period. UPS did exercise warrants in October 1991.

Mail Boxes enjoys the enviable position of having no long-term debt and a steady flow of cash from franchise fees, royalty and advertisement fees, and sales of supplies and equipment to a growing franchise base.

With earnings expanding at a 20 to 30 percent clip, Mail Boxes has attracted some attention. In September 1991, it earned a spot on the *Forbes* "Best 100 Small Public Companies in America" list.

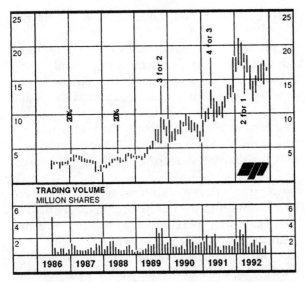

Chart 4-2 Mail Boxes Etc. stock chart. (*Reprinted by permission of Standard & Poor's Corporation.*)

In mid-1992, *Investor's Business Daily* ranked the relative strength of Mail Boxes' earnings per share as a 97, meaning its earnings per share growth outperformed 97 percent of the companies tracked by *Investor's Business Daily*.

However, its stock price has not reflected its track record and future possibilities. From an all-time high of $21 per share (adjusted for the 2-for-1 April 1992 stock split) in December 1991, Mail Boxes' stock price drifted lower, dropping to the $15 per share level in mid-1992. (See Chart 4-2.)

The company still sports a solid track record, increasing market penetration domestically and enjoying a wealth of opportunity in foreign markets as other economies become more service-oriented. The time to buy value and future earnings gains is when other investors fail to see the potential and undervalued situation.

Investing in Other Firms That Serve Unique Needs

RPM

Another company with a unique industry niche, RPM, Inc., based in Medina, Ohio, manufactures specialty protective coatings, sealants, and adhesives, as well as a line of do-it-yourself consumer, hobby, and craft products.

The specialty coatings products help other firms extend the life of their buildings, etc., making their purchase even more important during economic contractions. Likewise, the growing do-it-yourself and hobby markets add another degree of recession resistance to RPM's revenue and earnings streams.

I first covered RPM way back in 1985 in a *Barron's* "Investment News & Views" column. At the time, RPM boasted of $203 million in revenues, earnings of 55 cents per share, and a string of 39 years of consecutive record revenues and profits.

Since then, internal growth and a flurry of strategic acquisitions have more than doubled RPM's revenues to over $520 million for fiscal year 1992 ended May 31, 1992, extending its record of consecutive record revenues, earnings, and earnings per share to 45 years.

In addition to product and market-segment diversification, RPM adds a substantial degree of geographical diversification by marketing its products to approximately 75 countries from 44 operations facilities located in the United States, Canada, and Europe.

The firm has a long history of successful acquisitions, squeezing out productivity and market-share gains. In the past two years alone, RPM acquired Day-Glo Color Corporation in Cleveland, Ohio; Chemical Coatings, Inc., in Hudson, North Carolina; the European operations of Rust-Oleum Corporation; and a specialty protective coatings manufacturer in Belgium. In addition, it formed a 50:50 joint venture with a Swiss company to secure access to worldwide markets for the manufacture and marketing of specialty chemicals used in the concrete industry.

Adding to total return, RPM's board of directors voted a 10 percent increase in the firm's quarterly cash dividend, extending its dividend increase string to 18 consecutive years.

The company's stock is popular with investment clubs. According to the National Association of Investment Clubs (NAIC) in Royal Oak, Michigan, RPM ranks seventh of all publicly owned companies in the number of shares held by NAIC members. In fact, RPM is the only non-billion dollar company ranked in the top 25 listing of shares held.

Fiscal 1992 earnings of approximately $1.10 per share were negatively impacted by acquisition costs and the divestiture of the firm's Proko division. However, a look ahead shows that RPM should boost fiscal 1993 earnings over 22 percent to $1.35 per share.

Also adding to a bright future, RPM's new "green" products promise to help the company gain even more market share from companies with more toxic product lines.

RPM shareholders have fared well over the years. Since 1974, RPM faithful have earned an annual compounded rate of return on their investment around the 25 percent level. Previously, RPM was listed in Gene Walden's book, *The 100 Best Stocks to Own in the World.*

Environmental Firms

The environmental industry also provides substantial growth opportunities for well-situated companies. Of course, there are some caveats. A number of environmental firms ran into a heap of trouble, both operational and financial, that hurt their earnings and stock prices.

For example, in 1992, Chambers Development Company, Inc., took write-offs for accounting changes relating to the way it capitalized costs not directly associated with its landfill development projects. The stock market reacted violently, slashing the price of Chambers Development A stock from $33 per share in March to $6½ per share by the middle of June.

Other accounting developments led to the dismissal of the firm's chief financial officer and a change of outside certified public accountants—not a very comfortable situation for company shareholders.

Laidlaw Inc., a Canadian hazardous waste management company, also ran into a buzzsaw. Operating difficulties at waste facilities, environmental suits over unsafe conditions, and improper handling of waste plus poor performance at the firm's ADT subsidiary combined to drop earnings from $1.10 per share in 1990 to $0.51 per share in 1991.

A firm with a sterling record in the development of waste-to-energy facilities, Ogden Projects, Inc., originally spun off from Ogden Corporation back in 1985. (See Chap. 7, "Spin-Off Successes," for a discussion of spin-off investment opportunities.)

From a loss of 1 cent per share in 1987, Ogden Projects has accumulated a string of four consecutive years of record earnings. For 1991, the company improved earnings 20 percent to $1.19 per share. Based on an increasing proportion of service fees versus construction fees with lower gross margins, Ogden Projects promises to boost earnings to $1.35 per share in 1992 and $1.60 per share in 1993.

A new subsidiary, Ogden Recycling Systems, Inc. plans to tap the huge recycling market. In early 1992, Ogden Recycling entered into negotiations with the city of Chicago for the design, construction, and operation of an innovative materials recycling and recovery facility.

Tougher and tougher environmental legislation argues for strong industry growth in the years ahead. However, it won't be clear sailing. Recycling efforts are already bumping up against saturated demand for recycled materials. The NIMBY ("not in my back yard") syndrome makes new waste sites harder and more costly to establish.

According to a study by the University of Tennessee's Waste

Management Research and Education Institute, more than 32,000 sites are being considered for Superfund status. Cleaning up these sites could cost, depending on the stringency of the engineering requirements, from $484 million to $1.18 trillion over the next 30 years.

Other increased waste and environmental businesses will derive from regulations as more underregulated and currently unregulated materials come under the umbrella of environmental law.

The risks in this industry are far greater than those incurred in other, more stable, industries, but so are the potential gains.

Making Your Strategic Industry Investments

Look for fledgling industries and companies within attractive industries with market niches, specialized expertise, proprietary technology, etc. Search out that competitive edge and evaluate management's ability to deliver above-average returns.

Examples of some industries ripe for dramatic growth and superior investment returns include laser manufacturing, innovative optic technology, biotechnology, medical supplies, medical cost containment, regional banking, cosmetics and personal care, pharmaceuticals, soft drinks, and toys.

Look for new technologies or adaptations of old technologies that promise to help firms cut costs and/or improve efficiencies. While bar coding technology has been around for decades, a number of innovative applications and new technological improvements promise to push industry into more extensive use of bar coding technology.

This bodes well for firms that produce bar coding equipment, but it can also provide specific firms with an edge over their competitors. Not only search out firms that are developing the new technologies that will revolutionize the way firms conduct their operations, but find out who is getting a jump on competitors by putting the new technology to work.

If the economy finally recovers and people have more discretionary money to spend, look for opportunities in other fields such as leisure stocks like Carnival Cruise, the gaming industry, the hotel and travel industry, and toy companies.

The drastic drop in interest rates and the sluggish economy also put a favorable light on solid utility companies. They offer attractive yields in comparison with other interest-bearing securities, plus they possess capital appreciation potential as the service area economy recovers and industries boost their use of utilities.

Study the industry trade journals to learn who the major players are and which up-and-comers possess the staying power to make it big or be taken over by larger firms, either way delivering impressive investment gains for their shareholders.

The opportunities are virtually unlimited. All it takes is a commitment of investigative time and patience to buy right and sell timely.

5

Stock-Split Specials

Capitalizing on Stock Splits

You have all heard the old adage that the sum of the parts total more than the whole. While it may not make much sense on the surface, that often works out to be true in the case of stock splits.

Ever since the first stock split, brokers, analysts, investors, and financial academicians have spent countless hours debating the effects of the stock split on stock prices and overall investment returns.

All About Stock Splits

Strictly speaking, a stock split does not change your economic stake in the firm one iota. You still own the very same percentage of outstanding company shares after the split as you did before the stock split, only now each share is worth less. Theoretically, you are not any better off now then you were before; you just have more pieces of paper.

Think of it this way: If you have a $50 dollar bill and I swap you five $10 dollar bills, you still only have $50 in cash even though you now have five separate pieces of paper claiming ownership to the same $50 worth of value. A 5-for-1 stock split works in the same fashion.

To illustrate further, assume the data for XYZ Inc. as shown in Table 5-1.

Using these data, we can calculate several pieces of useful financial information. First of all, earnings per share work out to $5 per share ($10 million/2 million shares). Next, dividends amount to $2.5 million ($10 million × 0.25), or $1.25 per share ($2.5 million/2 million shares).

Table 5-1. XYZ Inc.

Outstanding common stock	2,000,000 shares
Par value per share	$1
Market price per share	$40
Dividend payout ratio	25%
Net income	$10 million

If you were fortunate to own 5000 common stock shares of XYZ Inc., the market value of your investment would total $200,000 (5000 × $40 per share). Your ownership percentage of the company would be ¼ of 1 percent ($5000/$2,000,000).

Now, let's assume that XYZ Inc.'s board of directors voted to declare a 2-for-1 stock split. In other words, every shareholder received two shares of XYZ common stock for each share of company stock he or she owned on the date of record.

When the stock split took place, since a doubling of outstanding shares occurred, each share after the split now had a market value of $20 instead of the presplit $40 per share value. What financial impact did the stock split have on the other items we previously calculated?

XYZ Inc.'s financial information now looks like this:

Table 5-2. XYZ Inc.

Outstanding common stock	4,000,000 shares
Par value per share	$0.50
Market price per share	$20
Dividend payout ratio	25%
Net income	$10 million

Recalculating earnings per share, we find they now stand at $2.50 per share ($10 million/4 million shares) since there are twice as many outstanding shares. Dividends still total $2.5 million, but the per share rate also drops in half to the $0.625 per share level.

Looking at your portfolio, you can see that you now own 10,000 shares of XYZ Inc. common stock worth $200,000 (10,000 × $20 per share), the same aggregate market value as before. Likewise, your percentage of ownership in the firm stays the same at ¼ of 1 percent ($10,000/$4,000,000).

With your 10,000 shares you still receive the same amount in cash dividends—$6250 (10,000 × $0.625)—as you did before (5000 × $1.25).

All the concrete financial evidence of the split itself clearly shows your financial stake in the company to be equal to that before the split took place.

If that's the case, then why all the commotion about stock splits? While you may not be better off in terms of your ownership stake in the company, many market pundits subscribe to the theory that a lower stock price makes the company's stock more accessible to the general public, thus generating higher demand and higher stock prices after the split.

There's reason to believe that an individual investor may be more willing to purchase 600 shares of a $30 stock versus buying only 200 shares of the same company at a $90 market price. Not only can you purchase more shares, but the commission charges get spread over more shares thereby allowing you to recoup investment expenses faster and improve your investment return.

The added accessibility of company shares to more individual share-holders after the stock split also works to broaden the company's share-holder base, making the firm less susceptible to price swings caused by traders and institutional investors.

Growth companies may also like to declare stock splits in lieu of rais-ing cash dividends because doing so conserves capital in the firm, mak-ing it available for operational requirements, research and development efforts, and strategic acquisitions that promise to increase shareholder value more in the long run.

Consumer-oriented and service companies often tend to view the ex-panded shareholder base as a captive customer base for its products and services.

Smaller companies traded over the counter or on the American Exchange may engage in a stock split to meet the listing requirements of the New York Stock Exchange where a member firm must have at least 1 million shares of common stock outstanding.

According to statistics from the *1991 Fact Book* put out by the New York Stock Exchange, Inc., stock splits in 1991 produced 2.9 billion new shares, compared with new listings of 4.8 billion shares. The peak year for the number of new shares from stock splits occurred in 1987 with 7.9 billion new shares deriving from stock splits of 50 percent or more. The year 1990 ranked second with 5.7 billion shares added, while the low-water mark during the past decade came in 1982 when only 600 million new shares resulted from stock splits.

In looking at the number of splits, 1983 proved to be the peak year with 300 splits, and 1988 produced the least splits in recent times with only 104.

In 1991, 107 companies on the New York Stock Exchange chose to split their stocks. As a matter of course, stock splits tend to occur more

Stock dividends and splits, 1982-1991

	Less than 25%	25% to 49%	50% to 99%	2-for-1 to 2½-for-1	3-for-1 to 3½ for-1	4-for-1	Over 4-for-1	Total
1991	18	8	33	46	1	—	1	107
1990	25	7	19	49	2	—	3	105
1989	28	9	34	66	2	2	1	142
1988	34	11	29	25	4	1	—	104
1987	36	18	59	118	10	1	2	244
1986	43	22	78	118	9	1	1	272
1985	40	17	43	60	6	—	—	166
1984	57	12	50	51	6	1	1	178
1983	54	21	80	131	12	—	2	300
1982	61	21	36	28	—	—	—	146

Note: Includes common and preferred issues. Data based on effective dates.

Annual number of stock splits*

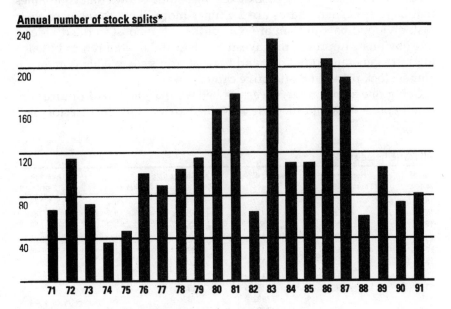

*Stock distributions of 3 for 2 or more.

Chart 5-1. Stock dividends and splits, 1982-1991. The graph below shows stock distributions of 3 for 2 or more. (*Source:* 1991 NYSE Fact Book. *Used with Permission of the New York Stock Exghange, Inc.*)

often during rising markets than at any other time. (See Chart 5-1.)

New York Stock Exchange statistics also seem to support the theory that individual investors prefer to purchase stocks in reasonable price ranges. Despite a prolonged bull market in the eighties and early nineties, the average share price tends to adjust itself downward after price run-ups.

For example, the average share price rose from $29.87 in 1981 to

$35.11 in 1983 before a flurry of stock splits dropped the per share price average to $32.31 in 1984. Again, the average share price rose, this time to $37.20 in 1985 before dropping to a $30.87 per share average in 1987. After the 1988 stock-split lull, the average share price rose to $36.51 in 1989. The large number of split shares in 1990 dropped the average price to $31.08. At the end of 1991, the average share price stood at $37.27— possibly getting ready for another flurry of stock splits. (See Chart 5-2).

A substantial body of research exists showing that in companies whose stock has split the value of investment holdings and/or the stock price of company shares may be worth more after the split due to real or perceived enhanced company prospects and/or psychological reasons.

First of all, a New York Stock Exchange study shows that companies that have split their shares are 2½ times more likely to increase their cash dividend payout than are nonsplitters. The boost in the dividend rate obviously improves the investor's yield and overall return but also works to generate added demand for that firm's stock which can mean higher stock prices and attractive capital gains.

Going one step further, investors believe that the board of directors won't vote a dividend increase on split shares unless the directors feel

All NYSE listed stocks

End of year	Number of companies	Number of issues	Shares listed (millions)		Average price •
			Number	Market value	
1924	N/A	927	433	$ 27,072	$62.45
1950	1,057	1,472	2,353	93,807	39.86
1960	1,143	1,528	6,458	306,967	47.53
1970	1,351	1,840	16,065	636,380	39.61
1975	1,557	2,111	22,478	685,110	30.48
1976	1,576	2,158	24,500	858,299	35.03
1977	1,575	2,177	26,093	796,639	30.53
1978	1,581	2,194	27,573	822,736	29.84
1979	1,565	2,192	30,033	960,606	31.99
1980	1,570	2,228	33,709	1,242,803	36.87
1981	1,565	2,220	38,298	1,143,794	29.87
1982	1,526	2,225	39,516	1,305,355	33.03
1983	1,550	2,307	45,118	1,584,155	35.11
1984	1,543	2,319	49,092	1,586,098	32.31
1985	1,541	2,298	52,427	1,950,332	37.20
1986	1,575	2,257	59,620	2,199,258	36.89
1987	1,647	2,244	7?,802	2,216,311	30.87
1988	1,681	2,234	76,175	2,457,461	32.26
1989	1,720	2,246	82,972	3,029,650	36.51
1990	1,774	2,284	90,732	2,819,778	31.08
1991	1,885	2,426	99,622	3,712,835	37.27

• This average cannot be used as an index of price trend due to changes in shares listed caused by new listings, suspensions, stock splits and stock dividends.
N/A-Not Available.

Chart 5-2. Average prices on New York Stock Exchange, 1924–1991. (*Source:* 1991 NYSE Fact Book. *Used with permission of the New York Stock Exchange, Inc.*)

confident that improved earnings will come into play to support the higher dividend payout.

The benchmark stock-split research study performed by Fama, Fisher, Jensen, and Roll (FFJR), reported in *International Economics Review* in February 1969, concluded that the New York Stock Exchange stocks studied during the period from 1927 to 1959 exhibited sharp price increases before a split. This supported the efficient market theory that the market instantaneously takes into account all available information and automatically discounts any implied favorable effects by the time the stock split is announced. The FFJR study concluded that investors purchasing stocks after their splits would earn normal returns.

A subsequent study (Reilly and Drzycimski) showed that investors earned higher-than-normal returns up to three trading weeks before the announcement date but no abnormal returns after that date.

However, more recent studies suggest a different scenario. In 1984, another study (Grinblatt, Masulis, and Titman) concluded that stock prices, on average, react positively to stock-split announcements (and dividend announcements) that are not contaminated by other simultaneous announcements such as earnings releases and merger information.

Later, Ohlson and Penman analyzed the behavior of stock return volatilities both preceding and following the split date. Their analysis indicated a 30 percent increase in the return standard deviations after the split date. More importantly, they concluded that the post-split-date excess returns were not temporary.

In July 1989, *The Accounting Review* published an article "Earnings and Stock Splits" by Paul Asquith and G. Palepu Krishna, both at the Harvard Business School, and Paul Healy of the Massachusetts Institute of Technology's Sloan School of Management. In addition to reviewing and discussing previous research, the authors examined whether stock splits convey information about earnings.

They tested the hypothesis that since stock-split announcements follow and are contemporaneous with stock price increases, they must reveal new information about the firm. The researchers examined three types of information that could be conveyed by stock splits: (1) favorable information about improved future earnings performance, (2) favorable information on presplit earnings, and (3) favorable information on increases in near-term dividends.

Asquith, Krishna, and Healy found that there are significant earnings increases in the four years before the stock-split announcement. These earnings increases appear to be permanent since the earnings changes after the stock-split announcement are either insignificant or positive for up to five years. Increases in presplit earnings stem from both industry and company-specific factors.

Firms that announce stock splits tend to be in industries that perform well, but outperform their industry counterparts in the year before the split date. The stock price reaction to firms' split announcements is related to their earnings increases in the two years before the splits, consistent with the belief that split announcements lead to an upward revision in investors' probability assessments that presplit earnings increases are permanent rather than temporary.

In conclusion, Asquith, Krishna, and Healy determined that there is indeed earnings information conveyed by stocks splits and that investors interpret the stock-split announcement as evidence that past earnings increases will be permanent. Since the study sample only included non-dividend-paying firms, results may differ for dividend-paying firms that announce stock splits.

What does this mean to the individual investor? It's sort of like the chicken and egg dilemma. Is the stock price action before and after the split announcement due to the anticipated or recent split, or is the stock splitting because of a stock price rise based on solid earnings performance?

Setting aside the reams of regression analysis and scatter diagrams that often produce conflicting results, it's clear that boards of directors vote stock splits because they do believe in the upward motion of their companies' fortunes. It's your job to uncover when the optimism is based in fact and can be supported and not sideswiped by external industry and economic factors or costly internal blunders.

Obviously, if you can divine potential stock-split candidates and invest in them before the announcement date, you can earn higher-than-normal returns. In this regard, you can research companies that have a record of successful operations and a past history of stock splits and accompanying cash dividend increases. Remember, if you're investing in the company for the long term, make sure it has strong enough fundamentals to keep the revenue, earnings, and dividend growth on track after the split.

"Typically, stocks will run up after a split announcement but will drift back or even fall after the split. Investors adopt a `wait and see' or `what are you going to do for me now' attitude. If you don't plan on sticking with the stock for the long term, the best time to bail out is right after the announcement," says Robert H. Stovall, president of the New York City money-management firm of Stovall/Twenty-First Advisers, Inc.

This may be especially good advice if the stock market has been hitting new highs and may be ripe for a tumble. But for the longer-term investor, a split announcement for the stock of a well-run company bodes well for future capital gains.

A Case in Point: Philip Morris

Take the case of Philip Morris Companies Inc., for example. After a 20 percent earnings increase in 1985, the stock jumped over 70 percent from $11 per share to $19.50 per share by the time the board voted a 2-for-1 stock split in mid-1986. Then the stock languished until early 1987. (See Chart 5-3.)

A sale of Philip Morris stock in 1986 would have locked in substantial profits, and your money could have been invested elsewhere until the stock started to show life again, rising to over $31 per share by October 1987. The October crash plunged the price of Philip Morris stock to under $20 per share, another buying opportunity for investors with strong conviction in the firm's earnings prospects and a rebound in the stock market.

As it turned out, the consumer products company turned in earnings gains before effects of an accounting change in excess of 20 percent in 1988 to $2.22 per share and over 43 percent to $3.18 per share in 1989. The stock market recovered from its jitters, and Philip Morris's stock price rebounded handsomely, jumping to $45 ⅞ per share in October 1989 when the stock split once again, this time 4 for 1.

Since its last split, Philip Morris boosted its 1990 earnings another 20 percent to $3.83 per share and its 1991 earnings over 10 percent to $4.24 per share before effects of an accounting change. Excluding the impact of restructuring the food business, net earnings grew 21 percent in 1991. This restructuring promises to generate $750 million pretax in savings through 1996.

Highlighting its transition from predominately a tobacco company to a full-fledged consumer products company, Philip Morris slotted Michael Miles into the chief executive office position. The move marks the first time a non-tobacco executive has held the firm's top post. Miles's experience in the food industry promises to hold Philip Morris in good stead, making the company more diversified and even more recession-proof.

His food industry background will come in handy in improving the operating performance of food operations acquisitions such as General Foods, Kraft, and Jacobs Suchard.

The stock market continues to act favorably to Philip Morris's bright prospects. In early 1992, its stock price hit an all-time high of $82 ½ per share, making the stock ripe for another stock split.

The company has also been taking care of its shareholders in the dividend category. Since 1987, when the company paid out 75 cents per share in annual cash dividends on its common stock, the dividend rate has nearly tripled to an annual rate of $2.10 per share.

PHILIP MORRIS NYSE-MO

RECENT PRICE	P/E RATIO	(Trailing: 14.9 / Median: 10.0)	RELATIVE P/E RATIO	DIV'D YLD	VALUE LINE
71	12.7		0.86	3.4%	318

TIMELINESS 2 Above Average (Relative Price Performance Next 12 Mos.)

SAFETY 1 Highest (Scale: 1 Highest to 5 Lowest)

BETA 1.05 (1.00 = Market)

1995-97 PROJECTIONS

	Price	Gain	Ann'l Total Return
High	160	(+125%)	25%
Low	130	(+85%)	19%

Insider Decisions

	S	O	N	D	J	F	M	A	M
to Buy	0	0	0	0	0	0	0	2	0
Options	1	2	0	0	0	0	5	2	0
to Sell	3	1	1	0	4	0	4	2	1

Institutional Decisions

	2Q81	4Q81	1Q82
to Buy	270	285	271
to Sell	262	255	297
Hld's(000)	544050	541874	520048

Target Price Range 1995 | 1996 | 1997 — scale: 200 160 128 96 80 64 48 40 32 24 16 12

Legends: 9.0 x "Cash Flow" p sh · Relative Price Strength · 2-for-1 split · 4-for-1 split · Shaded areas indicate recessions · Options: ASE

Percent shares traded: 9.0 / 6.0 / 3.0

Annual Price High / Low (1982–1993)

	1982	1983	1984	1985	1986	1987	1988	1989	1990	1991	1992	1993
High	6.9	8.5	9.0	10.4	11.9	19.5	31.1	25.5	45.8	51.8	81.8	82.4
Low	5.3	5.5	6.8	7.8	9.0	11.0	18.2	20.1	25.0	36.0	48.3	70.4

© VALUE LINE PUB., INC. — Per-Share Data

	1976	1977	1978	1979	1980	1981	1982	1983	1984	1985	1986	1987	1988	1989	1990	1991	1992	1993	95-97
Sales per sh A	4.51	5.43	6.67	8.33	9.84	10.85	11.63	12.98	14.22	16.72	26.71	29.26	34.35	48.20	55.25	61.38	69.45	79.55	115.00
"Cash Flow" per sh B	.35	.43	.53	.66	.77	.90	1.06	1.23	1.45	1.72	2.24	2.71	3.08	4.30	5.30	6.20	7.45	9.10	14.45
Earnings per sh C	.28	.35	.42	.51	.58	.66	.78	.90	1.06	1.27	1.55	1.96	2.22	3.02	3.83	4.54	5.60	6.95	11.25
Div'ds Decl'd per sh D	.07	.13	.16	.20	.25	.30	.36	.43	.50	.62	.71	.86	1.01	1.25	1.55	1.91	2.20	2.65	4.75
Cap'l Spending per sh	.23	.29	.57	.63	.76	1.02	.91	.57	.31	.36	.79	.76	1.11	1.34	1.46	1.70	1.90	1.95	2.30
Book Value per sh D	1.50	1.76	2.12	2.48	2.86	3.29	3.64	4.03	4.21	4.96	5.94	7.21	8.31	10.31	12.90	13.60	15.65	18.30	31.00
Common Shs Outst'g E	951.50	958.72	994.15	996.35	998.02	1003.2	1007.2	999.86	971.16	954.81	951.43	946.51	924.12	928.53	926.22	919.85	900.00	880.00	850.00
Avg Ann'l P/E Ratio	12.7	10.4	9.8	8.4	9.3	9.0	8.4	8.8	8.5	8.2	10.6	11.8	10.3	11.7	11.6	14.8			13.0
Relative P/E Ratio	1.63	1.36	1.34	1.22	1.14	1.13	.93	.74	.79	.67	.72	.79	.86	.89	.89	.95			1.00
Avg Ann'l Div'd Yield	2.0%	2.7%	3.1%	3.7%	4.0%	4.1%	4.6%	4.6%	4.7%	4.8%	4.8%	3.4%	4.5%	3.5%	3.5%	2.8%			3.2%

Bold figures are Value Line estimates

Financial Data (1982–1993, 95-97)

	1982	1983	1984	1985	1986	1987	1988	1989	1990	1991	1992	1993	95-97
Sales ($mill) A	11716	12976	13814	15964	25409	27695	31742	44759	51169	56458	62600	70000	98000
Operating Margin	16.5%	17.0%	18.3%	18.9%	16.8%	17.0%	16.3%	17.2%	18.2%	18.7%	19.1%	20.0%	21.0%
Depreciation ($mill)	283.7	327.0	375.5	424.0	655.0	704.0	779.0	1194.0	1367.0	1497.0	1625	1825	2650
Net Profit ($mill)	781.8	903.5	1034.1	1217.0	1478.0	1864.0	2064.0	2794.0	3540.0	4202.0	5100	6200	9650
Income Tax Rate	40.0%	43.0%	45.2%	46.0%	47.4%	44.3%	44.6%	41.6%	43.9%	43.4%	42.5%	43.0%	43.0%
Net Profit Margin	6.7%	7.0%	7.5%	7.6%	5.8%	6.7%	6.5%	6.2%	6.9%	7.4%	8.2%	8.9%	9.8%
Working Cap'l ($mill)	2236.5	1116.5	1288.6	1926.0	1432.0	1396.0	182.0	437.0	1007.0	770.0	950	1125	2175
Long-Term Debt ($mill)	3749.3	2514.7	2059.5	7331.0	5945.0	5222.0	15882	13646	15285	13420	13200	12000	5900
Net Worth ($mill)	3662.9	4033.7	4092.9	4737.0	5655.0	6823.0	7679.0	9671.0	11947	12512	14100	16100	26300
% Earned Total Cap'l	12.3%	15.8%	18.6%	11.3%	15.0%	17.4%	10.2%	14.1%	15.3%	18.4%	20.5%	23.5%	30.5%
% Earned Net Worth	21.3%	22.4%	25.3%	25.7%	26.1%	27.3%	26.9%	29.2%	29.6%	33.6%	36.0%	38.5%	36.5%
% Retained to Comm Eq	13.1%	13.3%	15.1%	15.6%	15.7%	16.3%	17.7%	16.3%	18.3%	20.2%	22.0%	24.0%	21.5%
% All Div'ds to Net Prof	39%	40%	40%	39%	40%	40%	43%	39%	38%	40%	39%	38%	42%

BUSINESS: Philip Morris Companies Inc. is a leading consumer products company with three major operating segments: tobacco (Marlboro, Benson & Hedges, Merit, Virginia Slims); food, including coffee (Maxwell House, Yuban, Maxim, Sanka, Brim), Post cereals, and packaged foods (Jell-O, Birds Eye, Kool-Aid, Oscar Mayer, Kraft, Velveeta, Miracle Whip, Sealtest), and beer (Miller High Life, Miller Lite, Sharp's, Miller Genuine Draft). Has about 42% share of domestic cigarette market. Acq. General Foods, 11/85; Kraft, 12/88; Jacobs Suchard AG, 8/90. Has about 166,000 emplys.; 99,200 stkhldrs. Insiders own less than 1% of stock. Chairman & C.E.O.: Michael A. Miles. Pres.: William Murray. Inc.: VA. Address: 120 Park Ave., New York, NY 10017. Tel.: 212-880-5000.

Chart 5-3 Philip Morris stock chart. (Copyright © 1992 by Value Line Publishing, Inc., used by permission. For subscription information to the Value Line Investment Survey, please call (800) 634-3583.)

Philip Morris represents a classic example of a well-run company with good future earnings prospects, solid cashflow, and a past history of stock splits and stock market performance that makes it an excellent candidate to deliver above-normal returns for the investor seeking an investment return boost from the firm's stock split.

The Gaming Industry

As a stock-split investor, you need to keep apprised of both company and industry factors and trends that can impact the future operating and stock price performance of the firm under consideration for purchase.

To illustrate, the exploding gaming industry has a lot going for it. More and more states are turning to various forms of gambling-generated revenues to help balance their budgets. In addition to states such as Nevada, New Jersey, South Dakota, and Colorado, which allow casino gambling in one form or other, some 20 other states are considering putting gambling initiatives on the ballot. On top of that, 12 additional Colorado cities are investigating gambling options and up to 100 Indian tribes across the nation are negotiating for legalized gambling.

Proposals range from the highly touted $2 billion complex in Chicago, to riverboat gambling, to Indian reservation bingo and video gaming. Obviously, the gaming industry stands to be one of the hot growth sectors well into the nineties.

With a rosy industry scenario in place, a look at individual gaming companies, those with the best prospects for capitalizing on the gaming explosion, makes good sense.

International Gaming Technology (IGT) appears well-positioned to be a winner. As the largest manufacturer and supplier of gaming machines, IGT already holds a better than 50 percent market share. Even more impressive, it is garnering a 60 to 80 percent share of the new business, a solid trend for future earnings increases.

Machine production figures also show tremendous possibilities. In mid-1992, IGT had around 100,000 machines operating world-wide. Industry machine production, which only totaled 10,000 in 1986, burgeoned to 32,000 machines produced in 1991. With the rapid expansion of gambling to new markets, an estimated 70,000 new slot machines will be required over the next several years.

Another plus, IGT's worldwide market (from North America to Europe to the Far East to Australia and New Zealand) provides a degree of geographical diversification and a buffer against regional recessions. Operating diversification comes in the form of the casinos it owns and operates, partnerships in a riverboat casino, and its owned and licensed multilocation progressive slot machine systems.

Since fiscal year ended September 30, 1989, IGT has boosted its revenue base from a little over $151 million to an estimated $280 million for fiscal year 1992. Earnings have followed suit, surging from 22 cents per share in fiscal 1989 to an estimated 80 cents per share in fiscal 1992 and 95 cents per share projected for fiscal 1993.

All this helped IGT parlay its stock price from a low of less than $1 per share in 1987 to a high near $35 per share in early 1992, after accounting for 2-for-1 stock splits in 1990, 1991, and 1992. The fact that IGT has already voted several stock splits indicates that it might be a candidate for future stock splits. Remember, stock-split companies enjoy a several-year period of excess returns before the split. Position yourself to get in well before the next split, if the right fundamentals are in place.

Check Out the Fundamentals

Request copies of industry annual reports to ferret out who has the best odds of outperforming the industry. Follow industry happenings in trade magazines. Call the companies and ask which publications they recommend for keeping up with new industry events.

"Since stock splits typically take place in conjunction with a pattern of higher earnings and stock prices, it's extremely important that the company have the staying power to continue higher earnings numbers to carry the stock even higher," says Garrett J. Nagle, with the money-management firm of Garrett Nagle & Company, Inc., in Boston, Massachusetts.

Nagle always checks out the firm's fundamentals when a stock split is announced. If the upcoming earnings over the next few quarters don't look impressive, he strongly considers selling the stock.

"Avoid the euphoria of the moment and investigate the fundamentals. This is even more important with cyclical stocks versus a company like Merck," says Nagle.

The strategy has paid off well for Nagle and his clients. For 1991, his model equity portfolio returned 51.0 percent, versus 20.3 percent for the Dow Jones Industrial Average and 26.3 percent for the S&P 500. Nagle's long-term results are equally impressive. Since its inception in 1989, the performance of his model equity portfolio has ranked in the top 8 percent of 700-plus reporting investment managers tracked by CDA Investment Technologies of Rockville, Maryland, for the three-year period 1989–1991. His all-equity portfolio is up an average of 35 percent annually since January 1989.

Case Study: Supercuts

At the present time, Nagle's portfolios own a lot of stock in Supercuts, Inc., a nationwide franchisor of hair-care salons. Supercuts went public in 1991 at $14 per share and quickly rose to $24 per share before the company's board of directors announced a 3-for-2 stock split effective April 1, 1992, to holders of record March 15, 1992.

"Each time, with a stock-split announcement, we step back and reanalyze as if we were making an initial investment. In the case of Supercuts, we found all the right numbers in place. Sales volume and income were rising plus interest expense was declining, all leading to an improved bottom line to support a continued stock price rise," says Nagle.

For 1991, Supercuts earned 48 cents per share before an after-tax extraordinary charge of $894,000, or 12 cents per share for costs associated with the early retirement of debt. Operating income also included another after-tax charge of $494,000, or 7 cents per share, due to a settlement agreement with a former executive. In comparison, Supercuts earned 43 cents per share in 1990 before the company went public.

Overall, Supercuts operates more than 600 stores in 36 states and Puerto Rico. Supercuts estimates that it performs approximately 3 percent of the haircuts given each year in the United States, plenty of room to grow. It has targeted a number of major markets for expansion, particularly the Northeast and Midwest, and anticipated opening 80 to 100 new stores in 1992 with strong penetration in the Boston and upstate New York (Buffalo, Rochester, and Syracuse) markets.

During 1991, revenues increased nearly 8 percent to the $32.1 million level. Interest expense dropped nearly 25 percent in 1991 and promises to drop further in the wake of the repurchase of $6 million of high-cost debt.

Since the split, Supercuts has continued its winning ways. The hair-care company earned first-quarter 1992 profits of 15 cents per share, or 50 percent more, even with 28 percent more outstanding shares, than results for 1991's first three months. The second quarter followed suit with earnings surging 111 percent to 19 cents per share from 9 cents per share a year earlier.

Its stock price hit a post-split spurt, rising to $18¼ per share in early 1992, up more than 40 percent for the year.

Case Study: Disney

"While stock splits in and of themselves don't have any real economic impact on the company, they tend to be very popular with individual investors, and boards of directors don't lose sight of this fact," says

Bradley E. Turner, senior vice president with McDonald & Company Securities, Inc., in Cleveland, Ohio.

According to Turner, companies like a fair amount of stock held by individuals to stabilize the shareholder base, plus individual investors tend to prefer stock in the $20 to $40 price per share range.

"The high price of Disney shares was mentioned a number of times by shareholders at the company's annual meetings," says Turner.

Either Disney's management and board of directors got tired of hearing requests for a stock split, or they saw the wisdom of lowering the price of their shares, because the board voted a 4-for-1 stock split effective May 18, 1992.

The news was received warmly. Disney's stock price jumped $3½ dollars to $146½ per share shortly after the announcement and eventually rose to a new high of $159½ per share before drifting down to the $150 per share level again.

Disney's first foray into the stock-split arena occurred back in 1986 with another 4-for-1 stock split. The stock had moved up from a late-1984 price per share of $60 until April of 1986 when it commanded around $200 per share. During that same period, earnings more than doubled from $0.75 per share in 1984 to $1.82 per share in 1986. Following the 1986 stock split, the stock renewed its upward price thrust, with a break following the October 1987 crash, until it peaked in 1992 at nearly $160 per share.

For the most part, strong earnings fueled the upward stock price rise, at least until 1990. From earnings of $1.82 per share in the stock-split year of 1986, Disney earnings per share rose steadily to hit $6 in 1990. But in fiscal 1991, lower park attendance and less-than-impressive film results caused concern in Fantasyland, dropping earnings to $4.78 per share.

After the 4-for-1 stock split on May 18, 1992, Disney stock initially traded in the $40 per share range before moving upward above the $41 per share level. Street estimates put Disney's earnings (adjusted for the recent 1992 4-for-1 stock split) at $1.55 for fiscal 1992 and $2 for fiscal 1993.

After suffering the first earnings decline in eight years, Disney redefined its film entertainment strategy and embarked on cost-cutting efforts. However, many positives still remain solidly in place. Despite a decline in attendance, spending per visitor at Disney's entertainment parks rose, a good indicator of increased revenues as attendance resumes its upward climb.

Another plus, 1991 attendance at Tokyo Disneyland did break prior records. In 1992, the grand opening of Euro Disney near Paris, France, promises to add new sparkle to Disney's revenues and earnings for years to come even though Disney admitted to abandoning its forecast of making a profit at France's Euro Disney in 1992. Within three years,

Disney plans to expand Euro Disney to include Disney MGM Studios Europe plus a Tokyo Disneyworld is also on the planning docket.

Whether or not the decline in Disney's 1991 earnings turns out to be an aberrant blip in its upward earnings projectile or a warning shot across the bow remains to be seen. During 1992, earnings resumed their upward track, and the smart money appeared to be betting on Mickey and the gang.

While many companies' stock prices continue to rise after their stocks split, as Nagle indicated earlier, there must be solid fundamental reasons behind the potential earnings gains to keep the ball rolling. Unless the economy, stock market, and competitive industry forces cooperate, the gains could be short-lived.

Case Study: Marriott

Even the best growth companies eventually face a slowdown or decline as their products' life cycles age, the economy stalls, new competition rears its ugly head, or management makes serious blunders that jeopardize the firm's market position and even its very own viability.

An examination of the stock price and earnings results of Marriott Corporation before and after its 1986 stock split serves as a good example of how changing circumstances can interrupt the stream of enviable financial results of an industry-leading firm.

Chart 5-4 illustrates a steady run of earnings growth from the early seventies right up through the time of Marriott's 5-for-4 stock split in mid-1986 and even beyond. Earnings per share nearly tripled from the $0.52 per share gained in 1975 to $1.40 per share in 1986, the year of the stock split.

Marriott's stock price followed suit, rising from just over $3 per share in 1980 to a high of $39 per share right after the stock split. From there, the stock drifted downward to end the year around $27 per share. Earnings improved more than 10 percent in 1987 to $1.67 per share, and the stock price hit a new high of $43⅞ per share, but the 1987 October crash slashed the stock price to $24 per share.

Despite a better than 20 percent jump in 1988 earnings to $1.95 per share, Marriott's stock meandered between $26 per share and $33 per share throughout the entire year before climbing to $41 per share in 1989.

This latest stock rise came on the heels of the start of an industrywide slowdown caused both by a saturation of lodging as overly optimistic hotel and motel developers overbuilt and by an overall slowing down of the general economy and decline in the number of consumers traveling by air.

MARRIOTT CORP. NYSE-MHS

		RECENT PRICE	17	P/E RATIO	22.7	(Trailing: 22.1 / Median: 17.0)	RELATIVE P/E RATIO	1.41	DIV'D YLD	1.8%	VALUE LINE 1784

TIMELINESS	4	Below Average
(Relative Price Perform-ance Next 12 Mos.)		
SAFETY	3	Average
(Scale: 1 Highest to 5 Lowest)		
BETA 1.25	(1.00 = Market)	

1995-97 PROJECTIONS

	Price	Gain	Ann'l Total Return
High	45	(+165%)	29%
Low	30	(+75%)	17%

Insider Decisions

	A	S	O	N	D	J	F	M	A
to Buy	0	0	0	0	0	0	0	0	0
Options	0	0	0	1	0	0	0	3	0
to Sell	0	0	1	0	0	0	0	3	2

Institutional Decisions

	2Q31	3Q31	4Q31
to Buy	40	54	41
to Sell	61	48	45
Hld's(000)	31937	33625	36083

	Percent shares traded	9.0 / 6.0 / 3.0

Target Price Range 1995 1996 1997 — scale marks: 100, 80, 64, 48, 40, 32, 24, 20, 16, 12, 8, 6

Shaded areas indicate recessions

5-for-4 split

7.0 x "Cash Flow" p sh

Relative Price Strength

Options: PHLE

1976	1977	1978	1979	1980	1981	1982	1983	1984	1985	1986	1987	1988	1989	1990	1991	1992	1993	© VALUE LINE PUB., INC.	95-97
4.88	5.60	6.38	9.41	13.72	15.29	19.14	22.60	27.37	32.38	40.32	54.88	67.77	73.30	81.69	87.24	86.00	91.20	Sales per sh A	108.70
.37	.43	.51	.76	1.02	1.17	1.36	1.57	1.82	2.13	2.55	3.28	3.98	3.73	3.75	3.71	3.50	4.25	"Cash Flow" per sh	5.70
.18	.20	.25	.39	.52	.64	.69	.83	1.00	1.40	1.40	1.67	1.95	1.77	1.40	.80	.75	1.35	Earnings per sh B	2.60
--	--	.02	.03	.04	.05	.06	.07	.09	.11	.14	.17	.21	.25	.28	.28	.30	.32	Div'ds Decl'd per sh C	.30
.82	.40	.56	.93	1.87	2.12	3.43	3.22	4.44	6.72	7.42	9.82	12.50	13.31	11.69	4.47	3.50	3.95	Cap'l Spending per sh	4.30
1.73	1.93	2.15	2.58	2.49	3.22	3.89	4.67	5.24	6.48	7.59	6.82	6.53	6.11	4.35	5.02	5.95	7.15	Book Value per sh	13.95
182.28	183.34	184.28	160.49	125.31	130.79	132.77	134.38	128.81	130.99	130.61	118.84	108.75	102.81	93.60	95.50	100.45	100.90	Common Shs Outst'g E	102.10
16.5	11.7	9.0	7.6	9.7	11.2	12.2	16.6	13.8	14.7	21.6	21.8	15.3	19.9	14.9	20.8	Bold figures are Value Line estimates	9.0	Avg Ann'l P/E Ratio	14.0
2.11	1.53	1.23	1.10	1.36	1.28	1.34	1.40	1.19	1.19	1.46	1.46	1.27	1.51	1.11	1.34			Relative P/E Ratio	1.10
--	--	--	1.1%	.8%	.7%	.7%	.5%	.6%	.6%	.5%	.5%	.7%	.7%	1.3%	1.7%			Avg Ann'l Div'd Yield	1.0%

1980	1981	1982	1983	1984	1985	1986	1987	1988	1989	1990	1991	1992	1993		95-97
2541.4		2541.4	3036.7	3524.9	4241.7	5266.5	6522.2	7370.0	7536.0	7646.0	8331.0	8720	9200	Sales ($mill) A	11100
12.0%		12.0%	11.5%	11.6%	10.4%	9.9%	9.3%	9.2%	8.5%	7.5%	7.7%	8.0%	8.0%	Operating Margin	6.5%
85.8		85.8	96.3	99.2	111.9	141.1	167.1	201.0	166.0	208.0	272.0	270	280	Depreciation ($mill)	300
94.3		94.3	115.3	135.3	167.4	191.7	223.0	232.0	197.5	143.0	82.0	100	165	Net Profit ($mill)	300
36.6%		36.6%	41.8%	42.7%	43.4%	46.8%	44.1%	39.4%	38.9%	38.6%	43.4%	42.0%	42.0%	Income Tax Rate	42.0%
3.7%		3.7%	3.8%	3.8%	3.9%	3.6%	3.4%	3.1%	2.6%	1.9%	1.0%	1.1%	1.8%	Net Profit Margin	2.7%
d46.4		d46.4	d92.5	d143.9	d162.3	d189.6	d203.6	d302.0	d243.0	d209.0	d312	d310	d310	Working Cap'l ($mill)	d310
889.3		889.3	1071.6	1115.3	1192.3	1662.8	2498.8	2857.0	3286.0	3553.0	3189.0	2900	2900	Long-Term Debt ($mill)	2600
516.0		516.0	628.2	675.6	848.5	991.0	810.8	710.0	628.0	407.0	679.0	800	920	Net Worth ($mill)	1625
10.2%		10.2%	9.5%	11.2%	12.2%	9.7%	9.4%	10.3%	9.4%	7.6%	6.2%	7.5%	9.0%	% Earned Total Cap'l	10.0%
18.3%		18.3%	18.3%	20.0%	19.7%	19.3%	27.5%	32.7%	31.4%	35.1%	12.1%	12.5%	10.0%	% Earned Net Worth	18.5%
16.7%		16.7%	16.7%	18.2%	18.0%	17.5%	24.8%	29.4%	27.3%	28.5%	11.5%	6.5%	16.0%	% Retained to Comm Eq	17.0%
9%		9%	9%	9%	9%	9%	9%	10%	13%	19%	33%	46%	10%	% All Div'ds to Net Prof	16%

BUSINESS: Marriott Corporation is a diversified lodging and food service company. Operates 698 hotels with about 161,000 rooms under *Marriott, Courtyard, Residence Inn* (acq'd 7/87), and *Fairfield Inn* names; supplies contract food services to institutions; operates restaurants and gift shops at U.S. airports and on highway systems. Acquired Saga Corporation, 6/86. Sold *Roy Rogers* restaurant chain (3/90); expects to sell *Allie's, Big Boy* chains in 1992. Sold In-Flite airline food businesses, 12/89. 1991 depreciation rate: 8.2%. Estimated facilities age: 4 years. Has 202,000 employees, 59,135 stockholders. Insiders own 30% of stock. Chairman and President: J.W. Marriott Jr. Incorporated: Delaware. Address: Marriott Drive, Washington, D.C. 20058. Telephone: 301-380-9000.

While Marriott's strategy to expand its lodging product line benefited revenues, earnings fell prey to high development, interest, and hotel-opening expenses. Management reacted to improve cashflow and reduce the firm's huge debt load by selling off assets including its Howard Johnson motels as well as its HoJo, Big Boy, and Bickford restaurants.

With earnings dropping from $1.95 per share in 1988 to $1.58 per share in 1989 and $0.46 per share in 1990, Marriott's stock price sank to a tad over $8 per share, levels not seen since 1982. (See Chart 5.4.)

Earnings rose a bit to $0.80 per share in 1991, and the stock recovered to a 1991 high of $22 ⅝ per share before once again retreating to the $17 per share level in 1992.

To be sure, the shakeout in the lodging industry will continue in the nineties. Pressure on Marriott's finances has been alleviated by mounting asset sales and the winding down of its aggressive hotel construction program.

Marriott has taken aggressive steps to adjust to the current economic environment. Management curtailed capital spending by canceling construction starts, eliminated administrative costs by some 20 percent, reduced working capital needs by over $110 million in 1991, repaid over $400 million in long-term debt, and negotiated the extension of maturities on another $700 million of existing debt.

The economy still remains the major question mark in the Marriott earnings and stock price equation. While aggressive promotion campaigns and discounting help boost the occupancy rates of Marriott's rooms, they do little to help improve the bottom line.

As you can see, unless the corporate and industry fundamentals fall into place, a stock split merely increases the number of pieces of paper you own and not the underlying value of those holdings.

Case Study: Bard

C. R. Bard, Inc., represents another company whose stock price did not react euphorically to its stock split. Back in 1988 when Bard split its stock 2 for 1, the company was on a string of 11 back-to-back earnings increases. Earnings more than doubled from $0.58 per share in 1984 to $1.38 per share in 1988.

The future looked bright for Bard as a leading international developer of health-care products. Demographics and the increasing level of spending for health-care products worldwide pointed to rising use of the firm's medical products; its international sales (which contributed 25 percent of company revenues) were growing at a 17 percent clip; and return on shareholder's investment had moved up to 19.8 percent by the late 1980s, compared with 12.5 percent 10 years earlier.

However in 1989, recall of the firm's angioplasty catheter in the United States contributed to an earnings decline to $1.18 per share. One-time charges for the angioplasty catheter recall, restructuring of a division, and write-down of a minority interest in a health-care products company amounted to approximately 20 cents per share.

That should have put the earnings dip in the past, but net income decreased another 38 percent in 1990 to $40.3 million, or 76 cents per share, with the continuing lack of angioplasty catheter sales in the United States on the back of additional catheter model recalls in early 1990. In fact, overall U.S. sales decreased by 6 percent in 1990.

Following the 2-for-1 split in late 1988, Bard's stock price hit a brief high of $24⅝ per share before closing out the year at $23 per share. In 1989, the stock price rose to a high of $26½ per share on reported earnings increases. After news of the recall hit the street, the stock dropped to $19¼ per share before closing the year out at $22⅛ per share on the optimism that the recall problems were a thing of the past.

Lower revenues and additional recalls in the first half of 1990 drove Bard's stock price even lower, hitting bottom at $13 per share in the third quarter of 1990.

The company's fortunes improved somewhat in 1991 when earnings recovered to $1.08 per share, but delayed approvals by the Food and Drug Administration and a shrinking of the fixed-wire balloon catheter market during Bard's absence still created a drag on the firm's earnings prospects. Look for Bard to eventually get back on track. Wall Street has already signaled its anticipation of better times ahead, pushing up Bard's stock price to a high of $31¾ per share in 1991 before allowing it to drift lower to the $25½ per share level in response to news of FDA approval delays.

Case Study: Tambrands

Tambrands Inc. effected a 2-for-1 stock split at the end of 1986 near its stock price high around $30⅜ per share. The stock briefly peaked at $35⅝ per share in the third quarter of 1987, just before the October 1987 crash called all bets off. By the end of the crash, Tambrands stock had fallen more than one-third to $22⅜ per share despite seven straight years of increasing earnings.

Over the next two years, Tambrands' stock price struggled back to hit a new high of $38⅜ per share in 1989 before a fourth-quarter charge for restructuring and other one-time items. The charge contributed to a sharp but brief earnings decline to $0.04 per share from $1.91 per share in 1988 before earnings rebounded to $2.30 per share in 1990.

The renewed earnings thrust saw Wall Street push up the firm's stock price to $45½ per share in 1990, and Tambrands' board of directors voted a 100 percent stock dividend (2-for-1 split) effective December 15, 1990.

Following the late 1990 stock split, Tambrands' stock price rose 54 percent to close 1991 at $66⅝ per share. In comparison, the Dow Jones Industrial Average only posted a 20 percent increase during 1991.

On top of the considerable stock price appreciation, Tambrands also bolstered shareholder returns by boosting its dividend payout to 34 cents per share quarterly during the fourth quarter of 1991, the fortieth consecutive year of dividend increases—a record matched by only two companies in the S&P 500.

Reconfiguration of Tambrands' manufacturing facilities worldwide accounted for a decrease in 1991 earnings to $1.92 per share from the $2.30 per share earned a year earlier.

The company held a solid 60 percent of the U.S.-Canadian market share, has taken aggressive marketing steps in Europe to capitalize on brand identity where its Tampax is the only brand of tampons sold throughout Europe, and continues expansion into tapping the huge market potential in developing countries such as Mexico, China, the former Soviet Union, and Brazil.

Tambrands enjoyed a healthy working capital in excess of $80 million entering 1992 and solid cashflow in excess of $3 per share.

In early 1992, the stock hit a new high of $70½ per share before drifting downward to the low $60s per share. Long-term prospects look bright, with rising earnings promising to drive Tambrands' stock price higher once again, potentially making it a stock-split candidate once again in the near future.

Case Study: Safety-Kleen

Four previous times in less than a decade from 1982 through 1990, Safety-Kleen Corporation, based in Elgin, Illinois, split its stock and followed those splits with both steady earnings increases and stock price gains. With that track record under its belt, investors once again looked with favor on the firm's proposed 3-for-2 stock split in April 1991.

Safety-Kleen, the world's largest recycler of contaminated fluids and provider of parts and tool-cleaning services, stood to benefit from stricter Environmental Protection Agency regulations, a more than threefold boost in recycling capacity, rapidly expanding European operations, and growing domestic market share.

Unfortunately, the recession intervened, causing the firm's 1991 earnings per share to decline more than 14 percent to $0.90 from the $1.05 per share earned in 1990. The 1990 earnings drop was the first in the company's 23-year history.

From a high of $37⅞ per share in the first half of 1991, the stock dropped to $22 per share before closing out the year at $25¾ per share in the wake of the disappointing 1991 earnings.

Looking behind the earnings numbers, a portion of it was attributable to a public offering of more than 5 million additional shares. In addition, a $1.2 million charge related to a settlement with the state of California and another $800,000 write-off associated with an unsuccessful attempt to permit construction for a proposed recycling facility in Nevada negatively impacted earnings.

Time will tell whether or not Safety-Kleen can get its earnings back on the upward projectile it previously enjoyed. Past stock-split history does provide a degree of comfort, but it must be tempered with a thorough knowledge of the present company and economic scenario. News of an impending stock split is no justification to jump right in and invest. It's only an invitation to investigate the situation to determine if the proper company fundamentals and outside economic factors are in place to allow management to make further revenue and earnings gains, leading, it is hoped, to higher stock prices.

Case Study: Merck

Merck & Company, Inc., represents an interesting stock-split study. Spurred by sharply rising earnings during the mid-eighties, Merck's stock price surged from $15 per share in 1985 to over $43 per share after its 2-for-1 split in mid-1986. Earnings for the pharmaceutical company jumped over 44 percent from $1.12 per share in 1984 to $1.62 per share in 1986.

After the split, Merck's stock continued skyward with a rise to a high of $74 ⅜ per share in September 1987. Like most other stocks, Merck felt the impact of the October 1987 crash, plummeting 46 percent to $48 per share.

But unlike other firms, Merck again split its shares in 1988, this time 3 for 1, despite being down quite a bit from former highs. While most companies like to split their stocks when encountering new highs, the unusual move didn't hurt Merck one bit. In fact, after the 1988 stock split, the stock resumed its upward climb as Merck's earnings growth steamrolled ahead.

By the end of 1991, Merck had put together an enviable stream of 20 percent-plus earnings per share growth years. The stock market followed suit, pushing up Merck's common stock price to a high of $169 ½ per share in early 1992 before giving up some of its gain to $148 per share. Merck's board of directors announced another stock split (3 for 1) effective May 26, 1992. The news of the latest stock split pushed Merck's stock price up $5 per share just before its split.

While the actual long-term impact of the latest stock split on Merck's stock price remains to be seen, the company was well positioned to post more earnings gains in the 20 percent-plus vein.

Merck pays close attention to enhancing shareholder value through stock repurchases (Merck repurchased 13 percent of outstanding shares between 1985 and 1991), increasing dividends (10 dividend hikes between 1985 and 1991) including a 21 percent rise in 1991, and strengthening operational performance. Over the same 1985–1991 time frame, Merck's shareholders realized a compound annual return of 43 percent on their investment.

Merck's product lines continue to expand in growing markets, a double bonus. In addition, it sports one of the strongest research and development product pipelines in the industry, backed by almost $1 billion in R&D. Merck's R&D expenditures account for approximately 10 percent of all research and development spending by U.S. pharmaceutical companies and 5 percent of all research spending by pharmaceutical companies worldwide.

The firm also taps into strategic partnerships with other corporate giants such as Du Pont, Johnson & Johnson, and AB Astra to expand its access to research, products, and markets around the world.

Stock-Split Investing and Insider Trading

Stock splits provide concrete evidence of a company's past record of successfully delivering revenue and earnings gains plus enhanced shareholder investment returns via rising dividends. The stock-split investor must be able to discern which managements can lead their companies to even higher operating results. Use the stock split as an early warning signal that more impressive stock prices gains may be waiting in the wings, ready for an encore. But investigate before you invest.

Taking management's concern over the future fortunes of the company one step beyond, investigate how much of the firm's stock is owned by management and other insiders such as directors.

High levels of inside ownership and insider trading activity (on the buy side) can provide that extra degree of assurance that management has full faith in the firm's ability to deliver higher earnings and excess returns. After all, managers and directors who purchase shares of the company in the open market must believe they can achieve higher returns by investing in their own firm's stock than they can from alternative investment options.

Insider trading information is regularly published in Standard & Poor's *The Outlook, Value Line Investment Survey, The Wall Street Journal, Barron's,* and *Vicker's Weekly Insider Report.* Search for trends in insider trading activity.

Overall, insiders tend to be net sellers, selling around 2.3 shares for every one they purchase. Therefore, heavy insider buying is a very good omen. One of the most comprehensive studies of insider trading, by H. Nejat Seyhun of the University of Michigan, concluded that insider trading can be a fairly active predictor of future stock prices and that following inside trading patterns can be an effective way to earn above-average returns.

Insider sales analysis can take into account the number of inside trades, the percentage of holdings purchased or sold, the number of company officers buying or selling, follow-up purchases or sales, and insider reversals.

Typically inside sales hold less predictive power since many factors can enter into the sale decision, completely unrelated to the fundamentals of the firm. For example, cash needed for college expenses or a new home purchase may trigger a sale of company stock by insiders.

Some investors even employ an insider trading indicator using a ratio of insider purchases to insider sales. When the ratio rises above a certain point, it is considered bullish and vice versa. While an insider indicator ratio may not pinpoint the exact time to buy or sell, it can provide useful information on the overall trend of insider transactions and whether or not it is bullish or bearish for a particular stock.

This chapter provided a number of case studies to illustrate both the upside and downside movement of stock prices, and some of the reasons behind them, in the wake of stock splits. Use the studies as guides for your own stock-split investment analysis. For stock-split information, check out *Value Line Investment Survey,* and Standard & Poor's *The Outlook,* as well as its *Dividend Record* publication which provides a yearly listing of stock dividends and stock splits.

6

Cyclical Stocks

Playing the On Again–Off Again Fortunes of Cyclicals

It doesn't take a brain surgeon to look at the economic pattern over a period of years and the track records of cyclical stocks to see where fortunes could have been made with timely purchases and sales. After all, news of economic recovery or an oncoming recession continually fills the headlines of national papers and business publications.

Simply put, cyclical industries and stocks are those that tend to follow the up-and-down moves of the overall economy. As the economy prospers, these industries and stocks enjoy great prosperity, recording record revenues and earnings. On the other hand, when the economy heads south, it's time to find greener pastures because these cyclical industries and stocks will be impacted to a greater extent than other industries and stocks. Their revenues and earnings will plummet like a rock as the economy contracts.

Purchasing Cyclicals: Going against the Flow

Patient, savvy investors learn to read the economic signals and purchase these stocks as others unload them and drive down their market price. As the economy recovers and the market prices of cyclical stocks rebound to former highs and beyond, shrewd investors start to unload their cyclical holdings at substantial capital gains.

It's long been a Wall Street adage that the best time to purchase good-quality cyclicals is after the midst of a recession. Many cyclical pundits believe two sure signs that we're approaching the backside of an economic recession occur when the President starts jawboning the Federal Reserve chairman to lower interest rates even more and the national news commentators, à la Dan Rather et al., delve into reasons why there's no end in sight to the current recession. As this book goes to press, these two great indicators are right on the mark.

It's not important to catch the exact market bottom or market top with your cyclical investing purchases and sales. In fact, that's nearly impossible, except by pure chance. The strategy lies in building and shedding your cyclical portfolio on the right side of the economic slope.

"On paper, it sounds very simple, but investing with hard-earned dollars at stake is more difficult. You have to possess the fortitude to purchase stocks in companies when revenues and earnings are still headed lower. Most industry and company projections will be forecasting a gloomy future, and other investors will be selling and driving the market price even lower," says Bradley E. Turner, senior vice president with McDonald & Company Securities, Inc., in Cleveland, Ohio.

While it's difficult to go against the flow, those investors that do buy on the way down and sell on the way up can earn significant profits. The key lies in proper timing and in purchasing the stocks of quality companies in a cyclical downturn. Unless you stick to companies with the market positioning, financial strength, and adept management to weather the economic downturn, your cyclical investing could turn into a disaster.

In order to employ your cyclical investment strategy successfully, you must adopt a contrarian attitude. After all, others will be fleeing the very industries and stocks in which you'll be investing. That involves being confident in your ability to determine the underlying value inherent in the stock. Often, during economic contractions, you can purchase cyclical stocks at or below book value, providing substantial downside protection. (See Chap. 1, "Value Investing").

You will also need to be aware of both industry and overall economic cycles and where you are within those cycles. Finally, you'll need plenty of patience. Since you won't know in advance when the market, industry cycle, or economic cycle will bottom out, you'll have to wait for the turnaround. Solid, up-front research and staying power go hand in hand and are crucial to successful cyclical investing.

All the intensive industry and company research won't do you any good if you chicken out and sell the stock while it continues to decline. All you will have accomplished then is locking in a sure loss.

You must thoroughly look at and understand your own investment temperament. Not everybody is cut out for contrarian investing. Those without the guts to stick it out should ignore cyclical investing and forgo the potentially large profits.

It's important to establish your cyclical holdings early, before the demand from other investors starts driving the stock price upward. Since cyclical investors will start accumulating shares on the downside of the recession, by the time recognizable signs of the industry or economic turnaround start to appear, it's too late to earn the large gains.

For example, even while the late 1991 and early 1992 economy had yet failed to make the surge out of its recessionary mode, stocks in many cyclical industries had already posted gains of 10, 20, and 30 percent from their cyclical lows. In some cases, individual stocks showed improvement, while in other cases entire industry sectors moved upward in anticipation of improved business conditions.

The move toward cyclicals in the automotive, rubber, natural resources, transportation, consumer hardgoods, chemical, steel, homebuilding, and textile industries rests on the premise that companies in these industries should post huge earnings gains over the depressed levels experienced during the economic trough.

This causes a shift in investment away from growth companies with earnings in the 20 to 25 percent growth range. The rationale is simple. Why invest in a growth company with compounded annual growth of 20 percent when cyclicals are delivering earnings jumps of 30, 40, and 50 percent or more?

A Case in Point: Chrysler

To illustrate, despite lackluster unit sales, automobile stock prices as evidenced by *Investor's Business Daily's* Auto Manufacturers-Domestic Index surged more than 30 percent in the first quarter of 1992, compared with an 8.5 percent decline for 1991.

Chrysler, which lost 82 cents per share in 1992's first quarter, experienced a better than 50 percent jump in its stock price. Ford and General Motors followed suit with stock price rises of 36 percent and 27 percent, respectively.

Chrysler's earnings fell steadily from $5.90 per share in 1987 to a loss of $2.74 per share in 1991. Likewise, its stock tumbled from a pre-October 1987 crash high of $48 per share to less than $10 per share in 1991. Cyclical investors who anticipated improving Chrysler fortunes in 1992 and beyond could have loaded up and rode the stock up above $21 per share in mid-1992, more than doubling their investment. (See Chart 9-1 in Chap. 9, "Tempting Turnarounds.")

Of course, such an investment would depend on more than the mere cyclicality of Chrysler's performance and stock prices. It should also take into account an analysis of the industry, foreign competition, the prospects of Chrysler's upcoming models, the firm's cost structure and competitiveness, and the management succession to Lee Iacocca.

Do Your Homework

Keep abreast of industry trends and events by reading several trade journals. Watching industry and company statistics such as production rates, plant capacity, number of day's inventory on hand, and price discounting help give you a feel for which way the industry and company are headed.

Overall economic indicators such as productivity gains, interest rates, factory capacity utilization, gross national product, and purchasing indices, give concrete clues to the general direction of the economy. You don't have to become enmeshed in a network of detailed numbers, but you should have a feeling for the general direction of the economy.

As more and more individual investors and professional money managers make the shift to cyclical stocks complete, the cycle will once again repeat itself. Eventually, the market price of cyclicals will exceed their underlying value and they will retreat from their highs. Over time, another cyclical downturn will rear its ugly head and cause lower stock prices as sales and revenues fall off. It is hoped that by then you will have shed your cyclical holdings at a handsome profit and are busy investigating new cyclical buying opportunities for the next downturn.

Be on the alert for companies that have done more than ride out the current recession. Investigate to see whether or not management has instituted cost-cutting programs, organizational restructuring, and a financial overhaul to make them more productive and cost-competitive when the economy improves. "Lean and mean" companies have a distinct competitive advantage over their still bloated competitors.

Gross margin improvements eked out via tough decision making in the midst of the recession will contribute to substantial profit improvement as the economy improves.

More than likely, the playing field will change from one complete cycle to the next. Companies that put their resources and talent to good use improving efficiency will gain market share while others will fall by the wayside, some permanently.

Search out those companies that have taken firm actions to capitalize on the economy's eventual improvement. Don't invest in companies with top management employing "bunker" or "wait and see" mentalities. As Lee Iacocca succinctly puts it in one of his Chrysler commercials, "In this business, you either lead, follow, or get out of the way."

Another Case in Point: Phelps Dodge

For a classic example of a cyclical company that not only made it through a severe industry recession but also cleared the decks to transform the firm into the industry low-cost provider, and into a more diversified and financially strong company, turn ahead to Chap. 9, "Tempting Turnarounds," and read about the resurrection of Phelps Dodge, the giant copper company beleaguered by huge losses in the early eighties.

While you can read the details in Chap. 9, suffice it to say that Phelps Dodge restructured, cost-cut, and diversified itself out of losses totaling more than $400 million, or $5 per share, from 1982 to 1984 to earn more than $500 million, or $7 per share, in 1989 alone. From the investor's standpoint, Phelps Dodge's stock price skyrocketed from a low of less than $6½ per share in 1984 to nearly $50 per share in 1992 (adjusted for the May 1992 2-for-1 stock split). (See Chap. 5, "Stock-Split Specials" and Chart 9-3.)

Investing in Aluminum

As mentioned in both Chap. 1, "Value Investing," and Chap. 9, "Tempting Turnarounds," aluminum companies worldwide offer unique investing opportunities. Not only have they been impacted by the economic cycles and downturn in aluminum demand, but aluminum producers have been negatively impacted by the former Soviet Union's dumping of aluminum ingots on the world market in order to generate hard currency for trade purposes.

Looking ahead, not only should the Russian aluminum dumping taper off and eventually cease, but demand should begin to outstrip production capacity since no new production facilities have been brought on line in recent years.

IMCO

In addition to traditional cyclical aluminum investments such as Alcan Aluminum Ltd., Aluminum Company of America (Alcoa), and Reynolds Metals Company, niche companies such as IMCO Recycling Inc. offer other ways to play the cyclical investment strategy.

IMCO, the world's largest independent aluminum recycler, derives its raw materials not from mining and milling operations but from recycled aluminum cans, scrap from the manufacture of aluminum products, and aluminum dross skimmed from melting furnaces. In fact, the tolling fee IMCO charges customers for its processing of metals contributes over 90 percent of company revenues, adding a bit of stability to company operations.

I first recommended IMCO back in an October 1989 cover story for *Changing Times* (now *Kiplinger's Personal Finance Magazine*) on the best stock buys in each of the 50 states. At the time, IMCO's stock traded at $7⅝ per share. Since then, the stock price hit a low of $4 per share in 1990 before hitting all-time highs in excess of $14 per share in mid-1992.

With the economic recovery apparently getting on track in late 1991 or early 1992, the growing use of aluminum cans, and new inroads into its customer base, IMCO increased its operating rate in 1992 to over 90 percent of capacity from 80 percent in 1991. In addition, IMCO inked an agreement with Barmet Aluminum Corporation to build a $16 million recycling plant adjacent to Barmet's Ohio rolling mill. The new facility, which will come on line in 1993, will boost IMCO's capacity by 50 percent to 800 million pounds annually.

Expanding its market and adding a tinge of diversification to its operations, IMCO acquired Interamerican Zinc, Inc., in Adrian, Michigan, for $5 million. The zinc recycling operations, the largest recycler of zinc dross in the country, should add $3 million to IMCO's annual revenues.

On the financial front, solid cashflow will allow capital expenditures to be internally financed. Long-term debt is also dropping to more acceptable levels, down from over 50 percent in 1989 to 36 percent at the end of 1991.

IMCO appears well-positioned to improve earnings as the economic recovery unfolds. But, remember, the cycle will eventually end and you want to take your profits and run before the next downturn.

Selling Short

You don't have to wait until a prospective positive turn in the economy to put your cyclical investment strategy to work. Instead of purchasing the stock of companies you expect to do well in the months and years ahead, you can go the short-selling route. In this way, you can take advantage of the falling fortunes of companies entering a down cycle.

A short sale is the sale of stock not owned in order to profit from its anticipated stock price drop due to an overbought condition or an upcoming downturn in its operating results and, therefore, its future stock price.

In effect, you borrow the stock from your broker to close the sale, for which you will be charged a small fee. You will also need to put up at least 50 percent of the value of the stock you want to sell short as collateral. Such collateral can be in the form of cash or other securities.

Short selling can involve a higher degree of risk than holding a long position. First of all, you must maintain the proper amount of collateral. In the event the price of the shorted stock rises, you may be subject to a margin call. If you fail to meet a margin call, your portfolio can be liquidated at a substantial loss to you.

Second, the downside risk of a stock purchase is limited to the difference between its price and zero, the amount you might end up with if the company goes bankrupt. On the other hand, shorting a stock carries with it a degree of unlimited loss to the extent that a stock's price rise theoretically could go on indefinitely. Of course, you always have the option of purchasing the stock to close out your short position.

Finally, many investors have a hard time psychologically selling something they don't yet own. Along those same lines, others consider it un-American to be betting against the good fortunes of companies vital to the country's economic well-being.

Short interest activity can be found monthly in *Barron's, Investor's Business Daily*, the *Wall Street Journal*, and elsewhere. Be aware of short interest trends overall and for particular stocks you follow. If a stock starts to advance, those who are in short positions may be forced to cover their positions by purchasing the stock, driving the market price up even higher and forcing more shorts to cover. This is termed a "short squeeze" and feels great if you own the stock and profit by the price surge but not so great if you are the one getting squeezed.

To illustrate how you can profit from a short sale, assume the following scenario. You have studied the economic environment and believe another downturn is just around the corner. Chrysler's shares have been bid up to a new high around $30 per share. Lee Iacocca has departed, and the new management team makes a few blunders in new models, pricing, etc., which promise to catch up to the company in the long run. However, the economy keeps chugging along, and Chrysler's earnings and stock price still move upward but not with as much gusto as earlier.

You firmly believe the end of the boom is coming and Chrysler's weaker finances will put it at a distinct competitive disadvantage to other domestic and foreign car manufacturers.

With the stock bouncing up and down around $30 per share, you decide to short 500 shares of Chrysler stock at $28 per share. Your current investment at risk amounts to $14,000 (500 × 28), ignoring commissions and fees associated with the short position. Now, your analysis proves correct, and car sales drop off, sending Chrysler's revenues, earnings, and stock price downward. Within six months, the stock trades at $24 per share. You can close out your short position and lock in your gain of $2000 (you have made a gain of $4 on each of 500 shares for a total profit of $200) or 14.4 percent (2000/14,000).

Still other ways to play the cyclical market involves the use of put and/or call options. An option is a security that provides the holder the right to purchase or sell a specified number of units of a particular security for a specified time limit. If the option is not exercised before the expiration date, it expires worthless and all monies paid for the option are forfeited.

A call option is a contract providing the holder the right to purchase the underlying security at a specific price during a specified period of time. A put option gives the holder the right to sell the underlying security at a specific price during a specified period of time. The exercise price of the option is termed the *striking price.*

The use of options provides leverage and the ability to greatly enhance investment returns. Instead of selling Chrysler short, assume that you decided to purchase a Chrysler put. Checking the option pages of the *Wall Street Journal*, you find:

Option & NY Close	Strike Price	Calls—Last			Puts—Last		
		Sep	Oct	Dec	Sep	Oct	Dec
Chryslr	26	2¼	r	2½	r	r	³⁄₁₆
28	28	⅛	⅜	½	½	¾	1½
28	30	r	⅛	⅜	2½	2¾	3½

The Chrysler call of 26 and the Chrysler put of 30 are said to be "in the money," which means that at the current Chrysler stock market price of $28 per share, those calls and puts have intrinsic value.

As in the earlier example, you believe Chrysler stock will drop below the $28 per share it trades at presently and that drop will occur before the expiration of the December puts. Since each put controls 100 shares of the underlying stock, a purchase of 5 puts would control 500 shares, the same number of shares you had planned on shorting.

Your investment would total $750 ($1.50 × 500), not including commission charges. If your prognosis proves correct and Chrysler's stock price drops to $24 per share before the December put expiration date, you will have earned a gain of $1250 ($4 below striking price × 500 shares less the $750 option cost). While the $1250 gain on your puts amounts to less than the $2000 earned on shorting Chrysler stock, your return on investment soared to 166 percent from 14.4 percent. That's the power of leverage inherent in option trading.

Case Study: Burlington Northern

Transportation companies stand to benefit from the increase in activity as the economy emerges from recession. As demand for products grows, shipments rise. The rising shipment levels mean that the profits of transportation companies will grow geometrically after their huge fixed costs have been covered.

Burlington Northern, a major hauler of western coal (approximately 33 percent of 1991 revenues), would benefit not only from hauling increased shipments of industrial products but also from the boost in coal usage by electric utilities. Another plus, the shift from high-sulfur eastern coal to low-sulfur western coal under stricter clean air environmental regulations bodes well for Burlington Northern coal shipments.

Lower labor costs also enter the picture. Guidelines specified by the Presidential Emergency Board in 1991 set the stage for the first real cuts in crew sizes in decades. With labor costs approaching 50 percent of revenues for many railroad firms, the savings can be tremendous.

With renegotiated labor agreements and operating costs on the downslope, railroad companies stand to regain market share from truckers, who are experiencing rising costs.

The international situation also promises to benefit Burlington Northern. As a major grain hauler (16 percent of 1991 revenues), the railroad stands ready to garner a good share of the grain traffic from the former Soviet Union's increased grain purchases.

Improvement in the cyclical forest products industry (10 percent of 1991 revenues) will also translate into higher rail shipments.

The economic contraction in the late eighties dropped Burlington Northern earnings to $2.12 per share in 1991 from $3.19 per share in 1989. During the same time period, Burlington's board of directors slashed the firm's cash dividend by more than 45 percent to $1.20 per share on an annual basis.

The firm cleared the decks for higher earnings with large write-offs in 1991 connected to cuts in management levels and crew sizes. The moves started to pay dividends in early 1992. First-quarter 1992 earnings, excluding nonrecurring charges, totaled $62 million, or 71 cents per share, versus a loss of $8 million, or 10 cents a share, for 1991's first three months. Burlington Northern's earnings are estimated to expand at a 15 percent clip for the next three to five years.

More importantly, operating expenses per ton-mile declined by over 10 percent while revenue ton-miles jumped 7 percent. As revenue ton-miles continue to chug ahead as the economy gathers steam, look for a much improved bottom line.

Expanding its market share and territorial reach, Burlington Northern entered into a joint venture to move freight into Mexico, a move that could add up to $30 million in annual revenues.

From a low of $21⅜ per share in 1989, Burlington Northern's shares have rebounded in anticipation of better times ahead. By mid-1992, the stock was posting new highs around $48 per share. (See Chart 6-1.)

Case Study: Union Carbide

Another cyclical player, Union Carbide Corporation, ran a deficit of $0.22 per share in 1991, down from profits of $2.19 per share in 1990 and $4.07 per share in 1989.

The basic chemical industry cycle may take a bit longer to play itself out. An oversupply of plant capacity will, in all likelihood, keep a lid on price increases. Earnings gains in the chemical business will be much harder to obtain than in other cyclical industries with tighter demand-supply relationships such as in the aluminum industry.

Despite tight market and pricing conditions for the foreseeable future, Union Carbide's restructuring and cost-cutting efforts will bring Union Carbide back into the profit side of the ledger in 1992 and help boost its earnings back above the $2 per share level by the end of 1993.

Part of the firm's restructuring involves the spin-off of its Industrial Gases division. (See Chap. 7, "Spin-Off Successes," for spinoff investment strategies.) That move leaves Union Carbide concentrating its efforts and resources in the basic chemicals industry segment. Other moves to streamline its operations and become more focused include the divestiture of nearly $500 million in nonmainline businesses.

News of the spinoff and divestitures combined with an improving economic scenario worked to push up Union Carbide's stock price from $17.50 per share in late 1991 to a high just below $29 per share by mid-1992.

The current excess industry capacity, and the chemical industry's track record of lagging the overall economy by six months on the average, means there's more time to stake out your claims in timely cyclical chemical industry stocks.

Union Carbide boasts of competitive advantages in its remaining core chemical businesses with advanced process technologies, efficient large-scale production facilities, and market leadership in key areas.

It's important to remember that not all cyclical industries and their stocks move in tandem. In addition, the action of the same industries and stocks will also vary from cycle to cycle due to changing industry conditions, the speed of each specific recovery, changes in the competitive playing field (higher foreign market penetration, etc.), and individ-

| BURLINGTON NO. NYSE-BNI | | | RECENT PRICE | 38 | P/E RATIO | 11.9 | (Trailing: 14.8 Median: 11.0) | RELATIVE P/E RATIO | 0.80 | DIV'D YLD | 3.2% | VALUE LINE | 285 |

TIMELINESS 3 Average (Relative Price Perform-ance Next 12 Mos.)

SAFETY 3 Average (Scale: 1 Highest to 5 Lowest)

BETA 1.10 (1.00 = Market)

1995-97 PROJECTIONS

	Price	Gain	Ann'l Total Return
High	90	(+135%)	26%
Low	60	(+60%)	15%

Insider Decisions

	S	O	N	D	J	F	M	A	M
to Buy	1	0	0	0	0	0	0	0	0
Options	0	1	0	1	0	3	1	0	4
to Sell	0	1	0	1	0	3	1	0	4

Institutional Decisions

	2Q'91	4Q'91	1Q'92
to Buy	85	123	110
to Sell	94	77	95
Hld's(000)	47623	58669	63752

High: 36.4 31.3 54.8 50.0 72.6 82.4 84.3 80.4 32.4 39.3 41.9 47.4
Low: 18.5 17.1 25.5 35.0 46.3 46.5 40.0 56.0 21.4 22.3 26.3 37.3

Target Price Range 1995 1996 1997

Relative Price Strength

Percent shares traded 9.0 / 6.0 / 3.0

Options: CBOE

Shaded areas indicate recessions

1976	1977	1978	1979	1980	1981	1982	1983	1984	1985	1986	1987	1988	1989	1990	1991	1992	1993	© VALUE LINE PUB., INC.	95-97
38.05	42.18	50.61	64.23	53.10	66.41	56.73	60.68	125.09	117.57	94.08	88.92	63.07	60.77	61.35	52.17	53.40	56.20	Revenues per sh A	72.20
3.08	3.29	4.10	5.30	4.32	5.20	4.02	8.91	13.43	14.52	11.39	11.98	7.57	7.28	7.46	5.86	7.30	8.45	"Cash Flow" per sh	12.15
1.42	1.44	2.13	3.28	3.78	3.51	2.28	5.40	7.15	8.03	3.41	4.93	2.76	3.19	2.89	2.12	3.20	4.20	Earnings per sh A B	6.40
.33	.40	.43	.49	.58	.77	.76	-1.12	1.10	1.45	1.55	2.05	2.20	1.20	1.20	1.20	1.20	1.20	Div'ds Decl'd per sh C	1.60
3.59	5.53	5.13	6.71	5.20	5.35	4.17	8.87	12.73	15.38	8.02	6.50	5.57	4.92	5.26	5.82	6.10	6.20	Cap'l Spending per sh	7.00
33.75	34.58	36.28	38.77	32.64	35.37	38.33	50.76	56.98	63.13	47.90	50.80	12.31	14.25	16.29	13.76	15.70	18.75	Book Value per sh	30.45
49.83	50.01	50.03	50.61	74.46	74.32	74.00	74.30	73.20	73.58	73.78	73.46	74.58	75.80	76.19	87.39	88.50	89.00	Common Shs Outst'g D	90.00
7.3	7.9	4.6	3.9	5.6	8.0	10.4	7.9	6.2	7.4	18.8	14.1	24.9	8.0	11.2	15.3	Bold figures are Value Line estimates		Avg Ann'l P/E Ratio	11.5
.93	1.03	.63	.56	.74	.97	1.15	.67	.58	.60	1.27	.94	2.07	.61	.83	.98			Relative P/E Ratio	.90
3.1%	3.5%	4.3%	3.9%	2.7%	2.7%	3.2%	2.6%	2.5%	2.4%	2.9%	3.0%	3.2%	4.7%	3.7%	3.7%			Avg Ann'l Div'd Yield	2.1%

						4197.6	4508.2	9156.3	8650.9	6941.4	6620.9	4699.5	4606.3	4674.0	4559.0	4725	5000	Revenues ($mill) A	6500
						9.7%	22.5%	20.7%	21.3%	20.5%	23.9%	22.1%	21.0%	20.1%	18.9%	21.0%	22.0%	Operating Margin	25.0%
						128.3	257.4	450.9	475.6	596.4	534.0	360.7	309.2	346.0	347.0	360	375	Depreciation ($mill) E	520
						178.0	413.3	608.1	658.3	277.4	369.3	207.2	243.0	222.0	165.0	285	375	Net Profit ($mill)	575
						22.3%	39.0%	45.8%	43.2%	44.8%	43.7%	41.5%	37.8%	37.6%	37.5%	37.5%	37.5%	Income Tax Rate	37.5%
						4.2%	9.2%	6.6%	7.6%	4.0%	5.6%	4.4%	5.3%	4.7%	3.6%	6.0%	7.5%	Net Profit Margin	8.9%
						568.1	46.3	d14.8	d222.9	d343.9	d399.4	d154.1	d491.0	d545.0	d717.0	d800	d650	Working Cap'l ($mill)	d150
						1333.3	2930.1	2453.9	3118.0	3393.8	3001.1	2722.6	2219.6	2083.0	1834.0	1675	1700	Long-Term Debt ($mill)	2350
						2941.3	4479.7	4868.3	5163.9	3596.1	3839.6	932.1	1093.8	1253.0	1213.0	1400	1680	Net Worth ($mill)	2750
						5.7%	6.5%	10.4%	9.8%	6.1%	7.6%	9.1%	11.1%	10.4%	9.5%	12.5%	13.0%	% Earned Total Cap'l	13.5%
						6.1%	9.2%	12.5%	12.7%	7.7%	9.6%	22.2%	22.2%	17.7%	13.6%	20.5%	22.5%	% Earned Net Worth	21.0%
						4.0%	8.5%	10.8%	10.7%	3.5%	5.8%	4.6%	12.4%	10.5%	5.8%	13.5%	16.0%	% Retained to Comm Eq	16.0%
						36%	22%	26%	25%	55%	41%	80%	45%	41%	58%	34%	29%	% All Div'ds to Net Prof	25%

BUSINESS: Burlington Northern, Inc., a holding company, owns the Burlington Northern Railroad, which operates about 25,000 miles of track connecting the Midwest, the Pacific Northwest, and the Gulf of Mexico. Also serves the Powder River Basin coal mines in Wyoming. Chief freights: coal, 33% of 1991 revenues; agricultural commodities, 16%; industrial products, 15%; intermodal, 15%; forestry, 10%; food and consumer products, 9%; auto, 2%. All non-rail assets (Burlington Resources) spun off to shareholders, 12/88. Depreciation rate: 3.9%. Has about 31,760 employees, 30,700 shareholders. Insiders own less than 1% of common stock. Chrmn., Pres. & C.E.O.: Gerald Grinstein. Inc.: Delaware. Address: 777 Main Street, Fort Worth, Texas 76102. Telephone: 817-878-2000.

Chart 6-1. Burlington Northern stock chart. (Copyright © 1992 by Value Line Publishing, Inc., used by permission. For subscription information to the Value Line Investment Survey, please call (800) 634-3583.)

ual company management efforts to improve productivity and efficiency.

In order to take advantage of cyclical investment opportunities, you must keep abreast of these fluctuating economic, industry, and company developments.

Case Study: Phillips Petroleum

An even more complicated cyclical investment scenario, the integrated petroleum industry remains battered by weak demand, excess capacity, near-record crude supplies, and a return to the market of higher Kuwaiti production as restoration efforts brings war-damaged wells back on stream.

In the midst of declining oil prices, Phillips Petroleum Company, based in Bartlesville, Oklahoma, initiated moves to make the firm more competitive and financially stronger. Sales of select assets helped to generate excess cash and shed nonessential businesses. In addition, the 1992 public offering of up to 51 percent of the company's gas gathering and processing subsidiary (GPM Gas Corporation), the largest domestic producer of natural gas liquids, will help unlock the value of that business segment while providing the oil company with a much stronger capital structure and lower interest expenses.

Cost-cutting efforts will trim some 1100 employees from the payroll, with savings estimated at around $150 million annually. On the operations front, a new 50-percent-owned Texas facility will add 1.5 billion pounds of ethylene and 600 million pounds of propylene capacity. Around 80 percent of the new facility's estimated production is already committed under long-term contracts.

Phillips's earnings fell from $3.13 per share in 1990 to $0.99 per share in 1991. While 1992 won't bring a lot of improvement, the future looks brighter as the economy moves toward a strong economic recovery in the mid-1990s.

During 1991, Phillips's shareholders experienced a decline in their investment of 4 percent, including reinvested dividends. However, for the five-year period 1987–1991, shareholders did much better, with a total return of 21 percent.

From a high of just above $31 per share in 1990, Phillips's stock price dropped to a low of around $22 per share in both 1991 and 1992.

To be sure, the oil industry still suffers from major demand-supply imbalances and thus depressed prices that threaten to keep stock prices from rising much higher in the near future. But for the cyclical investor with an eye to an eventual strong recovery, it's an opportune time to establish a position in the petroleum industry before other investors push up the stock price. In the meantime, sit back and enjoy the solid 4½ percent dividend yield.

Case Study: Worthington Industries

In the steel-related business, Worthington Industries, based in Columbus, Ohio, represents a classic cyclical play. Worthington's earnings record follows the ups and downs of the large economic cycle, increasing as the economy gathers steam and firms in many industries order processed steel and then retracting as the economy downshifts and companies cut back on material orders.

Operating from 28 manufacturing plants in the United States and Canada, Worthington stands to benefit from an improving economy as industrial producers beef up their production schedule. Signs of a turnaround in the economy showed up in its fiscal 1992 earnings ended May 31, 1992. Revenues increased to $974 million from $875 million a year earlier. Earnings followed suit. After declining from $1.05 per share in fiscal 1989 to $0.75 per share in fiscal 1991, earnings rose to $0.94 per share in fiscal 1992.

From a 1990 low stock price of $12⅝ per share in 1990, Worthington's common share rose to an all-time high of $26⅜ per share in early 1992.

With evidence of better times ahead for Worthington firmly in place, cyclical investors can still hop on the bandwagon and participate in the stock's potential upswing with anticipated future earnings gains. In fact, *Value Line Investment Survey* estimates Worthington could earn as much as $2.20 to $ 2.40 per share by 1995–1997.

Adding even more impetus to Worthington Industries' ability to outperform the market, the firm invested in new state-of-the-art processing equipment at its Porter, Indiana, steel plant, making it the most advanced steel pickling facility in the world.

Case Study: Magma Copper

Like Worthington Industries, Magma Copper, San Manuel, Arizona, has paid a lot of attention to cutting costs and improving efficiency. Primed for an economic recovery, Magma Copper stands ready to benefit from its streamlined operations at the largest and most modern copper smelting and refining complex in the nation.

Key ore deposits will keep its smelting operations humming with low-cost ore reserves. In addition to building solid operating facilities, Magma also worked to clean up its balance sheet and lower interest expenses with debt refinancing to eliminate high-cost debt.

Case Study: OEA

Expand your research beyond the industry giants. There are plenty of smaller niche companies with the ability to react faster to changing economic and industry conditions. For example, while the majority of investors and a myriad of analysts track the fortunes of General Motors, Ford, and Chrysler, other industry companies that supply the giants receive relatively little coverage. Your chances of scooping other investors on the Big 3 remain proportionally lower than if you concentrated your investigative skills on smaller companies.

For example, small Denver-based OEA, Inc. gets tracked mainly as a defense supplier due to its line of explosive propulsion devices for escape systems from military and commercial aircraft. However, OEA also serves the automotive industry as a leading manufacturer of air bag initiators. Despite cutbacks in defense and a sluggish automotive industry, OEA continues to post new revenues and earnings highs.

I first recommended OEA in a *Changing Times* article in June 1990. Since that time, OEA has increased revenues from $77 million to an estimated $95 million in 1992 in the face of military cutbacks. Earnings gains followed suit from 47 cents per share in 1990 to an estimated 70 cents per share in 1992 and 85 cents per share in 1993.

Another plus, OEA moved from the American Stock Exchange to the Big Board, thereby increasing its exposure to individual investors and institutions.

From a stock price of around $12 per share, adjusted for a 2-for-1 split in 1991 and a 3-for-2 split in 1992, OEA's stock price dropped below $8 per share on defense cut worries, creating buying opportunities for investors with the fortitude to hang in there. By the end of 1990, the stock price recovered to close above $13 per share. Since then, OEA's stock price hit a new high of $28 per share in 1991 and $37 per share in 1992 before losing ground to the $25 per share level in mid-1992.

With 75 percent of the air bag initiator market in both the United States and Japan, OEA figures to be a major beneficiary of the resurgence in the economy and auto sales. Demand for its air bag product is estimated to rise to 25 million units by 1996 from 4 million units in 1991.

On top of that, fears about OEA's defense business appear to have been overblown. Its aircraft ejection systems remain secure, and efforts to expand its commercial business lines are also gaining market acceptance.

While others jump on the bandwagon, look for overpricing situations, such as OEA's price rise to $37 per share. They represent opportunities to shed your holdings at significant capital gains plus the chance to short specific stocks for even more cyclical-based profits. If you feel comfortable with options, use their leverage to enhance your investment returns.

Of course, if bears start driving the cyclical stock price below its intrinsic value and the fundamentals remain solid, it may be time to reestablish your position.

Some Points to Keep in Mind about Cyclicals

Cyclicals aren't buy-and-hold investments. You must continually reassess the economic environment, industry trends, and company activities to keep on top of the game. Cyclicals offer superior returns for those investors willing to do their homework.

Cyclicals typically lead the market in economic recoveries as their depressed earnings begin to rebound. This usually lasts between a year and 18 months. Search for cyclical firms that will not only outperform the market during this period but also outperform other cyclical stocks due to actions taken by management to improve efficiency, cut costs, and expand market share.

Be alert for global raw material glut which could hamper the comeback efforts of certain cyclical industries and companies, such as was the case with chemicals and major equipment manufacturers in the eighties.

Other industry factors also come into play. Banks, while traditionally cyclical stocks, are coming out of a period of severe earnings depression following huge loan losses as well as undergoing a major industry consolidation. These factors will impact how and which banks will emerge from the economic recession best positioned to prosper in the years ahead.

In this light, emerging superregional banks, such as Bank One and Norwest, with the financial wherewithal to gain market share and enhance internal efficiencies, promise to outperform their industry counterparts.

There's plenty of opportunity to beat the market in the cyclical arena. Study the economic cycles, look for early signs of an economic turnaround, and investigate those companies that can deliver impressive earnings gains and much higher stock prices.

7

Spin-Off Successes

The Parts Perform Better Than the Whole

Why Companies Undertake Spin-Offs

Companies have been spinning off divisions, subsidiaries, and other corporate units for decades. But today a number of events combine to make spin-offs even more attractive to company management.

First of all, Congress's 1986 overhaul of the tax system eliminated the general utilities doctrine, which permitted companies to liquidate unwanted businesses for cash and avoid paying any taxes on the gain in appreciated value. This left the corporate spin-off as the only tax-free alternative for the shedding of assets that no longer fit into the firm's long-term strategic planning. Under the spin-off arrangement, companies distribute stock in the new corporate entity as a tax-free stock dividend to existing shareholders of the parent firm. The shareholders only incur and pay taxes after they sell their shares in the new entity, and the parent company avoids paying any tax whatsoever on the stock dividend.

The flurry of takeover activity in the late eighties also spurred many company managements to shed company assets via spin-offs in efforts to thwart unfriendly takeovers. While the pace of takeovers has slowed a bit since the eighties, companies continue to shed excess and nonvital assets to make themselves less susceptible to corporate raiders seeking undervalued assets.

Another external factor, the collapse of the "junk bond" market, contributed to making spin-offs more attractive. Firms could no longer attract buyers to pay inflated prices for company assets not considered crucial to the future direction of the firm.

Internal factors also came into play. By transferring debt related to the spun-off firm's operations, the parent company helped spruce up its own balance sheet while freeing up needed borrowing capacity. Another plus, if the parent company owned at least 80 percent of the subsidiary and included it in its consolidated financial return, the parent could have that subsidiary borrow funds and pay it a dividend, which would be totally tax-free under current tax legislation.

To qualify for the tax-free spin-off status, the corporation must distribute all its stock in the company or at least 80 percent of its ownership, and both the parent company and the spun-off business must have been in active existence for at least five years before the spin-off. In addition, the spun-off company could not have been purchased by the parent during that same five-year period.

Savvy individual investors can use the plight of companies divesting corporate assets to their own advantage. While some corporate "orphans," or spin-off companies, truly represent dogs that are being shed solely for the purpose of eliminating the drag they inflict upon overall corporate financial results, others reflect opportunities for investors to capitalize on the unrecognized value of the spun-off assets or the unrealized potential of the spun-off business once it has been unshackled by a less-than-enthusiastic or -supportive management team back at corporate headquarters.

To be sure, not all spin-off companies turn out to be success stories. But the world of corporate spin-offs is a fertile field, offering ample opportunities for huge capital gains for the investor willing to do some investigative work on his or her own.

Seeking Spin-Offs in Unlikely Places

"Spin-off investing just makes good, common sense. It ties in with my investment view as a contrarian searching for value where others fail to recognize it," says Charles W. Neuhauser, vice president with Investment Counselors of Maryland in Baltimore.

Neuhauser, who specializes in ferreting out special situations, maintains that the best investment opportunities are often found in the most unlikely and unpopular parts of the market.

"The big-name companies are picked over by a myriad of analysts and investors. After all, what investment advantage can you expect to uncover on a company already being followed by 15 other analysts? New stocks, such as spin-offs, represent new ground. There are no major brokerage houses doing research on spin-offs. Wall Street analysts just don't bother with these corporate cast-offs. It's time-consuming work and their time is more profitably spent producing research on companies that their institutional clients will pay for," says Neuhauser.

Spin-Offs and Initial Public Offerings

There's an important distinction between spin-offs and initial public offerings (IPOs). While both spin-offs and IPOs bring new stock to the public market, they arrive under completely opposite circumstances.

IPOs hit the scene with a lot of fanfare. Underwriters make extensive efforts to make sure investors know about the company, its business, management depth, etc. The required SEC red herring provides a lot of in-depth corporate information on the new firm. Investment bankers strive to get these documents into the hands of as many potential buyers as possible, well in advance of the offering date.

On the other hand, the poor, orphan spin-off has a hard time getting its story told. Typically, it's dumped on the market with little information, a paucity of publicity (usually only a brief press release or two), and little if any following. These conditions make the spin-off a perfect candidate for undervaluation and the perfect investment vehicle for exceptional profits.

"Spin-off companies don't enjoy the luxury of investment bankers singing their praises and beating the bushes to drum up investment interest. Likewise, the lack of institutional research hampers getting the real story out," says Neuhauser.

On top of that, information on the spin-off company's prior operating history and even its main lines of business often remains scarce since its financial results were buried in the parent's consolidated financial reporting. Documents relating to the soon-to-be-independent company are often only available upon special request to the SEC.

While the lack of information on and understanding of the firm's business causes the spin-off company to be ignored by most research analysts and major market players, that's exactly the reason individual investors can take advantage of the undervalued spin-off special situation.

Misconceptions and Realities Regarding Spin-Offs

In order to determine how spin-offs get undervalued in the first place, it's important to look at some of the misconceptions and realities about spin-offs and the real reasons companies spin off certain operations.

Too often, it's assumed that the only reason a parent company sheds an operation is that it's a real dog with little chance of improving earnings or that the new firm operates in a lackluster industry with little chance for growth. However, a bevy of valid reasons exist for casting off a spin-off company to shareholders which do not reflect poorly on the new firm or its ability to succeed or even flourish under its newly found independence.

As mentioned earlier, outside forces such as takeover threats, financial maneuverings, and tax considerations help convince management a spin-off might be in the best long-term interest of the parent company.

A number of other major factors impact the decision to spin off a company operation. Analysts tend to specialize in market niches or industries and have trouble valuing nonmainline assets. As a result, diversified companies fall victim to valuations that as a whole would be less than the separate valuations of the sum of the corporate parts.

The spin-off is one way management can unleash the value of those operations to shareholders by releasing them from the shadow of the corporate umbrella.

To illustrate, when Burlington Northern, whose principal business fortunes lie in its railroad operations, spun off its natural resources business as Burlington Resources in July 1988, management hoped that the market would more fairly value its resource assets. In effect, Burlington Northern's massive railroading operations overshadowed its resource assets, causing analysts to either vastly undervalue them or disregard their value altogether.

The strategy proved prophetic. Burlington Resources stock more than doubled its initial price of $25.50 per share before topping out at $53⅝ per share in late 1989. Market value of Burlington Resources surged nearly $5 billion, a clear indication of hidden value unlocked by the spin-off.

The strategy worked so well that Burlington Resources management announced a spin-off of its own, moving to shed its El Paso Natural Gas pipeline subsidiary in 1992. Shareholders received one share of the new company stock for every four shares of Burlington Resources stock owned. This spin-off contained a twist in that Burlington Resources first made a public offering of 14 percent (5 million) of the shares of the new company before distributing the remaining 86 percent of El Paso Natural Gas shares tax-free to shareholders. El Paso's shares were offered at $19 per share in the March 1992 public offering, rapidly rising above $22 per share.

Burlington Resources management cited several reasons for the spin-off. First of all, the spin-off would result in the removal of regulatory restrictions disadvantaging both the oil and gas exploration and production and interstate transportation of natural gas business units. It also offered investors pure plays on the distinct businesses and provided greater access to capital markets for each separate company.

Other spin-off reasons include cutting loose operations either too small or not closely aligned with the parent's major business and, of course, the desire to shed money-losing operations.

But don't give up on a spin-off just because it lost money under the corporate umbrella. The removal of headquarter's restrictions on capital, equipment, and human resources often allows the new company to flourish instead of flounder as it did under stifling corporate restraints. The newly gained entrepreneurial spirit of spin-off management teams can unleash actions needed to get the company moving again.

Spin-Offs Come in a Variety of Sizes

Barbara Goodstein, managing analyst of *The Spin-off Report*, explains that spin-offs come in all sizes (by market capitalization) ranging from, for example, large multibillion dollar companies splitting off $900-plus million subsidiaries (e.g, the Burlington Resources/El Paso Natural Gas spin-off), to companies separating smaller operating units (such as the November 1991 spin-off of $143 million Bio Whittaker from the Whittaker Corporation), to companies spinning off early-stage technologies. *The Spin-off Report* is published by an independent research firm that provides continuous coverage of all spin-offs in progress and issues research reports, valuations, and investment recommendations on individual subsidiaries about to be divested as new publicly traded companies.

"The smaller [$100 million–$200 million market capitalization] spin-offs have traditionally been underfollowed by Wall Street during the early stages of independence. The absence of rigorous coverage by `the Street' results in inefficient pricing of the shares of the spin-offs, and the inefficiency, consequently, provides significant investment opportunity," asserts Goodstein.

It can take up to one year from the time the parent company announces the proposed spin-off to the time the subsidiary's shares are distributed. On occasion, an announced spin-off may not materialize. Not many analysts and institutional research companies are willing to spend time tracking something that may or may not happen. As a result, for many spin-offs, there's a scarcity of information and in-depth analysis.

This lack of information, combined with the downside price pressure created by institutional investors who find themselves stuck with unwanted shares of a company that does not fit into their investment parameters, makes investing in spin-offs a profitable occupation for the patient investor. There's plenty of research to back up the claim that spin-offs significantly outperform the market during the first three years of trading.

Research on Spin-Offs

Most recently, separate studies at both the Smeal College of Business Administration at the Pennsylvania State University and the Graduate School of Business at the University of Texas concluded that spin-offs deliver higher-than-normal investment returns.

In the University of Texas study, Keith C. Brown, associate professor of finance, and Van Harlow, a vice president with Fidelity Management Trust Company in Boston, used a sample of 74 spin-off events covering a 10-year span beginning in January 1980.

The Brown and Harlow research tested the hypothesis that the need for institutional investors to rebalance their portfolios by liquidating newly created corporate spin-off shares generates a substantial, but temporary, selling pressure in these spin-off securities.

Pressure on institutional investors to sell their spin-off shares derives from several factors. Most importantly, the new shares may not meet the investment policy of the bank trust department, insurance company, mutual fund, pension fund, or other institutional investor in regard to industry exposure, liquidity, or credit constraints. In reality, the investment manager may not have any choice but to sell the newly acquired spin-off shares, without regard to investment potential, in order to resolve any violation of investment policies.

In other words, factors completely external to the spin-off itself and the future prospects of the spin-off company can contribute to negative price pressure. In fact, a study by Seifert and Rubin (1989) documented that newly created spin-off shares experienced abnormal losses by as much as 10 percent in the first several months following their initial trade.

Brown and Harlow's data clearly illustrate that indeed there exists an observable tendency for institutional investors to reduce their spin-off holdings substantially after a restructuring. For a sizable number of spin-off firms, this reduction leads to a significant, seller-induced price-pressure effect that is largely temporary. In addition, the size of the initial price decline and the size of the subsequent rebound were both significantly related to the extent to which institutional investors liquidated their spin-off positions.

Finally, Brown and Harlow found that the tendency for institutions to sell their spin-off shares could be explained to some extent by investment constraints that could be observed in advance, the most notable being the presence of the parent firm in the S&P 500 index (See Chart 7-1).

In the Penn State research, Patrick J. Cusatis, James A. Miles, and J. Randall Woolridge evaluated the investment performance of a sample of 146 spin-offs covering 27 industries over the 1965–1988 time frame. Since spin-offs represent new corporate entities and are analogous to IPOs in terms of newly traded stock in the marketplace, the Penn State study compared their performance with that of IPOs over the same period.

While prior research by others (Ibbotson, Sindelar, and Ritter, 1989) illustrates that investors in IPOs earn, on average, superior returns on the day that IPOs come to market, still other research (Aggarwal and Rivoli, 1990, and Ritter, 1991) concludes that investors who purchase at the close of the first day of trading in the IPOs' shares and hold for up to three years achieve negative abnormal returns.

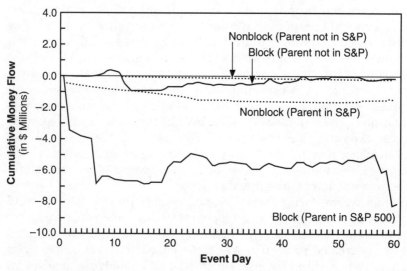

Chart 7-1. Parent in S&P 500. (*Source: Brown & Harlow Study, University of Texas, Austin, Texas*)

The conjecture is that investors overvalue IPOs in initial trading and that their market price adjusts over time to their intrinsic value, thereby creating the long-term negative returns.

On the other hand, unlike the overenthusiastic reception of highly touted IPOs, the merits of the typical newly launched spin-off company get pushed aside as institutional selling puts substantial negative pressure on the firm's stock price.

As seen earlier, much of the selling pressure has little to do with the intrinsic value and potential of the spin-off firm, stemming instead from unrelated internal institutional investment policies.

Not surprisingly, the Cusatis, Miles, and Woolridge research found that initial returns for spin-offs proved to be primarily negative. But long-term performance analysis indicated that spin-offs provide superior return to investors.

Comparing spin-offs with IPOs on a matched-firm-adjusted basis, the Penn State study found an average raw buy-and-hold return in excess of 74 percent for spin-offs over the first three years. Spin-offs outperformed firms matched by industry and capitalization by 30 percent over this three-year period. The most favorable performance typically occurs between years one and two following the spin-off.

Cusatis, Miles, and Woolridge cite a number of reasons for the significantly better performance of spin-offs over IPOs. First of all, as indicated earlier, IPO prices need to adjust downward after the initial upward spurt. Second, as time goes on, the organizational changes usually associated with spin-offs start to induce superior operating performance, Third, the improved operating results get recognized by the market, resulting in higher demand for the shares and higher share prices. Finally, a number of spin-offs attract takeover bids from suitors who recognize their undervalued situation.

Along with the superior returns garnered by the spin-off companies, the Penn State study found that the spin-offs' parent firms earned in excess of 60 percent raw buy-and-hold returns over the three years following the spin-offs, significantly outearning market returns for the same period. Again, as in the case of the spin-offs themselves, a high incidence of takeover activity contributed to the parent company's higher-than-market returns.

Cusatis, Miles, and Woolridge conclude their report by stating that it is unclear why investors incorrectly price both IPOs and spin-offs. While research and debate on those reasons will undoubtedly continue for decades, it is precisely that irrational behavior of market forces that spells opportunity for the investor willing to investigate and ferret out attractive spin-off companies poised to capitalize on rejuvenated management unshackled by the home office.

York International: A Successful Spin-Off

"It's an open field. Analysts don't cover these companies. If everybody followed them, there would be no hidden values to uncover. That's why I find these corporate cast-offs an attractive investment alternative with unique opportunities for substantial gains," says Investment Counselors of Maryland's Neuhauser.

Neuhauser cites the Borg-Warner 1986 spin-off of York International (in York, Pennsylvania) as a classic example of a successful spin-off.

At the time, York International was a wholly owned subsidiary of Borg-Warner Corporation as well as one of the world's largest suppliers of air conditioning, heating, and related equipment, serving the large building, shipbuilding, and industrial process markets.

In the three years before the spin-off, the York International subsidiary produced net proforma losses totaling nearly $13 million. York's operations were negatively impacted by a number of factors including increased global competition; reduced domestic margins resulting from increased competition and higher production costs; declining sales in the Middle East market affected by lower petroleum-related revenues for countries in that region; and the relative strengthening of the U.S. dollar, making York International products less competitive in international markets.

On the plus side, in the years before the spin-off Borg-Warner invested nearly $50 million in capital improvements geared to improving York International's production efficiency. Most notable, a flexible machining system and plasma arc flame cut system promised to cut operating costs and make the firm more competitive.

In addition, efforts to cut inventories and outstanding accounts receivable benefited the firm's working capital, improving its current ratio to an enviable 2 to 1.

The company also enjoyed a good reputation for quality products and excellent service, a solid base from which to build additional revenues and profits.

Another plus, unlike a number of other spin-off parents, Borg-Warner did not load York International up with tons of debt. In fact, long-term debt totaled a paltry $31 million, only about 15 percent of overall capital.

Borg-Warner originally acquired York Corporation back in 1956. Over the years, Borg-Warner operated two separate air-conditioning operations before combining them in 1983.

"It was a case where the subsidiary no longer fit into the long-range strategic plans of the parent company," says Neuhauser.

The spin-off took place in April 1986 with Borg-Warner shareholders receiving 1 share of York International common stock for each 10 shares of Borg-Warner common stock owned on the record date. York International directors and executive officers ended up with approximately 19 percent of the outstanding common stock shares upon the distribution.

That's always a good sign to look for in spin-offs. The more direct financial interest by directors and top management there is, the more likely they will work harder to ensure the spin-off's success. After all, their own money is at stake.

To make a long story short, the spin-off shares of York International initially traded around $14.38 per share. Company revenues increased to $963 million in 1987 from $637 million in 1985. More importantly, management took the company from a loss position in 1985 to earnings of $27.6 million, or $2.82 per share, for 1987, and 1988 looked even more promising with six-month earnings reported at $24.3 million, or $2.27 per share.

At this time, Citibank and others started engineering a leveraged buy-out which took place near year-end 1988 at $57.50 per share for a total capitalization around $760 million.

Borg-Warner shareholders who kept their York International stock and savvy investors who purchased York International common stock shortly after the spin-off saw their investment more than triple in less than three years.

But that's not the end of the story. In October 1991 York International went public, again offering 12,065,000 shares at $23 per share. Then in March 1992, the company sold another 5,040,000 shares to the public at $31.75 per share. Pro forma 1991 financial statements show York International earning $50 million, or $1.36 per share, on revenues of $1.7 billion. (See Chart 7-2.)

"It's been a win-win situation for everybody involved. Today, the firm's capitalization stands approximately twice what it was in 1986 when Borg-Warner spun off the operation," says Dean T. DuCray, vice president and chief financial officer for York International.

Intelogic Trace: A Less-Than-Successful Spin-Off

Obviously, not every spin-off works to the advantage of investors. Some truly are dogs shed by the parent company, while others come loaded with debt and inherent operating problems that promise to hamper earnings potential for years.

Take the case of Intelogic Trace, for example. Spun off from

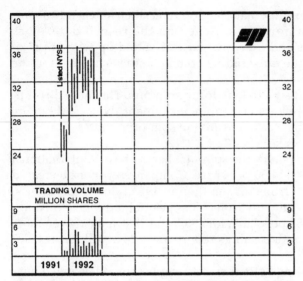

Chart 7-2. York International stock chart. (*Reprinted by permission of Standard & Poor's Corporation*)

Datapoint's domestic computer customer service division in 1985, Intelogic suffered from a rapid decline in its user base and unsuccessful efforts to penetrate the IBM computer service segment. From earnings of $0.56 per share in 1987, Intelogic dropped into the red to the tune of $2.15 cents per share in fiscal 1990 and another $1.59 per share in fiscal 1991.

From a high of $18⅛ per share in 1986, the computer maintenance firm's common stock plummeted below $1 per share by 1990 and has not risen above $1 per share since.

You Need to Continually Assess What's Happening

As you would any investment, you need to thoroughly investigate and understand the risk and reward potential of spin-off companies. Furthermore, should you be fortunate enough to single out a successful spin-off candidate and ride the stock price upward, your analysis doesn't stop there. You need to constantly review that investment for fundamental changes in the company and its industry's future prospects.

Ask yourself the following questions: Has competition made inroads into the firm's market share? Have technological advancements made the major product or service less desirable? Have profit margins eroded with competition and higher raw material costs? Is management making the appropriate capital investments to ensure that its operations are on the industry's cutting edge? Is the firm's financial position secure with ample cash and credit facilities in place, or is it getting debt-heavy? Etc.

Unless you have already sold out your stock position, it's wise to keep a pulse on the company's vital signs and outside factors that can impact its performance.

A. P. Green Industries

To illustrate how changing circumstances can take its toll on an attractive spin-off company, let's take a look at the fortunes of A. P. Green Industries, a Mexico, Missouri, manufacturer of refractory products used to line high-temperature equipment such as boilers, furnaces, incinerators, and kilns.

Originally purchased by USG Corporation in 1967, A. P. Green was later spun off to USG shareholders in February 1988. The new company also came away with seasoned industry management talent including its CEO, Harry M. Stover, who had retired as vice chairman from USG shortly before the spin-off. During Stover's tenure with USG, he once headed the A. P. Green operations.

A. P. Green was one of the top half-dozen firms in a 200-company industry serving the mature $1.6 billion refractory market. It had pioneered many new refractory products as well as developed new distribution and production methods over the years. Its lime subsidiary also prepares lime for use in road construction and process industries such as paper manufacturing.

Stover and his management team immediately took decisive action to improve A. P. Green's earnings by eliminating nearly 90 marginal products and adding 25 new refractory products, by trimming unneeded production capacity, and by slashing overhead by a whopping 30 percent.

The firm also took steps to improve its international competitive position and expand its product line with the United Kingdom acquisition of Detrick Refractory Fibers. In other words, A. P. Green was making all the appropriate moves toward higher profitability.

Boosted by higher capacity utilization rates at key customers, A. P. Green's strategies started to pay off and big. From a net income of $2.1 million on revenues of $174.3 million in 1987, A. P. Green's earnings surged 307 percent to $8.6 million, or $3.29 per share, on a 9 percent revenue increase to $191.4 million. The momentum also carried over into 1989 when the refractory company earned $2.94 per share.

Of course, by now the market had started to take notice. In mid-1988, the stock traded around the $25 per share level, about a 25 percent discount to book value and less than seven times its estimated 1989 earnings of $3.60 per share. By the end of 1989, investor demand drove the stock to a high of $40 per share.

The A. P. Green spin-off story proved to be a great success. Earnings rose substantially over pre-spin-off days, and investors in the spin-off company had a right to be proud of their financial prowess and stock profits. An investment in mid-1988 at $25 per share would have yielded a better than 60 percent return, including the reinstated dividend of 10 cents quarterly, if you were foresighted enough to sell at the $40 per share peak price.

That's where your continual assessment of investments comes in to play. A review of the refractory industry and the customers it serves would have shown that the oncoming recession would have disastrous implications for A. P. Green and other industry companies.

In fact, with the slowdown in the global economy, A. P. Green's earnings sunk like one of its refractory bricks to 4 cents per share in 1990. It got worse in 1991, with the company losing money. Likewise, its common stock stumbled, closing out 1991 at $13¼ per share, down nearly 70 percent from its $40 per share high.

Investing is not a static activity. It takes time, patience, and endurance. This holds especially true in the unique world of spin-off investing. You worked hard to sift through the dozens of spin-off companies to uncover those with the best potential for both rising financial results and higher stock prices. Don't give up your hard-earned gains by failing to recognize when to sell your spin-off investments.

Investing in Spin-Offs

How do you get started in spin-off investments? First of all, you must be aware of upcoming spin-offs. The *Wall Street Journal* routinely covers most, if not all, proposed spin-offs in its daily dividend announcement section. Likewise, *Investor's Business Daily* and other financial publications regularly report on proposed spin-offs.

Once you're on the spin-off trail, one of the best sources of information on spin-off companies is the parent company of the proposed spin-off. Contact the firm's financial or legal department and request a copy of the SEC Required Information Statement, SEC Form 10, which includes a five-year history of the newly created company. Then find a comfortable chair and get prepared to wade through some 100-plus pages of data, a great deal of it stultifying, boring, legal verbiage.

Also request copies of the parent company's annual reports and SEC Form 10Ks for the past three years as well as news releases pertaining to the spin-off.

All this information will provide you with a solid foundation for your spin-off analysis. It includes data on the spin-off company's main lines of business, business history, business properties, affiliated companies, competition, depth of management experience, amount of director and executive participation in company ownership, debt structure, liquidity, and capital resources, along with factors impacting operating results and company outlook.

"You have to be eagle-eyed, looking for those items that spell opportunity," says Neuhauser.

Look for advantages that can give the spin-off company an edge over industry competitors. Does it possess patents or trademarks? Does its market niche allow it to command higher-than-normal prices and margins? Do high entry costs prevent additional competition from entering the industry picture in the future? Does it have the financial wherewithal to capitalize on the industry's consolidation through strategic acquisitions and/or aggressive marketing actions to capture additional market share?

Are capital expenditures keeping the company's equipment and production processes state-of-the-art? Are research and development expenses geared to the development of new products? Does the firm's future depend on a few major customers or government contracts susceptible to the budget-cutting process? How do current backlogs compare with previous years' backlogs? Is the trend upward or downward?

Does the company have alternative raw material sources to alleviate interruptions in raw material supplies or significant rises in raw material prices? How will cyclical economic forces impact future operations and profitability?

What has been the firm's history of labor relations? Is the company unionized? What is the recent strike history? Will the company be able to implement cost-cutting strategies without incurring extended and costly work interruptions?

Does management possess the industry knowledge and expertise to make the right decisions? Is this the same management that produced the lackluster performance in past years, or has there been an infusion of new blood and corporate restructuring to improve operations?

Take a good, hard look at the financial statements. Have revenues and margins held steady, or are competition and higher costs taking their toll on profitability? Will the firm generate adequate cashflow to fund needed capital expenditures, research and development, and market expansion?

Is the company debt-heavy? Will debt servicing cause a cash crunch if planned revenues fail to materialize? How secure are the company's lines of credit. When do they expire, and how do their rates compare with the current interest environment? After all, the rates lenders charge reflect the degree of confidence they have in the company's ability to repay the amounts borrowed.

Review the reasons behind extraordinary charges or credits to company financial results. Are they likely to happen again in the future? Do they promise to improve or hinder future financial performance?

How successful has the company assimilated past acquisitions? Have the acquisitions gone smoothly, or has the company had to charge write-offs for past acquisitions gone awry?

Evaluate how external forces can impact the spin-off company's operations. Will the firm take on significant legal liabilities as the result of the spin-off? Can environmental actions or a change in government regulations impact the firm's cost structure or ability to remain a competitive force in the industry?

It's also a good idea to get a handle on the competition and industry trends. Request copies of the annual reports and Form 10Ks from major competitors. How does their financial performance in terms of revenues, costs of goods sold, administrative and selling overhead, margins, and net income compare with that of the spin-off company? What differences are there in capital structure and debt load, and how will that affect the spin-off company's competitive position?

Read both managements' discussions of operating results and their perspectives of major trends in their industry carefully. Are they similar or on opposite ends of the spectrum? Investigate reasons for the differences. Also take a look at their strategies. Ask yourself: Why the differences and can they be explained rationally?

For independent appraisals of industry trends, read industry trade magazines as well as investment analysis reports on specific industries and companies found in financial reference sources such as *Value Line* and Standard & Poor's *The Outlook*. General-interest business magazines such as *Business Week, Forbes, Fortune,* and *Industry Week* routinely cover industry trends and what's happening to companies in those industries.

In other words, keep yourself well-informed on factors that can affect your spin-off company and its chances of success. Ask yourself tough questions and find out the answers before you invest in the spin-off. Remember, sometimes the best investment decision is the decision not to invest, thereby protecting your capital from erosion due to a costly mistake.

Goodstein on Spin-Offs

"You need not be pressured into making a spin-off investment decision. There's plenty of time to make a thorough review and analysis before committing your funds. It usually takes several months to a year or more from the time of the initial spin-off announcement until the deal gets finalized," says Barbara Goodstein. As noted earlier, Goodstein is managing analyst of *The Spin-off Report* in New York City. *The Spin-off Report*, published by Hunstrete Corporation, probably offers the most in-depth coverage of spin-off opportunities, and Hunstrete is the only firm on Wall Street to focus exclusively on spin-off investing. (Hunstrete Corporation can be contacted at 55 Liberty Street, Suite 9B, New York, New York 10005, 212-233-0100.)

Approximately once per month, Goodstein publishes a comprehensive report on a new spin-off opportunity. Valuation techniques used include discounted cashflow, earnings per share, and asset value analysis.

On top of that, Goodstein also publishes a monthly *Spin-off Calendar* that tracks the progress of spin-offs from announcement date until well after the new public company begins to trade. According to Goodstein, the *Spin-off Calendar* represents the only spin-off product of its kind in the investment community. (See Chart 7-3.)

Goodstein reports that the rate of announced corporate spin-offs has increased to three times the historical norm in the first half of 1992. Since 1978, the percentage of companies with only one business segment has risen to 54.3 percent from 35.6 percent.

Fisher-Price

"The Fisher-Price spin-off by Quaker Oats Company in June 1991 represented a spin-off that promised to benefit both the spun-off toy company and the parent firm," says Goodstein.

The Spin-off Report, at the time of the divestiture, predicted a strong turnaround for Fisher-Price after disappointing results in both 1990 and 1991 with losses exceeding $2.50 per share each year, its first losses since the early 1930s during the Great Depression. The new spin-off company has plenty going for it. It boasts of one of the most recognizable brand names in the world. Its infant/juvenile/preschool toy lines dominate both the U.S. and Canadian markets as well as command number one or number 2 market shares in European markets.

THE SPIN-OFF CALENDAR

Continuous Coverage of All Newly Announced Spin-offs and Spin-offs In Progress

Barbara Goodstein (212) 233 - 0100
Darren M. Bagwell   (212) 233 - 0150

JULY 1992

PARENT/ SPIN-OFF	STATUS	DESCRIPTION
ADOLPH COORS COMPANY	**ANNOUNCEMENT DATE:** 5/14/92	**COORS BREWING COMPANY,** Adolph Coors' largest subsidiary and the only business that will remain with the parent, is the third largest brewer in the U.S. with net sales of $1.53 billion in 1991. The Coors line of malt beverages includes a range of high quality premium and lower priced beers, as well as non-alcoholic beverages which are marketed nationwide through over 600 independent distributors and eight subsidiary-owned distributors.
(NASDAQ - ACCOB)	**SPIN-OFF DATE:** Targeted for late 1992.	
Price (7/1/92): $19 5/8		
Pre-Announcement (5/13/92):	**TAX STATUS:** The company will file a request with the IRS for a tax-free ruling.	
Price: $18 3/8		
S&P 500: 416.45		
52 Week Range: $23 5/8 - $17	**SPIN-OFF RATIO:** Undetermined.	**AC TECHNOLOGIES** will include all of the parent's technology companies:
Div/Yld: $0.50/2.5%		Coors Ceramics Company is the largest U.S. manufacturer of advanced ceramics for diversified industrial applications. Sales and operating income in 1991 were $180.1 million and $1.98 million, respectively. In June, the division signed a cooperative R&D agreement with National Renewable Energy Laboratory to experiment with the use of NREL's solar-powered furnace in the production of CCC's silicon carbide powder in an attempt to lower production costs.
1991 Revenues: $1.92 billion	**PREREQUISITES:** Spin-off is contingent on final approval by the board, and a tax-free ruling from the IRS.	
1991 Earnings: $25.5 million		
1991 EPS: $0.68		
Shares Out: 37.5 million (includes 1.26 mil closely held "A" shrs.)	**SEC APPROVAL:** Plans for filing information documents have not yet been disclosed.	Golden Aluminum Company uses a patented technology to manufacture aluminum for the rigid packaging industry. Sales and oper. income in 1991 were $196 million and $6.35 million, respectively.
Market Cap: $736 million		Graphic Packaging Corporation produces high performance folding carton and flexible packaging for major manufacturers - 1991 sales and oper. income were $188.1 million and $17.2 million, respectively.
AC TECHNOLOGIES CO.		Various developmental companies, including ventures in biotechnology, advanced electronic modules, and other emerging technologies, have significant commercial potential. Although 1991 sales were $111.3 million, operating losses incurred by these developing entities totaled $44.2 million.
(Exchange/Symbol-Unassigned)		
		PURPOSE OF THE SPIN-OFF: The immediate effect of the separation of the non-brewing businesses will be to eliminate their current drag on the parent's bottom line. Preliminary data indicate significant growth potential for AC Technologies, which, as an independent entity, will be better able to raise the capital required for the growth and development of its promising businesses.

PARENT/ SPIN-OFF

BAXTER INTERNATIONAL

(NYSE - BAX)
Price (7/1/92): $35 7/8
Pre-Announcement (4/23/92):
  Price: $36
  S&P 500: 409.02
52 Wk. Range: $40 7/8-$31 1/2
Div/Yld: Nil
1991 Revenues: $8.92 billion
1991 Earnings: $591 million
1991 EPS: $2.03
Shares Out: 279.4 million
Market Cap: $10.02 billion

CAREMARK INC.

(Exchange/Symbol - Unassigned)

STATUS

ANNOUNCEMENT DATE: On 4/24/92, BAX announced its intention to explore various methods of divestiture. On 6/12/92, the company's Board approved the spin-off of "new" Caremark's shares to shareholders of the parent company.

SPIN-OFF DATE: Targeted for year end 1992.

TAX STATUS: Expected to be tax-free.

SPIN-OFF RATIO: Not yet determined.

DESCRIPTION

BAXTER INTERNATIONAL is the leading worldwide manufacturer and marketer of health-care products, systems and services for hospitals, clinical and medical research laboratories, blood and dialysis centers, rehabilitation centers, nursing homes, patient-at-home laboratories, doctors offices and manufacturing facilities. The company offers more than 120,000 products to health-care providers in 100 countries.

CAREMARK INC., will include the former Caremark Inc. unit, the Orthopedic Services Division, the Prescription Service Division, and two managed care facilities in Puerto Rico. The company will be a market leader in providing Alternative Site Health Care including products and services for home health care, infusion therapy, physical therapy, AIDS care, women's health care and prescription services. Revenues for these divisions increased by 25% in 1991 to approximately $1.2 billion and have been growing more than 20% per year for the last four years.

ONE PURPOSE OF THE SPIN-OFF is to eliminate the perceived conflicts of interest that BAX, in its current configuration, experiences when, through its alternate site health care facilities, it provides services that take patients away from the hospitals which are its largest medical supply customers.

It is expected that, as a separate entity, the faster growing alternate site businesses will be valued at a higher multiple than the parent. In 1991, the spin-off's net sales growth was over three times that of Baxter's remaining businesses.

The market has shrugged off the impending structural changes, no doubt due in part to concerns stemming from both (1) adverse publicity associated with quality of service and pricing in the home infusion therapy industry as a whole and (2) pricing pressure exerted by major insurers who insist that they pay less for the services. Caremark's home infusion therapy unit's market share approaches 25 - 30% of the rapidly expanding $3 billion business.

Chart 7-3.

125

Seasoned industry management with turnaround experience came on board with the hiring of Ronald J. Jackson as president and chief executive officer. Back in the mid-eighties, Jackson engineered a successful turnaround as president and chief executive officer of Kenner Parker Toys, a spin-off from General Mills.

Jackson's first decision lay in getting rid of the new promotional toy line initiated by previous management, an ill-advised diversification strategy that diverted valuable corporate human and financial resources away from Fisher-Price's main product lines and bread-winners. Over $114 million in charges from inventory and accounts receivable write-offs, plant consolidations, and employee terminations helped clear the financial decks for clear sailing ahead.

Quaker Oats shareholders, as of July 8, 1991, received one share of Fisher-Price common stock for every five shares of parent common stock they owned.

"Fisher-Price began its new corporate life with a markedly reduced cost structure, a competitive debt position, improved operating efficiency, and a renewed emphasis on its dominant product lines. We expected a strong recovery with Fisher-Price returning to its historic profitability with gross margins of 40 percent to 42 percent and net earnings in the $1.20 per share to $1.60 per share range by fiscal year 1993," said *The Spin-off Report.*

Before the spin-off, *The Spin-off Report* indicated that Fisher-Price could certainly become a takeover target in the consolidating toy industry. In fact, Mattel expressed an early interest in the Fisher-Price operations and signed an 18-month stand-still agreement even before the spin-off took place. In June 1991, *The Spin-off Report* estimated Fisher-Price's private market valuation in the case of a takeover at $30 per share.

Fisher-Price stock initially came to market at $25 per share and has since hit a 52-week low of $22 per share and a high of $40¾ per share, already exceeding its anticipated takeover price. The higher stock prices came on the heels of healthier earnings than originally anticipated. For example, for the first six months of fiscal year 1992, Fisher-Price earned 80 cents per share, considerably higher than street estimates.

On the parent side of the coin, earnings per share in 1991 for Quaker Oats rose to $2.65 per share from $2.15 per share a year earlier, and 1992 looked even better. As Quaker Oats chairman, president, and chief executive officer, William D. Smithburg, stated in the company's 1991 annual report, "With the successful spin-off of Fisher-Price, Quaker is now focused solely on grocery products for the first time in over 20 years." It has been a win-win situation for both Quaker Oats and Fisher-Price.

Selling Short

On the other side of the coin, spin-off analysis can present opportunities for uncovering prime candidates for shorting if the market initially overprices a particular company's prospects.

Although the classic spin-off presents investment opportunities for investors interested in long-term growth, as the Fisher-Price example illustrates, the market performance of the typical spin-off also provides opportunity for short-term traders, "short" traders, and value players, as well.

Shortly after trading in the new public spin-off company begins, often a significant price depression occurs due to indiscriminate selling by institutional investors. The selling pressure, unrelated to fundamentals of the spun-off companies, arises when institutional investors find themselves recipients of spin-off shares that do not fit the investment parameters of their portfolios.

For example, index funds that own the parent company must sell the spin-off if it will not, like the parent, be included in the index. Pension funds, which generally are allowed to hold only dividend-paying stocks, must sell the spin-off if it will not, like the parent, pay a dividend. If the business of the spin-off is very different from that of the parent company, portfolio managers unfamiliar with the industry of the spin-off company will simply dump the newly acquired shares.

Bio Whittaker

The spin-off of Bio Whittaker, a company that sells medical research supplies, diagnostic test kits, and endotoxin kits, from parent Whittaker Corporation, a defense industry firm, serves as a case in point. The company opened when-issued trading at $13½ per share on November 8, 1991. During the month that followed, the spin-off's stock price was beaten down to $7½ per share, a 44 percent drop.

Short sellers (investors who believe that a company's shares will decline, and go out and borrow shares in order to sell, pocket the short sale proceeds while waiting for the price decline, buy the shares back at the lower price, return the borrowed shares, and profit from the drop in prices), counting on selling by portfolio managers who had originally purchased shares in a business 85 percent concentrated in defense and didn't want to own a stock that had "bio" in its title, earned handsome profits.

At the same time, value investors (those who seek to invest in good quality companies that are undervalued by the market for one reason or other) had the opportunity to buy the anticipated growth of the spin-off at bargain-basement price levels, relatively speaking. Three months after the stock hit its low of $7½ per share, the stock was once again trading above $13 per share.

GFC Financial Corporation

Another close follower of corporate spin-offs, Bradley E. Turner, senior vice president with McDonald & Company Securities, Inc., in Cleveland, Ohio, views the Dial Corporation's spin-off of its financial business, GFC Financial Corporation, as benefiting both entities.

"Dial management believes the price-earnings ratio accorded to financial-oriented stocks is far less than that of consumer products stocks. In addition, research analysts tend to specialize in investment niches, and diverse companies with unrelated businesses find it difficult to attract sponsorship in the research and investment community. The spin-off provides management an opportunity to unlock the undervalued portions of firms like Dial and enhance shareholder value," says Turner.

In March 1992, Dial shareholders received one share of spin-off stock for every two shares of parent stock owned. Restructuring moves before the spin-off promised to deliver an improvement in profits of 50 cents per share for the parent company and a boost of 20 cents per share for the spin-off company.

Other efforts taken before the spin-off helped put GFC Financial on more solid footing. Nonperforming loans were sharply reduced to just over 3 percent of assets, versus an industry average of 6 percent. The company's efforts were rewarded with upgrades from the financial rating agencies, helping to minimize the costs of funds.

GFC Financial's net income for 1991 totaled nearly $30 million, a better than 9 percent improvement over 1990 results. To be sure, GFC Financial still faced a tough competitive environment and difficult economic conditions in the commercial lending and mortgage insurance arenas.

While the long-term effects of the spin-off for Dial, GFC, and their respective shareholders remain to be seen, the strategy to increase shareholder value is well in place.

Your Turn

Spin-offs offer unique investment opportunities. In your analysis of new spin-offs, don't ignore the enhanced profit potential and potentially higher stock prices of the parent company. As indicated by McDonald's Turner and others, too diverse companies often suffer from lack of coverage or a substantial undervaluation of specific parts of their operations. With a more focused corporate strategy, the market could place a more realistic value on the parent's common stock as well.

Reviewing past spin-off performance can prove helpful in ferreting out lucrative spin-off investment opportunities (both spin-off and parent) in the future. Use the spin-off listing in Table 7-1 to develop and fine-tune your own spin-off investment strategy.

Request copies of past annual reports and 10Ks to use in your analysis. Evaluate what went right or what went wrong with each spin-off and the subsequent market reaction. Good luck.

Table 7-1. Spin-Offs

Parent/Spin-off	Spin-off business
Ametek/Ketema	Diversified industries
Borg-Warner/York International	Air conditioning
Burlington Northern/Burlington Resources	Natural resources
Burlington Resources/El Paso Natural Gas	Oil and gas
Castle & Cooke/Dole	Processed foods
Community Psychiatric Centers/Vivra	Home health care
Datapoint/Intelogic Trace	Computer services
Dial/GFC Financial	Financial services
Dresser Industries/NEWCO	Industrial and mining equipment
Ethyl/Tredegar	Aluminum, plastics, energy
First Illinois/Mercury Finance	Consumer finance
First Mississippi/FirstMiss Gold	Gold mining and exploration
Henley/Fisher Scientific	Scientific products
Household International/Eljer	Building products
Lucky Stores/Hancock Fabrics	Fabric stores
Quaker Oats/Fisher-Price	Toys
RLC Corp/Matlack	Bulk trucking
SmithKline/Allergan	Eye care
Teledyne/United Insurance	Insurance
Thiokol/Morton International	Chemicals
Universal/Lawyer's Title	Title insurance
USG/A. P. Green	Refractory products
Whittaker/BioWhittaker	Biotechnology
Zayre/Waban	Merchandise warehouse

8
Defensive Stocks

Finding Stocks to Own
When the Market Heads South

As the stock market and economy go through their cycles from boom to bust, it's extremely important to shift your portfolio mix from growth companies to companies and industries with good track records in recessionary times. In many cases, defensive stocks perform well during economic downturns because they supply those goods and services we simply can't do without. No matter how much the economic situation deteriorates, we still need to eat, seek medical care, etc.

On the corporate scene, those companies with little or no debt, adequate cash, niche markets, and strong revenue and earnings track records often outperform the cyclical, growth, and high-technology sectors as the economy and stock market head south.

"The dominant theme in defensive investing lies in focusing on quality. Accumulate a number of choice equities over time to take advantage of lower prices as the market declines," says Bradley E. Turner, senior vice president with McDonald & Company Securities, Inc., in Cleveland, Ohio.

Falling Back on Utilities

Among traditional equities that investors have fled to during the onset of a recession, utilities used to be "no-brainers." In other words, most utilities offered a conservative haven in which to comfortably sit out the recession. They provided downside protection and attractive income via generous dividend yields. In addition, when the economy started to show life again, increased utility usage helped boost revenues, earnings, and capital gains prospects.

While the concept still remains valid, the list of worthy utilities has shrunk in the wake of nuclear risk exposure, hostile rate environments, high debt and interest burdens from overly aggressive construction programs, slashed dividend payouts, etc.

Obviously, the defensive investor must be more cautious than ever in his or her choice of utilities with which to weather the economic storms.

To help investors navigate today's more treacherous utility waters, I launched the *Utility and Energy Portfolio* investment newsletter in the fall of 1992. The newsletter covers timely industry topics and information, profiles of utility and energy companies with attractive investment opportunities for investors, plus a special annual investment review of every major U.S. utility company. The newsletter costs $95 for an annual subscription. Look for subscription information and for special discount offer at the end of this book.

As the recession deepens and the Federal Reserve Board lowers interest rates to prime the economy, interest rates for certificates of deposit and other investments decline. This, in turn, causes investors to seek securities paying higher yields. As a result, many investors flock to utilities with their attractive yields.

Don't wait for other investors to beat you to the punch. Anticipate the economy's downturn and establish your utility portfolio early. In this way, you preserve the high yield and can participate in the price rise of the utility stock as increased demand pushes the market price upward.

Many solid utilities also have long records of dividend hikes, working to increase your overall return. *Value Line Investment Survey*'s "High Yielding Stocks" list makes an excellent place to begin your search for quality utilities that deliver protection against recession in the form of attractive dividend income and capital appreciation potential.

Don't limit yourself to electric utilities. There's plenty of opportunity in the other utility companies such as gas, telephone, and water firms.

Should you prefer to let others make the utility investment decisions for you, a bevy of utility funds such as Dean Witter Utilities, Fidelity Select Electric Utilities, Fidelity Utilities Income, Financial Strategic Utilities, IDS Utilities Income, Liberty Utility, Midwest Strategic Utility Income, SLB Income Utilities, and Vanguard Equity Income target this market segment.

High Dividends—A Possible Warning Sign

"Don't be enticed by a high dividend payout; it may signal that the utility company is ripe for a dividend cut. More than 30 electric utility companies have slashed their dividends in recent years and in every case these companies sported high yields before the ax fell," says John Slatter, senior vice president and senior portfolio manager with Hickory Investment Advisors in Cleveland, Ohio and author of *Safe Investing: How to Make Money without Losing Your Shirt* (Simon & Schuster, 1991).

To support his warning against investing in high-yield electric utilities, Slatter offers the following information. For the three-year period 1985–1988, comparisons of high-yielding electric utilities and low-yielding utilities reflected a wide disparity in total return. (See Chart 8-1.)

As you can see, investors in the initially high-yielding companies paid dearly in terms of total return. Dividend cuts combined with poor stock market performance to drop total returns far below that of the initially low-yield companies studied by Slatter.

For example, initially high-yielding Commonwealth Edison and Ohio Edison compiled a three-year growth in total returns of 12.3 percent and 15.3 percent, respectively. That compared with initial low-yielding utility company returns of 37.7 percent for TECO Energy, 35.8 percent for Wisconsin Energy, and 24.5 percent for Baltimore Gas & Electric.

Other initially high-yielding companies fared even worse. Detroit Edison delivered only a 2.2 percent three-year growth in total return,

Company	Initial yields year-end 1978	10-year dividend total	Capital appreciation value	Total return	3-year growth in total return
Detroit Edison	11.3%	$12,302	$12,874	$25,176*	+2.2%
TECO Energy	7.5	11,933	27,146	39,079†	+37.7
Commonwealth Edison	10.1	10,943	12,804	23,747*	+12.3
Wisconsin Energy	8.6	11,886	31,158	43,044†	+35.8
Ohio Edison	11.8	12,365	12,684	25,049*	+15.3
Baltimore G&E	9.4	12,733	25,554	38,287†	+24.5
Philadelphia Electric	11.6	13,339	11,207	24,546*	0
Northern States	9.2	13,351	27,870	41,221†	+23.6
Niagara Mohawk	10.3	12,253	9,282	21,535*	−36.6
Duke Power	9.3	12,198	23,865	36,063†	+30.7

*Stocks with an initial high yield.

†Stocks with an initial low yield.

Chart 8-1. High and low-yield companies (total returns).

Beginning dates	Region	Low ratio groups	Net spread	High ratio groups
Oct. 1, 1982	Eastern	+ 137.2%	+ 107.3%	+ 29.9%
Dec. 10, 1982	Western	+ 77.4	+ 14.2	+ 63.2
Dec. 31, 1982	Eastern	+ 104.3	+ 71.9	+ 32.4
Apr. 1, 1983	Eastern	+ 88.7	+ 42.7	+ 46.0
June 10, 1983	Western	+ 50.6	+ 12.5	+ 38.1
June 29, 1984	Eastern	+ 110.9	+ 42.1	+ 68.8
Oct. 26, 1984	Midwest	+ 107.8	+ 87.6	+ 20.2
Dec. 7, 1984	Western	+ 29.2	− 0.6	+ 29.8
Group averages		+ 88.3%	+ 47.3%	+ 41.0%

Chart 8-2. Comparison of price-to-revenues ratios price appreciation to July 31, 1988.

Philadelphia Electric's came in at no change, while Niagara Mohawk turned in a negative 36.6 percent over that three-year time frame.

Instead of using yield as a decision factor for purchasing utilities, Slatter recommends a different approach for ferreting out undervalued situations. Slatter's research on several different groups of power companies in eight different time spans supports his conclusion that using price-to-revenues ratios can help uncover value much of the time.

On average, the gains of the low-ratio utility stocks more than doubled the gains of their high-ratio utility brethren. (See Chart 8-2.)

Admittedly, Slatter's price-to-revenues ratio strategy carries a speculative bent since utility companies experiencing financial and operating difficulties can affect the price-to-revenues ratio dramatically. However, it does provide another unique evaluation tool for your war chest.

For the more conservative value hunter, investigate the utility's financial strength: cashflow versus debt repayment; interest expense, dividends, and capital spending requirements; revenue and earnings stability; and rate environment. Pay attention to construction programs, nuclear exposure, and the economic scenario of the utility's service area.

In the past, too many utilities diversified into areas too far afield from their expertise, only to shed them later or write them down at substantial losses. Study the track record of past diversification efforts. Ask yourself: Were the moves successful? What are the risks?

Which Utilities to Choose?

The following utilities have proved to be adept at delivering value to their shareholders in the past. Use them as a guide to uncover more utility values for your portfolio, especially when a threat of recession rears its ugly head.

Connecticut Energy Corporation. Despite a slow regional economy, warmer-than-normal winters, and low home construction, Connecticut Energy Corporation continues to post strong financial performance. Heavy stress on cost containment and increased success in converting oil customers to gas are keeping earnings on an upward slope.

Currently paying dividends yielding around 6 percent, the natural gas company has paid dividends since 1850, the longest record of any nonfinancial company listed on the New York Stock Exchange. The board of directors has increased the annual dividend 13 times in the past 15 years.

Looking to the future: A return to more normal weather patterns, an eventual regional economic upturn, and additional conversion customers bode well for Connecticut Energy.

Shareholders have been rewarded for their confidence in the natural gas company's operations. Over the past 10 years through the end of 1991, the annual total return averaged 20.5 percent.

Since the end of 1990, the market price of Connecticut Energy stock has traveled an upward path, hitting new highs along the way.

Citizens Utilities. Among utilities, Citizens Utilities Company, headquartered in Stamford, Connecticut, ranks as one of the most diversified. It provides electric, gas, water, wastewater, and telecommunications services in a wide variety of service locations including Arizona, California, Colorado, Hawaii, Idaho, Illinois, Indiana, Louisiana, Ohio, Pennsylvania, Utah, and Vermont.

In addition to a well-diversified operation to guard against revenue and earnings declines, Citizens Utilities sports strong financials. Its bonds garner AAA ratings, cashflow is strong, and management has delivered 47 consecutive years of increased earnings, dividends, and shareholders' equity.

The company plans to continue its successful acquisition strategy, purchasing utility firms in growing markets with the ability to deliver economies-of-scale efficiencies. In fact, in a study of 776 companies, Citizens ranked higher that 745 companies in terms of earnings productivity per employee and first among 19 major telecommunications firms.

Back in early 1990, Citizens quit paying cash dividends and initiated stock dividends instead. The stock dividend rate around 1.5 percent quarterly is equivalent to a bit less than 60 cents per share quarterly and can be tapped through a stock dividend sale plan.

A move to the New York Stock Exchange in the third quarter of 1991 provides more liquidity and better exposure to investors. Since the shift to the Big Board, Citizens B stock has been on a roll, rising from the mid-$20s to new highs around $40 per share.

In the telecommunications sector, which accounts for 36 percent of company revenues and over 60 percent of pretax income, telephone access line growth of 7 percent more than doubles the national average of 3 percent.

Acquisitions in the natural gas industry have boosted that segment's percentage of customer connections from 4 percent at the end of 1989 to almost 40 percent at the end of 1991. More record years are in store for Citizens. Higher stock prices and stock dividends promise a safe haven for recession-weary investors.

California Water Service Company.   Drought conditions negatively impacted earnings at California Water Service Company over the past few years. But things are starting to look up. Customer water rationing has declined to 35 percent in mid-1992 from 60 percent in 1991. Customer growth and anticipated rate relief in 1992 should boost earnings over the foreseeable future.

Healthy cashflow and strong finances bolster the dividend payout, averaging in excess of 70 percent. In January 1992, the board of directors raised the cash dividend 6 cents annually, the twenty-fifth year of consecutive increases.

California Water's stock price has treaded water over recent years, finally breaking the all-time high of $32⅜ per share (reached back in 1988) during the first half of 1992. A yield around 6 percent, combined with potential capital gains as economic and weather conditions improve, makes California Water a solid defensive pick.

Pick Companies with Little or No Debt

Little or no-debt companies represent another safe haven for defensive investors. Low-leveraged firms possess a lot more flexibility to deal with economic downturns, thereby gaining a tremendous operating advantage over competitors burdened with debt and interest payments.

Low-debt companies provide a significant degree of protection against downside risk. Even though the firm can encounter slumping revenues and decreasing earnings, it has the resources and staying power to tough it out and the ability to bounce back faster as the economic picture improves.

Debt-free companies come in all shapes, sizes, and flavors. Take International Flavors & Fragrances Inc., for example. This leading creator and manufacturer of flavors and fragrances uses its substantial capital resources and strong cashflow to make sweet-smelling profit gains year in and year out.

Steady stock price gains and dividend increases have kept shareholders happy over the years. With the stock price over $110 per share, International Flavors & Fragrances should be a good candidate for a stock split. (See Chap. 5, "Stock-Split Specials.") Since the October 1987 crash, its stock price has nearly tripled despite the onset of a recession.

Tambrands, a company we discussed in detail in Chap. 5, is another debt-free company with a consistent track record of rising revenues and record earnings per share. With a 60 percent market share, plenty of cash, and product-pricing flexibility, Tambrands can outmaneuver any competitor in good times and bad.

Choose Convertibles

Shifting a portion of your assets from plain vanilla common stocks to convertible securities offers another way to take a defensive stance. In essence, convertible securities are hybrid investments combining the best aspects of both stocks and bonds. Under conversion privileges, both convertible bonds and convertible preferred stock are exchangeable into common stock at the option of the holder under specified terms and conditions.

The conversion ratio spells out the number of shares the holder receives upon surrender of the convertible security. The conversion price is the effective price paid for the common stock when conversion occurs.

Since convertible securities pay a fixed rate of interest, their yield remains constant after purchase. An attractive yield can be locked in while waiting for the stock price of the underlying common stock to increase in value. This income-yield feature helps support the convertible's market price, and thus will decline slower and less than the market price of the underlying common stock.

On the other side of the coin, the ability to convert the security into common stock helps the price of the convertible bond correlate closely with the price increase of the underlying stock once the conversion price has been attained. This hybrid combination allows the investor to earn a more attractive yield while waiting out the recession plus gives him or her the opportunity to participate in upside moves in the common stock.

In addition to offering both higher yields and price appreciation, convertibles also occupy a senior position in the firm's capital structure in relation to common stock. This provides even more defensive protection. First of all, interest on convertible bonds and dividends on convertible preferred stock must always be paid before the issuance of any common stock dividends. Even more important, in the event of liquidation or bankruptcy, convertible securities possess a superior claim to company assets over common stock.

Firms offering convertible securities range from struggling new firms offering kickers to entice buyers, on the one hand, to the bluest of the blue chips, on the other. Companies like to issue convertibles because they typically carry a lower coupon or dividend rate than straight bonds or preferred stock. On top of that, the convertible provision causes them to sell at a premium.

As with any investment, analyze the track record, underlying value, and future prospects of the issuing company. Look for the "cv" symbol in *Barron's, Investor's Business Daily,* and the *Wall Street Journal* that denotes a convertible security.

A number of mutual funds specialize in the convertible arena, and many convertible issues are not available to the general public. Pay attention to the convertible terms and conditions. As with many bonds, some convertibles carry a redemption clause that allows the issuing company to redeem or call the convertible before maturity. If the convertible security trades above the call price, you could stand to lose the difference between what you paid and the redemption price. Check out the call price and the earliest call dates. Avoid any issues with unfavorable call terms.

You can combine your convertible strategy with your turnaround strategy. See Chap. 9, "Tempting Turnarounds," for a more detailed discussion.

Start your research with *Value Line Convertibles,* found at many public, university, and business libraries. Then expand your analysis to examine the company's prospects and value just as you would analyze a value investment as discussed in Chap. 1, "Value Investing."

Pick Companies That Have Been Around

Success breeds success. This is certainly true of the companies listed in Table 8-1. Despite a preponderance of banking companies in this listing of the nation's 50 oldest publicly owned companies, the group outperformed both the Dow Jones Industrial Average and the S&P 500 in 1991.

Table 8-1. Fifty Oldest Public Companies in the United States

Company	Established business		Company	Established business	
Dexter Corp.	1767	Spec. chem.	Old Stone Corp.	1819	Banking
Bowne & Co.	1775	Fin. printing	Society for Svg.	1819	Banking
Core States	1782	Banking	Merrill Lynch	1820	Investment
Bank of Bost.	1784	Banking	Vt. Finl. Ser.	1821	Banking
Bank of N.Y.	1784	Banking	Con Edison	1823	Utility
Fleet/Norstar	1791	Banking	Chemical Bank	1824	Banking
Cigna Corp.	1792	Insurance	Courier	1824	Banking
Shawmut Natl.	1792	Banking	Bos. Five Banc.	1825	Banking
State St. Bos.	1792	Banking	KeyCorp	1825	Banking
Bird Corp.	1795	Bldg. matl.	NBB Bancorp	1825	Banking
Dixon Ticon.	1795	Writ. prod.	CSX Corp.	1827	Rail Trans.
Chase Man.	1799	Banking	NESB Corp.	1827	Banking
Alex. Brown	1800	Investment	Miners Natl.	1828	Banking
WA Trust	1800	Banking	SmithKline	1830	Pharmaceut.
duPont	1802	Chemicals	Amoskeag Co.	1831	Textiles
Midlantic	1804	Banking	Keystone Her.	1831	Banking
Colgate-Pal.	1806	Consumer	Poughkeepsie Svg.	1831	Banking
Valspar Corp.	1806	Paints	Belding Heming.	1832	Textiles
Lukens Inc.	1810	Steel	Houghton Mifflin	1832	Publishing
Citicorp	1812	Banking	Rogers Corp.	1832	Electronics
Constell. Bank	1812	Banking	Star States	1832	Banking
First Fidel.	1812	Banking	Brown & Sharpe	1833	Machine Tool
Baltimore Gas	1816	Utility	Cooper Indus.	1833	Indl. Eq.
Meritor Sav.	1816	Banking	McKesson Corp.	1833	Pharmaceut.
Reliance Grp.	1817	Insurance	Reading Co.	1833	Real estate

Since you don't have to buy the whole group, search the list for those firms particularly well situated to perform well in a down economy and outperform the market substantially when the economy improves.

There's quite a bit of diversity in the list. In addition to such banking stalwarts as State Street Boston (1792), you can choose from pharmaceutical giant SmithKline Beecham (1830) and paint and coatings manufacturer Valspar Corporation (1806).

Some of the banks and other companies make better turnaround candidates than defensive holdings, while still others listed in the table represent cyclical plays.

Look for Companies That Provide Services and Support to Other Companies

Companies that help other businesses improve productivity and efficiency stand to do much better in a down economy. As other firms, hit hard by a recession, work to trim costs and improve operations, they turn to specialists for help. In addition, even during good economic times, intense global competition makes it paramount that companies employ the most productive tools and processes available.

Structural Dynamics Research Corporation

That leads us once again to Dublin, Ohio-based Structural Dynamics Research Corporation (SDRC). As discussed in Chap. 3, "Small-Cap Gems," SDRC has been a stellar performer for years.

It holds a worldwide leadership position in a niche market, developing mechanical design automation software and providing engineering services for the automotive, aerospace, and industrial manufacturing industries.

Besides aiding other companies in improving their operations and cost structure, SDRC pays a lot of attention to its own productivity performance.

Back in 1986, SDRC enticed Ronald J. Friedsam to join the firm as chairman, president, and chief executive officer. Friedsam, with 20 years of industry experience at Burroughs Corp. (now Unisys), helped transform SDRC from a firm with a heavy focus on research and development to an operating company with a strong marketing thrust. He brought to the table a strong emphasis on profit and performance goals and cost and financial controls.

Friedsam didn't shackle research and development efforts. In fact, R&D expenses increased over 30 percent while he created a balance in company operations. Before he instituted strict financial and marketing controls, product costs often outstripped projected costs, and the final product often failed to meet market needs.

Earnings have increased from 18 cents per share in 1987 to 60 cents per share in 1991, adjusted for 2-for-1 stock splits in both 1990 and 1991. (See Chap. 5, "Stock-Split Specials.") During that same time frame, revenues have more than doubled to $146 million from $61 million.

SDRC estimates that the worldwide market for its mechanical computer-aided engineering software products and services continues to grow at a 25 percent clip. SDRC has the best of both worlds. During economic slowdowns, companies turn to the firm for its productivity-enhancing software; and during economic recovery, demand increases for the firm's engineering services.

Over the past five years through the end of 1991, SDRC revenues compounded at 24 percent annually while net income surged with a 49 percent annual increase. Keeping the company in the forefront of the industry, SDRC's research and development efforts have increased at a compound rate of 39 percent per year.

The firm also runs a tight financial ship. With nearly $50 million in cash and cash equivalents plus a current ratio of 3 to 1, SDRC has plenty of resources to capitalize on market opportunities. The firm is completely debt-free, adding even more ability to outmaneuver any economic constrictions.

Another plus, management and directors own nearly 10 percent of company shares, giving them a huge stake in the firm's success. In addition, they also have options to acquire another 10 percent of company stock.

A diversified customer base, both by industry and by geography, shields the company from single-customer and regional disruptions. Over 30 percent of company revenues derive from Europe and the Far East, while domestic customers account for 38 percent of company revenues. In 1992, the company had more than 50,000 software licenses installed at more than 6600 customer sites worldwide.

New major releases of software and expanded distribution channels during 1991 bode well for future market penetration, higher revenues, and enhanced earnings. During the first quarter of 1992, SDRC increased net income by 42 percent on a revenue rise of 19 percent. Samsung Group, Korea's largest corporation, chose SDRC's software as the standard for its mechanical design automation in the first quarter of 1992, providing evidence of SDRC's growing international market penetration.

Despite higher revenues and surging earnings, SDRC's stock price slumped 40 percent from an all-time high of $30 per share in early 1992 to the $18 per share level by midyear. Savvy investors can use price pullbacks in this solid company to acquire additional shares for even greater investment returns. (See Chart 8-3).

Cintas Corporation

Cintas Corporation helps keep other companies looking neat and trim through its sales and leasing of company uniforms and everything else from dust mops to entrance mats.

The Cincinnati-based company has weathered many a recession with

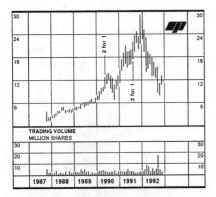

Chart 8-3. Structural Dynamics Research stock chart. (*Reprinted by permission of Standard & Poor's Corporation*)

a string of 22 consecutive years of uninterrupted growth in revenues and earnings. Over the 22-year period, revenues grew at a compound rate of 26 percent, and net income surged ahead at a compound rate of 37 percent. A look ahead indicates that heavy investment in two new plants and a new distribution center will pay off in increased efficiencies for years to come.

Shareholders have also done well. Since the company went public in 1983, the value of its shares has compounded at an annual rate of around 30 percent. Dividend growth is also impressive, increasing at a compound rate in excess of 40 percent since 1983.

Taking an aggressive acquisition posture in a highly fragmented industry promises to bolster Cintas's market share. Over the past two years, Cintas acquired 15 businesses. In addition, in 1991 it rolled out a new work shoe program and new catalog direct-sales program. In 1992, Cintas operated uniform-rental operations in 28 states including three manufacturing plants and four distribution centers. It's no secret that management fully intends to be the nation's uniform supplier.

Adjusting for stock splits in both 1991 and 1992, Cintas's stock price rose from a low of $12⅞ per share in late 1990 to an all-time high of $32⅛ per share in early 1992. (See Chap. 5, "Stock-Split Specials.")

Choose Drug-Related Companies: Arbor Drugs

Drug-related firms have long been considered defensive stocks to own during economic contractions. Arbor Drugs, Inc., headquartered in Troy, Michigan, ranks as Michigan's second largest drugstore chain and holds the nation's twenty-first largest spot.

Its discount format holds it in good stead, especially in hard times. High-tech point-of-sale scanning cash registers provide tight inventory controls and merchandise sales tracking information to keep a pulse on shifting consumer buying patterns.

For the five fiscal years ended July 31, 1991, Arbor Drugs's revenues increased at a nearly 22 percent compounded rate, while net income rose at a compounded 19.7 percent pace. First-half fiscal 1992 net income jumped nearly 24 percent on a 16 percent sales increase. From just a 13.5 percent market share in the metropolitan Detroit market in 1986, Arbor boosted its presence to 26.2 percent market share in March 1992. Management targets further penetration of the southeastern Michigan area, which constitutes the nation's fifth largest drugstore market.

Arbor Drugs's prescription for success includes a commitment to wide product assortments, discounted prices, and exceptional service. In comparison with industry competitors, Arbor Drugs stands out in key benchmark measures. For example, Arbor Drugs generates average sales per selling square foot of $449 versus only $270 for the industry average. Likewise, average store sales of $3.7 million exceed the industry average by 59 percent, and net margin for Arbor Drugs outpaces that of all other publicly held drugstore chains in the nation.

From a low of $8⅞ per share in late 1990, the stock price for Arbor Drugs rose to hit an all-time high of $25¼ per share in early 1992 before drifting downward to near its 52-week trading low under $18 per share.

Ample opportunity exists for savvy investors to purchase the stock both as a defensive investment should the economy continue to flounder and as a growth opportunity ready to participate as the economy rebounds.

Look for earnings growth in excess of 20 percent as Arbor Drugs capitalizes on the nation's aging population, increased market penetration, and a well-balanced product mix.

Make Your Choice on the Basis of Demographics: American Greetings

Demographics also plays a large role in the promising future of American Greetings. As the nation's baby-boom generation ages, unit greeting card sales should rise since older consumers typically purchase more greeting cards than younger consumers.

Another demographic plus, the larger number of women in the workplace translates into higher card sales since women account for in excess of 90 percent of card sales. Increased time demands also favor purchasing in mass-merchandise outlets where American Greetings maintains a strong presence.

A strong focus on everyday cards that sell all year long keeps American Greetings's mass-merchandise retail customers happy. Of the 63 percent of company revenues derived from greeting cards, everyday cards generate about two-thirds of the total. A strong emphasis on merchandising and displays aims at enhancing retailers' sales in order to cement customer relationships.

On the financial front, cost-cutting efforts and operations restructuring by American Greetings have resulted in a decline in the percentage of operating expenses in relation to revenue, a plus for the bottom line and the firm's ability to compete. For fiscal year ended February 28, 1992, operating expenses declined to 41.1 percent of revenues from the 43.0 percent experienced in fiscal 1990.

Net income increased 18 percent in fiscal 1992 on a 10 percent revenue rise. Look for continued double-digit earnings per share gains and record results through the late nineties, recessions or no recessions.

To date, foreign operations contribute less than 20 percent of company revenues. While foreign greeting card markets traditionally have been dominated by specialty stores versus the mass merchandisers preferred by American Greetings, the foreign markets offer significant future growth opportunities.

Ever since American Greetings stock recovered from the effects of the October 1987 market crash, the stock price has been on an upward escalator. From a low of $13 per share in late 1987, its stock price rose to an all-time high of $43¾ per share in early 1992.

Some Final Advice

Keep your value focus intact when searching for defensive investments. Look for solid track records in good times and bad, and look for good future prospects. Table 8-2 lists some of the companies that have managed to deliver higher earnings per share for each of the past 19 years or longer.

When the economic storm clouds start accumulating, shift to more defensive investments based upon solid values and bright prospects.

Table 8-2. Companies That Have Delivered High Earnings per
Share over the Long Term

Company	Business	Company	Business
Abbott Labs	Pharmaceuticals	Food Lion	Grocery
Albertson's	Grocery	Hubbell, Inc.	Elec. equipment
American Home Products	Pharmaceuticals	Jostens, Inc.	Recreation Awards
Auto. Data Processing	Payroll processing	McDonald's	Fast food
Banc One	Banking	Philip Morris	Consumer products
H&R Block	Tax Preparation	UST	Smokeless tobacco
Emerson Electric	Electrical Products	Walmart	Retailing
First Hawaiian	Banking		

9

Tempting
Turnarounds

Cashing In on Corporate Rebirth

Stalking the corporate turnaround can pay big dividends for the patient investor. As at the racetrack, betting on the dark horses often delivers higher returns on your money. Of course, investing in turnarounds, like horse racing, has its own set of risks. However, you can limit those risks with careful investigative work.

Avoiding the herd instinct and ferreting out unique turnaround investment opportunities where others fear to tread can help you beat both the odds and the market.

Too often investors link turnaround situations with bankrupt companies. While a bankrupt firm can indeed make an excellent turnaround candidate, a company does not have to be in bankruptcy to qualify as a money-making turnaround situation for the contrarian investor.

What Is a Turnaround?

Simply stated, a turnaround represents a positive change in the fortunes of a company which can stem from many different factors, both internal and external to the firm.

The turnaround is truly a special situation where the individual investor can beat the professionally managed institutions to the punch and earn substantial profits as the rest of the market moves to properly value the successful turnaround in process.

145

A bevy of problems can contribute to the company having fallen on hard times. Ineffective top management can be squandering market opportunities and market share with inappropriate product, marketing, and operation strategies; undercapitalization, excessive debt, and poor financial planning can lead to cashflow crises; and lost expansion opportunities and technological innovation can leave the company in the dust with outmoded production facilities and/or outdated product lines.

Outside factors can also negatively impact the firm's ability to compete and result in declining revenues and profits. Of course, general economic and industry conditions impact a firm's financial results. As illustrated by the OPEC oil cartel, price hikes for scarce raw materials or the sudden unavailability of key raw materials can spell doom for those companies without adequate contingency material sources.

Other reasons for company economic misfortunes include loss of a major customer due to competition, bankruptcy, or other reason; governmental regulation such as newly enacted stringent environmental requirements; natural disasters such as earthquakes or fires that disrupt production operations; shifting customer preferences (from branded to unbranded products, for instance); labor problems; and, as many American companies found out in the eighties and nineties, more intense foreign competition.

It's important to remember that not all distressed companies represent turnaround situations. Some companies' operating results and stock prices have been driven down for good reason and without a realistic chance of recovery. You must learn to separate the wheat from the chaff.

Turnaround situations provide the opportunity for you to profit from new and unusual developments occurring both within the firm and in its surrounding environment. Unlike most other investment situations, the individual investor can learn about them and invest in these special situations before the general market and institutions bid up the stock prices.

Turnarounds routinely take many months and years to orchestrate. There's typically plenty of time to do your thorough up-front analysis before committing investment funds. Declining earnings and falling stock prices, lackluster near-term prospects, negative publicity, and uncertainties clouding the future of troubled companies drive away most potential investors. These stocks are shunned because few investors desire to perform the work necessary to find the winners.

On the institutional front, many mutual funds and other institutional investors abide by investment guidelines that prohibit their investing in companies that don't pay dividends or meet some other specific criteria.

This places downward pressure on the stock prices of potential turnaround candidates, increasing the disparity between market valuation and intrinsic value.

Likewise, as the turnaround company's fortunes improve and institutions can once again take a position in the stock, increasing institutional demand translates into upward price pressure. All this works to the benefit of the turnaround investor who initiated his or her position after selling pressure drove the stock down and before newfound demand started to drive the stock price back up again.

Why the Turnaround Is a Good Deal for the Individual Investor

Several factors make the turnaround a perfect investment vehicle for the individual investor. As mentioned earlier, you are not at a time disadvantage to the large institutions. In fact, the opposite may be true. Most institutions want to invest in firms with secure futures now and typically don't have the patience to wait for the eventual turnaround.

Second, the firm's stock has already been beaten down to new lows in the wake of negative financial or other news or mounting losses, making the possibility of an undervalued situation more likely.

Third, since many distressed companies already sell below book value, there's some downside protection in the event the turnaround attempt proves unsuccessful.

Fourth, with time at your side, you have just as much access to research material as institutions do. Your analysis can be just as thorough as theirs, leveling the investment playing field.

As Always, Do Your Homework

There are plenty of places to start your search for the right turnaround. Peruse the lists of stocks making new lows in *Barron's, Investor's Business Daily,* or the *Wall Street Journal.* Look at cyclical companies in industries presently nearing the bottom of their current trough, and read *Forbes, Fortune,* and Standard & Poor's *The Outlook* for listings of companies with low price-earnings ratios or low price–book value compared with their industry benchmarks or the market in general.

A management change signals one of the sure signs of a turnaround attempt in process. Routinely follow the shuffling of the corporate elite in the financial papers. Announcements of restructuring, shedding of divisions or subsidiaries, plant consolidations, mass employee layoffs, and large write-offs also indicate a drastic shift from "business as usual" to a "we mean business" attitude required for the successful turnaround.

Many kinds of developments can create the turnaround special situation, such as a new technological breakthrough; a new product or service line; a change in management or ownership; the discovery of a new mineral deposit or raw material source; a merger, acquisition, or takeover; a favorable piece of legislation impacting operations or taxes; international currency fluctuations; strategic joint ventures; or an improvement in the economic environment.

Concentrate your search on industry giants or small-fry with unique niches. The larger firms can dictate the industry pace and can often effect a turnaround by selling off underutilized assets. The smaller firm tends to be more flexible and able to react faster to changing market conditions and opportunities, providing they have access to adequate capital. Middle-size firms, on the other hand, get locked into pricing and policies set by the big boys in the industry, butting heads for market share with those with far more financial, personnel, and operating resources.

"First of all, you need to focus on companies with a solid-core business. It may not currently be their major product or service line, but you must have something to build upon," advises George Putnam III, editor of *The Turnaround Letter* published by New Generation Research, Inc., in Boston.

In the same vein, according to Putnam, turnarounds generally favor companies with more than one line of business. For example, if a fast-food company falls out of favor or consumers decide to eat at home more, it leaves company management with few alternatives to turn the firm around.

There are always exceptions to the rule though. Consider Lee Iacocca's amazing rejuvenation of Chrysler back in the early eighties or Stephen Wolf's herculean efforts to get both Republic Airlines and Tiger International off the ground and flying high again. Turnaround investors in any of these three companies would have profited handsomely for their patience and confidence in the ability of these two corporate magicians to perform their magic.

Chrysler

For example, in its darkest days, Chrysler wallowed in losses, hitting the bottom with a $11.56 per share loss in 1980. Its stock price plummeted to less than $3 per share. A $3000 investment for 1000 shares of common stock would have grown to 2225 shares following 3-for-2 stock splits in March 1986 and April 1987. Just before the October 1987 crash, the $3000 investment would have peaked at $106,800 (ignoring commissions), not a bad return on investment. (See Chart 9-1.)

Republic Airlines

No less impressive, Wolf pulled Republic Airlines out of its nosedive and took faithful investors' profits sky-high. Rising fuel costs, high labor expenses, and airfare wars combined to drop Republic's financial results into the red. By 1983, the airline piled up losses in excess of $220 million, causing its stock to drop from a five-year high of $11⅞ to around $3 a share. Republic's convertible bond traded at $550, a deep discount reflecting the investment community's lack of confidence in the firm's ability to emerge from troubled waters.

Armed with tough labor contract renegotiations, stricter financial controls, slashed operating expenses, new route structures, and a shift to more fuel-efficient aircraft, Wolf pulled Republic out of its downward spiral. Later, when Wolf engineered the sale of Republic to Northwest Airlines, the stock could be converted to $17 per share, and the 10⅛ 2007 convertible bond commanded $1270 per bond.

Tiger International

At Tiger International, Wolf inherited a company with a long tradition as the nation's oldest and largest air cargo carrier but saddled with debt and a negative net worth. For the four-year period ended December 1985, Tiger International piled up losses in excess of $520 million.

Wolf negotiated 25 percent pay cuts with the pilots' union to keep the carrier flying. Then he embarked on a program of restructuring, including refinancing equipment debt, thereby slashing long-term debt and trimming interest expenses by an estimated $100 million over five years. A partnership profit-sharing program geared to distribute 15 percent of company profits after the first $10 million helped guarantee that full-time employees would work hard to make the turnaround a success.

As at Republic, Wolf installed an information reporting system that let him know the status of key corporate indicators on a day-to-day basis. Quality became paramount, with quality-control reports tracking each shipment from point of origin to destination. A stickler for details and for monitoring progress, Wolf was known to show up at key company operations across the nation at 2 A.M. to see how smoothly operations and shipments were going.

CHRYSLER NYSE-C

| | | | | | RECENT PRICE | 21 | P/E RATIO | NMF | (Trailing: NMF Median: 8.5) | RELATIVE P/E RATIO | NMF | DIV'D YLD | 2.9% ... 1.4% | VALUE LINE | 103 |

TIMELINESS 3 Average (Relative Price Performance Next 12 Mos.)
SAFETY 3 Average (Scale: 1 Highest to 5 Lowest)
BETA 1.30 (1.00 = Market)

1995-97 PROJECTIONS

	Price	Gain	Ann'l Total Return
High	50	(+140%)	27%
Low	30	(+45%)	14%

Insider Decisions
Institutional Decisions

Percent shares traded 12.0 / 4.0

Options: CBOE

Target Price Range 1995 1996 1997

Relative Price Strength

3-for-2 split
3-for-2 split

Shaded areas indicate recessions

Statistical Array — © VALUE LINE PUB., INC.

	1982	1983	1984	1985	1986	1987	1988	1989	1990	1991	1992	1993	95-97
Revenues per sh AF	56.17	48.31	71.61	93.31	104.23	118.78	152.42	156.53	136.48	100.55	101.70	115.25	152.55
"Cash Flow" per sh	.56	2.16	6.41	8.34	7.57	7.93	9.88	7.42	6.53	2.74	5.00	7.25	11.45
Earnings per sh B	d.57	1.91	5.22	6.25	6.31	5.90	5.08	1.36	.30	d2.74	Nil	2.00	5.70
Div'ds Decl'd per sh C	.38	.45	.45	1.00	1.00	1.20	1.20	1.20	.60	.60	.60	.60	2.00
Cap'l Spending per sh	1.47	2.34	2.93	4.58	6.06	5.79	7.01	7.33	8.00	7.74	6.25	6.45	6.80
Book Value per sh D	d1.84	4.17	12.10	18.50	24.67	29.40	32.58	32.42	30.53	20.91	20.10	21.50	28.00
Common Shs Outst'g E	178.82	274.08	273.31	227.80	216.69	221.22	232.74	223.10	224.36	292.09	295.00	295.00	295.00
Avg Ann'l P/E Ratio		5.8	2.4	2.6	4.0	5.8	4.8	17.9	NMF	NMF		--	7.0
Relative P/E Ratio		.49	.22	.21	.21	.39	.40	1.35	NMF	--			.55
Avg Ann'l Div'd Yield		--	3.1%	2.7%	3.2%	2.9%	4.1%	4.9%	8.1%	4.7%			5.0%
Revenues ($mill) AF	10045	13240	19573	21255	22586	26277	35473	34922	30620	29370	30000	34000	45000
Market Share	8.6%	9.2%	9.5%	11.2%	11.5%	10.8%	11.2%	10.5%	9.3%	9.0%	9.5%	11.0%	11.0%
Operating Margin G	2.8%	8.2%	12.8%	10.4%	9.0%	9.4%	14.8%	14.8%	19.1%	7.9%	9.0%	9.5%	10.0%
Net Profit ($mill)	d68.9	525.8	1496.1	1635.2	1403.6	1289.7	1143.3	315.0	68.0	d665.0	Nil	590	1680
Income Tax Rate	NMF	48.0%	40.5%	34.8%	45.5%	48.6%	37.9%	42.9%	53.7%	NMF	36.0%	36.0%	36.0%
Net Profit Margin	NMF	4.0%	7.6%	7.7%	6.2%	4.9%	3.2%	.9%	.2%	NMF	NMF	1.7%	3.7%
Working Cap'l ($mill)	256.5	d700.1	d135.8	584.3	243.0	d467.1	14266	11181	9208.0	7609.0	7450	7715	8925
Long-Term Debt ($mill) F	2189.0	1104.0	760.1	2366.1	2334.1	3333.2	16636	17002	12750	14980	15370	15570	15570
Net Worth ($mill)	991.0	1365.3	3305.9	4215.3	5344.8	6502.9	7582.3	7233.0	6849.0	6109.0	5930	6345	8255
% Earned Total Cap'l	1.4%	23.5%	33.0%	26.2%	19.8%	14.6%	8.1%	4.7%	4.8%	1.3%	NMF	6.5%	10.5%
% Earned Net Worth	NMF	38.5%	45.3%	38.8%	26.3%	19.8%	15.1%	4.4%	1.0%	NMF	NMF	9.5%	20.5%
% Retained to Comm Eq	NMF	35.8%	41.6%	36.1%	23.0%	16.5%	12.1%	.6%	NMF	NMF	NMF	6.5%	13.0%
% All Div'ds to Net Prof	22%	8%	8%	7%	13%	17%	20%	85%	NMF	NMF	NMF	30%	35%

BUSINESS: Chrysler Corporation is the third largest automobile and truck manufacturer in the United States. Builds Plymouth, Dodge, and Chrysler cars and Dodge trucks. Also produces automotive parts and accessories, and defense-related products, primarily for the U.S. government. Imports and sells Mitsubishi cars. Acquired American Motors Corporation in 1987. Sold Gulfstream Aerospace Corporation in 1990. Labor costs: 14% of sales; foreign sales: 7%. 1991 depreciation rate: 11.3%. Estimated plant age: 12 years. Has 99,950 employees, 213,450 stockholders. Insiders own 1% of stock. Kirk Kerkorian 9.6%. Chairman & CEO: Lee Iacocca; Vice Chmn: Robert J. Eaton. Incorporated: Delaware. Address: Highland Park, Michigan, 48288. Telephone: 313-956-5252.

Chart 9-1. Chrysler stock chart. (Copyright © 1992 by Value Line Publishing, Inc., used by permission. For subscription information to the Value Line Investment Survey, please call (800) 634-3583.)

In addition, he beefed up marketing programs, putting them to work wooing back customers who fled the cargo carrier when news of financial difficulties leaked out.

Again, Wolf's strategies salvaged a wounded air carrier from crashing. By the end of 1986, Wolf reduced Tiger International's net loss to $45.1 million versus $72.7 million a year earlier. In 1987, rising revenue ton-miles returned Tiger International to profitability with a vengeance.

For 1987, Tiger International earned $58.7 million, or $1.61 per share, versus a loss of $1.45 on revenues of $1.1 billion for the previous year. While Wolf later moved on to climb into the cockpit of United Air Lines and its parent company, Allegis (now UAL Corporation), Tiger International's improved fortunes attracted a takeover bid from Federal Express in 1989.

Investors in the Tiger International turnaround earned impressive profits. From a low of $3⅝ per share in 1986, shareholders received $20⅞ per share with the completion of the Federal Express takeover of Tiger. Likewise, Tiger International convertible bond holders, who purchased their convertibles at a steep discount, experienced handsome investment gains as Federal Express paid off the bonds at $1000 par plus interest. (See Chart 9-2).

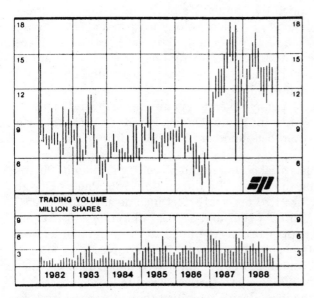

Chart 9-2. Tiger International stock chart. (*Reprinted by permission of Standard & Poor's Corporation*)

Phelps Dodge

In the cyclical arena, G. Robert "Bull" Durham had his work cut out for him at giant copper producer Phelps Dodge Corporation in Phoenix, Arizona. The future looked bleak in 1984. Losses totaled more than $200 million, or $11.27 per share, that year and more than $400 million for the period from 1982 to 1984. Phelps Dodge's huge debt ate up valuable cash in interest expenses, foreign competition cut into domestic markets, and high operating costs kept the company from remaining competitive.

Durham took the bull by the horns, closing excess and high-cost mine and smelter operations, forcing the union into a strike situation leading to union decertification, and selling a 15 percent stake in the firm's Morenci, Arizona, copper facilities to Japanese interests.

Operating costs were slashed, with employee ranks trimmed some 40 percent in the wake of the union battle. Another $10 million in annual savings came from making cuts in management levels and moving the corporate headquarters from costly New York offices to more economical Phoenix space.

Realizing you can't save yourself into prosperity, Durham invested more than $40 million at the Morenci facilities to improve operating efficiencies. The installation of in-pit crushing and conveying operations eliminated the high-cost, labor-intensive maintenance of track, dump cars, and locomotives previously utilized.

Durham also accelerated the company's push into using solvent extraction/electrowinning (SX/EW) technology for producing low-cost, high-quality copper. The SX/EW process bypasses high-cost conventional milling, smelting, and refining operations, dropping operations costs to below 30 cents per pound versus 57 cents per pound under conventional copper mining techniques.

As the saying goes, "A penny saved is a penny earned," and that gets multiplied many times over for Phelps Dodge. For every 1 cent the firm squeezed out of operation costs, another $10 million dropped to the bottom line.

With production costs slashed to around 57 cents per pound, Phelps Dodge started turning the corner. By the end of 1986, Phelps Dodge earned $61.4 million, or $1.79 per share. Net income surged to $205.7 million, or $6.48 per share, in 1987 and $420.2 million, or $13.15 cents per share, in 1988 as copper prices continued to rise from market bottoms around 65 cents per pound to new highs approaching $1.30 a pound as the world economic situation improved and Durham's cost-cutting and production efficiency strategies kicked in.

Like the Phoenix, the legendary Greek bird that consumed itself in fire and rose, reborn, from the ashes, Phelps Dodge confounded the naysayers and perfected the ultimate turnaround. With the recovery well in hand, the company's stock recovered from a 1984 low of less than $13 per share to $56 per share in 1987, eventually posting a new high of $79¼ per share in 1991. (See Chart 9-3).

But that's not the end of the story. Durham didn't remedy problems at the copper company just to make it susceptible to another economic downturn in the copper industry. Instead, he took his strategy several steps further. Durham made giant strides to expand the firm's noncopper business lines in order to make it more recession-proof.

For example, the $240 million acquisition of Columbia Chemicals Company made Phelps Dodge the world's second largest producer of carbon black—a reinforcing agent used in rubber tires, printing pigments, and other industrial applications. Another acquisition, Accuride Corporation, brought with it the number one market share in wheel rims for medium-sized and heavy-duty trucks.

As an added bonus to shareholders, Phelps Dodge's board of directors reinstated the quarterly cash dividend in 1987. As of 1992, the stock paid out $3 per share in quarterly dividends, yielding an attractive 4.5 percent. In May 1992, the board also voted to split Phelps Dodge stock 2 for 1 and raise its quarterly dividend 10 percent to 82.5 cents per share, presplit. (See Chap. 5, "Stock-Split Specials.")

Keep a Careful Eye on Management

"While new management may not be the all-clear signal to jump right in, it is a great indicator that you should begin looking seriously at the particular company's turnaround prospects. Only by tracking the new management's strategies and actions will you be able to tell how the turnaround attempt is progressing," says Putnam.

You can see evidence of a management shake-up or the infusion of new management blood by keeping an eye on changes in the corporate suites reported in *Barron's, Investor's Business Daily,* and other business publications. Also keep tabs on the whereabouts of those unique individuals such as Stephen Wolf who make a career rescuing companies from the brink of disaster.

Of course, don't discount the ability of existing management to get back on top of events and turn their corporate performance around after achieving a period or two of dismal results.

PHELPS DODGE NYSE-PD

| | | RECENT PRICE | 87 | P/E RATIO | 11.1 | (Trailing: 12.2 Median: NMF) | RELATIVE P/E RATIO | 0.69 | DIV'D YLD | 3.4% | VALUE LINE | 1245 |

TIMELINESS 3 Average (Relative Price Perform- ance Next 12 Mos.)

SAFETY 3 Average (Scale: 1 Highest to 5 Lowest)

BETA 1.50 (1.00 = Market)

1995-97 PROJECTIONS
	Price	Gain	Ann'l Total Return
High	215	(+145%)	26%
Low	145	(+65%)	17%

Insider Decisions

	M	J	J	A	S	O	N	D	J
to Buy	0	0	0	0	0	0	0	0	0
Options	0	2	1	0	0	0	2	1	1
to Sell	0	2	2	0	0	0	1	1	1

Institutional Decisions

	2Q31	3Q31	4Q31
to Buy	82	75	97
to Sell	80	81	77
Hld's(000)	25351	24403	24236

Options: ASE

© VALUE LINE PUB., INC.

Target Price Range 1995 1996 1997

Shaded areas indicate recessions

Relative Price Strength

7.0 x "Cash Flow" p sh

| High: | 48.5 | 66.17 | 68.97 | 61.82 | 68.69 | 42.35 | 44.94 | 39.81 | 44.02 | 39.34 | 36.93 | 32.67 | 31.14 | 52.40 | 76.06 | 77.98 | 76.53 | 69.93 | 71.15 | | |
| Low: | 31.1 | | | | | | | | | | | | | | | | | | | | |

	1976	1977	1978	1979	1980	1981	1982	1983	1984	1985	1986	1987	1988	1989	1990	1991	1992	1993	© VALUE LINE PUB., INC.	95-97
	45.68	46.42	48.69	61.82	66.97		44.02	39.34	36.93	32.67	31.14	52.40	76.06	77.98	76.53	69.93	71.15	76.30	Sales per sh	100.00
	4.45	3.22	4.01	8.30	7.55	6.08	d0.99	1.3%	d1.85	2.64	2.60	7.13	17.12	18.29	17.07	11.83	12.45	17.45	"Cash Flow" per sh	25.00
	2.07	.64	1.16	5.06	4.20	2.61	d3.59	67.5	d0.41	.21	.57	4.51	13.15	14.24	13.12	7.86	8.25	13.00	Earnings per sh^A	20.00
	2.20	1.80	.60	1.20	1.55	1.60	.30	d0.43	d0.41		.15	.95	B2.85	3.00	3.00	3.00	3.00	3.00	Div'ds Decl'd per sh^B	5.00
	6.50	5.41	4.66	5.16	6.07	6.79	4.60		2.65	1.25	1.71	4.86	5.88	6.28	8.47	10.28	8.55	8.55	Cap'l Spending per sh	10.00
	43.34	42.35	42.92	46.78	49.30	50.09	44.94	39.81	29.16	28.78	30.36	35.37	47.10	39.00	48.86	53.41	58.45	58.45	Book Value per sh^C	107.85
	20.63	20.67	20.69	20.72	20.88	21.74	21.76	24.64	24.64	27.17	27.17	30.76	30.50	34.62	34.44	34.81	35.00	35.00	Common Shs Outst'g^D	35.00
	19.9	44.9	19.0	5.2	8.4	14.7			NMF	NMF	41.6	8.3	3.2	4.3	4.4	8.5	Bold figures are		Avg Ann'l P/E Ratio	9.0
	2.55	5.88	2.59	.75	1.12	1.79			NMF	NMF	2.82	.55	.27	.33	.33	.55	Value Line estimates		Relative P/E Ratio	.75
	5.3%	6.3%	2.7%	4.6%	4.4%	4.2%	1.2%			2.8%	2.1%	3.0%	3.0%	4%	2.3%	B4.7%	5.2%	4.5%	Avg Ann'l Div'd Yield	2.8%

	957.8	963.9	910.1	886.6	845.9	1611.7	2319.8	2699.6	2635.7	2434.3	2490	2670	Sales ($mill)	3500
	NMF	1.3%	NMF	13.9%	15.1%	22.6%	32.2%	34.0%	33.3%	24.7%	25.5%	33.0%	Operating Margin	36.0%
	56.6	67.5	59.8	55.3	54.9	60.7	116.9	133.4	133.0	138.9	145	155	Depreciation ($mill)	175
	d74.3	d63.5	d97.4	18.9	28.6	150.6	420.2	504.0	454.9	272.9	290	455	Net Profit ($mill)	700
	NMF	NMF	NMF	40.6%	39.3%	35.2%	24.1%	32.3%	33.0%	32.5%	33.0%	34.0%	Income Tax Rate	34.0%
	NMF	NMF	NMF	2.1%	3.4%	9.3%	18.1%	18.7%	17.3%	11.2%	11.6%	17.0%	Net Profit Margin	20.0%
	163.0	132.5	112.6	170.3	204.2	305.4	431.5	212.2	349.3	341.7	370	550	Working Cap'l ($mill)	1300
	667.2	600.3	591.2	448.1	609.8	398.2	449.7	431.5	403.5	382.0	375	375	Long-Term Debt ($mill)	300
	1026.3	1022.3	863.0	918.4	955.2	1337.8	1676.2	1350.1	1682.9	1859.3	2045	2295	Net Worth ($mill)	3775
	NMF	NMF	NMF	2.8%	3.0%	10.1%	20.9%	29.6%	22.6%	13.2%	13.0%	17.0%	% Earned Total Cap'l	17.5%
	NMF	NMF	NMF	2.1%	3.0%	11.3%	25.1%	37.3%	27.0%	14.7%	14.0%	19.0%	% Earned Net Worth	18.5%
	NMF	NMF	NMF	1.9%	2.6%	12.3%	20.9%	20.9%	20.9%	9.1%	9.0%	17.0%	% Retained to Comm Eq	14.0%
	NMF	NMF	NMF	.7%	45%	11%	11%	9.1%	23%	38%	36%	23%	% All Div'ds to Net Prof	25%

BUSINESS: Phelps Dodge Corporation is the largest U.S. copper producer in terms of domestic output. Nearly all of output is derived from low-cost, open pit mines. 1991 copper production: 538,100 tons. Average price: $1.05 lb. Has extensive copper fabricating operations. Company owns 44% of Black Mountain Ltd. 16% of Southern Peru Copper. Acquired Columbian Chemical 12/86. Ac-

quired Corporation 2/88. Hudson International 11/89. Officers and directors own about 1% of common stock. '91 depreciation rate 4.0%. Estimated plant age: 11 years. Has 13,931 employees, 28,000 shareholders. Chairman, President, C.E.O.: D. C. Yearley. Incorporated: New York. Address: 2600 North Central Avenue, Phoenix, Arizona 85004. Telephone: 602-234-8100.

Chart 9-3. Phelps Dodge stock chart. (Copyright © 1992 by Value Line Publishing, Inc., used by permission. For subscription information to the Value Line Investment Survey, please call (800) 634-3583.)

Michael Stores

Putnam cites the case of Michael Stores, Inc., the specialty retailer based in Irving, Texas, which saw earnings drop from more than $5 million, or 50 cents per share, in fiscal 1988 to a mere $13,000, or zero cents per share, in fiscal 1989 ended January 28, 1990.

Looking behind the earnings numbers, a number of out-of-the-ordinary factors contributed to the poor performance. First of all, legal and other expenses associated with a failed buyout offer totaled in excess of $4 million. In addition, a noncash charge for closing and relocating several older stores also negatively impacted earnings. Finally, preopening costs of new stores more than doubled in 1989 to $1.8 million.

In anticipation of the announced buyout, the price of Michael's stock ran up from a low of $3⅞ per share during the first quarter of 1988 to a high of $10¼ in 1989. The combination of the failed buyout, due to the inability of the proposed purchasers to arrange adequate financing, and poor earnings forced Michael's stock to plummet. During the third quarter of fiscal 1990, the stock hit a low of $2⅞ per share.

A close follower of Michael Stores would have seen the signs of the potential turnaround. With the failed buyout now in its wake, Michael's top management could devote its full attention to running the business. The one-time legal charges were also a thing of the past.

The company still commanded an industry leadership position as the largest retailer of arts and crafts. Improved store layouts promised to more prominently display merchandise and attract more customers. Increased advertising and enhanced merchandising programs put into place began to pay off and big.

By the end of fiscal 1991, revenues rose to record levels of $410 million, more than $120 million over fiscal 1989 revenues. Even more important, fiscal 1991 operating income more than doubled that achieved in fiscal 1989. Net income, before an extraordinary item related to early redemption of debt, rose to $10.7 million, or 87 cents per share.

Investors finally took notice, boosting Michael's stock price to a high of $24 per share in the fourth quarter of fiscal 1991. In conjunction with increased investor interest, the company moved to NASDAQ from the American Stock Exchange in September 1991.

Further improvements appear in store. With the proceeds of a secondary offering which raised $61 million, the company paid down virtually all its long-term debt and had plenty left for store expansion and operations. The move also slashed interest expenses, which had been running nearly $10 million annually as recently as fiscal 1990.

Unlike other retailers, Michael's actually prospered from the economic contraction, with consumers shifting from store-bought items to a recession-inspired return to homemade gifts, decorations, and crafts. A 1990 survey conducted by Hobby Industries of America, the industry trade group, found that 77 percent of all U.S. households participated in some sort of hobby or craft in 1990, up from only 64 percent in 1988.

While it's too late to participate in the Michael's turnaround, it represents a good case study.

Beverly Enterprises

Putnam cites another classic turnaround that took some three years to accomplish. Plenty of time to get your investment stake well-positioned to make a killing. In fact, this turnaround offered several opportunities to take advantage of the market's lack of respect for the ongoing turnaround.

Back in 1989, Beverly Enterprises, Inc., a long-term health-care company, looked like a terminal case itself. It had suffered three straight disastrous years, losing $31 million, or 54 cents, per share, $24 million, or 47 cents per share, and $ 104 million, or $1.96 cents per share, in 1987, 1988, and 1989, respectively.

In January 1988, the company announced it was in technical default of its revolving credit agreement and other credit agreements totaling approximately $800 million and as a result had to suspend payment of cash dividends on both its common and preferred stock.

The stock market evidently disliked Beverly Enterprise's vital signs, sending the stock into a trauma of its own. From a high of $22½ per share in mid-1986, the stock hit a low of $3⅞ per share as 1988 drew to a close.

"Hard-pressed firms must be willing to make tough choices and shed assets to get cashflow back into equilibrium," advises Putnam.

In the Beverly Enterprises case, actions taken in 1988 to stem the hemorrhaging included a restructuring of the $800 million in debt, a decision to sell up to 20,000 long-term beds, sales and leaseback of certain assets, and sales of notes receivable from prior asset sales.

It also placed into motion recommendations from the management consulting firm, McKinsey & Company, Inc., to compress Beverly Enterprise's management organization, completely eliminating three layers. This move not only slashed operations and overhead costs; it also streamlined communications and made local managers more responsive to their community's needs.

In addition, formation of a new management team of executive vice presidents oversaw the critical functions of operations, finance, marketing, administration, and development.

By the third quarter of 1989, the efforts started to pump life back into Beverly Enterprise's earnings picture. Likewise, the stock market took notice, driving up the stock to $10 per share.

However, despite continuing improvement in 1990 (earnings for the year rose to nearly $13 million, or 19 cents per share), investors lost faith, and the stock once again plummeted to less than $4 per share in the first quarter of 1990. Thus another great opportunity for the turnaround investor to take advantage of the market's lack of conviction presented itself.

In 1990, management took additional steps to ensure more efficient use of its remaining facilities by doubling the marketing effort. From January 1990 through December 1990, average occupancy rates rose from 86.4 to 87.7 percent.

Also in 1990, the company consolidated senior management personnel in a central location with the relocation of the firm's corporate headquarters to Fort Smith, Arkansas, from Pasadena, California. Later in 1991, other senior company staff positions were relocated from Virginia Beach, Virginia, to the Arkansas headquarters.

Industrywide trends such as our nation's aging population (during the next 25 years, the over-65 population will grow by 61 percent and the over-85 population will more than double), demand for nursing homes rising faster than supply, and a 1990 favorable government ruling on Medicaid payments bode well for industry participants.

The good news continued in 1991. Beverly Enterprises and Lincoln National Insurance entered a joint venture under which Beverly will provide care for over 4 million acute Lincoln policyholders and Beverly entered a separate joint venture with RehabCare Corporation to develop units in Beverly nursing homes to provide inpatient rehabilitation. The increase in non-Medicaid patients means higher margins for Beverly and less susceptibility to government actions in cutting Medicaid payment rates.

The restructuring actions put into place back in the late 1980s came to fruition in 1991. Net income surged to $29.2 million from $12.9 million in 1990, and earnings per share nearly doubled to 37 cents per share, versus only 19 cents per share a year earlier, even though 15 million more shares were outstanding at the end of 1991 than at the end of 1990.

The fickle stock market once again took notice, driving up the price of Beverly Enterprises common stock above $12 per share, its highest level since it tumbled from around $16 per share to less than $8 per share during the October 1987 crash.

Three Important Variables to Assess

Robert Natale, research director for Standard & Poor's equity division, looks at three major variables in the turnaround scenario. First of all, he considers the financial viability of the troubled company. In other words, does it make sense to spend valuable time, effort, and money to track the fortunes of a particular company if its chances for survival are minimal.

This often means keeping close tabs on who the company's largest creditors and stockholders are. These players often assume a pivotal role in the ultimate success or failure of the turnaround. Also look good and hard at the debt-servicing and banking relationships that will be vital to the firm's survival.

Next, Natale assesses the likelihood that company earnings can make a successful comeback. This involves analyzing reasons for the firm's misfortunes. Is an economic contraction, industry cycle, or product life cycle at the root of the problem, and how will anticipated changes in those scenarios impact the company and its ability to bounce back?

"You have to remember that some companies are beaten down like dogs because in reality they really are dogs possessing no real chance to prosper again," says Natale.

Finally, Natale works at deciphering management and its actions. What restructuring strategies is it undertaking to correct the situation? Are there key acquisitions in the works? What new and innovative marketing avenues is it trying? Look at the changes to determine whether or not the turnaround seems plausible.

A host of questions need to be answered. Evaluate each of the company's crucial operations from manufacturing to marketing and from finances to research and development to get a feel for how the company is handling problem areas. Equally important, get a feel for factors external to the company that can impact, either positively or negatively, the firm's operational and financial standing.

Successful Turnarounds

Case Study: Informix

Natale points to Informix Corporation—a Menlo Park, California, supplier of database information management software—as a completed successful turnaround that the overall market misjudged.

Following earnings of 48 cents per share in 1989, the software company made a voluntary accounting change, taking a more conservative approach to recognizing revenue in 1990. Unfortunately, the accounting decision change came after the company had already reported three quarters' worth of earnings for 1990, and the adjustment included the cumulative change for all previous years of operation.

The move contributed to a loss of $46 million, or $3.65 per share; however, even without the accounting change, Informix would have reported a loss for 1990 due to a slowdown in revenue growth and higher costs. On a pro forma basis, Informix would also have reported a loss for the years 1989 and 1988 if the more conservative accounting position had been in effect earlier.

Faced with the flip-flop in earnings, an industry slowdown brought on by the international economic contraction, and pricing pressures, investors took flight. From a high of $15⅜ per share in the fourth quarter of 1989, Informix's common stock plunged to $3⅝ per share during 1990's fourth quarter and below $3 per share in early 1991.

Despite the earnings bomb Informix dropped on shareholders, the gloomy situation contained some bright spots that foretold better times and higher stock prices ahead.

"While the solidness of Informix's earnings was called into question with the accounting change, the fundamental revenue base was still essentially intact. The market clearly misperceived the company's prospects," says Natale.

For example, during the fourth quarter of 1990, Informix and ASCII Corporation signed an exclusive distribution agreement for the Japanese market. As part of the agreement, the Japanese firm purchased 5 percent of Informix's common stock at $10 per share, far above the current market price.

Later, in early 1991, Hewlett-Packard committed to purchase up to 5 percent of Informix common stock in the open market, with Informix having the option to sell an additional 5 percent to Hewlett-Packard in the form of newly issued shares. The agreement also included a joint development, marketing, and sales arrangement.

These deals not only provided for an influx of capital but also set the stage for powerful strategic business partnerships with access to new markets and/or technology.

Four new technologically advanced product introductions in 1989, including a graphical presentation spreadsheet and the industry's first fault-tolerant on-line transaction processing database engine to support multimedia databases, set the stage for increased market penetration and sustained revenue growth. In fact, the company's graphical spreadsheet, called Wingz,™ earned all four of the top 1989 software awards in the Macintosh sector.

In 1989 and early 1990, Informix strengthened its management team with the addition of a new chief executive officer and new vice presidents in marketing, customer service, human resources, finance, North American sales, and Asia/Pacific operations.

At the same time, the firm realized it needed to cut costs and reestablished a single corporate headquarters. A January 1991 restructuring also reduced the firm's work force by some 15 percent.

With streamlined operations, heavy sales efforts, and continued new-product introductions, things began to take shape. By the second quarter of 1991, the company turned a quarterly profit and by the end of 1991 had earned record annual revenues and profits. On a sales increase of nearly 23 percent, net income rose to $12.6 million, or 84 cents per share, versus the loss of $46 million, or $3.65 per share, in the accounting-adjusted results of 1990.

Finally, the stock market caught up with the realities of the Informix rejuvenation and drove the stock price up to a 1991 high of $15⅞ per share, a nice rise from its low of $2⅝ per share less than a year earlier. However, the best was yet to come. For the first quarter of 1992, Informix posted sharply higher earnings of 73 cents per share. That performance nearly eclipsed the 74 cents per share from continuing operations in all of 1987, the best year on record before 1991.

The Informix story is still being written as this book goes to press, but its stock was surging to new highs daily in excess of $36 per share. To be sure, turnaround investing pays off big.

Case Study: Magna International

Magna International Inc., a leading Canadian manufacturer of advanced automotive systems and assemblies such as bumper systems, transmissions, automotive interiors, and chassis stampings, represents another classic cyclical turnaround.

Following the automotive industry recession of 1981–1982, Magna embarked on a significant expansion move to become a major supplier of automotive components to North American original equipment manufacturers and later took a more global market approach. The strategy fit hand in glove with the automobile industry's trend to increased outsourcing and the establishment of plants in the United States by foreign automotive firms.

Revenues grew from Can$200 million in fiscal 1982, to nearly Can$2 billion for fiscal 1989. Overall, Magna International operated 126 North American and 4 European manufacturing and product development facilities.

For the most part, earnings also grew steadily from fiscal 1982's Can$0.48 per share to a peak of Can$1.93 per share generated in fiscal 1986.

Earnings dipped to $0.70 per share in fiscal 1988 from $1.56 per share a year earlier but recovered to Can$1.21 per share in fiscal 1989.

In order to expand in both the North American and global markets simultaneously plus acquire new technologies, Magna took on a huge debt load. Long-term debt ballooned from Can$61 million at the end of fiscal 1982 to nearly Can$1.1 billion in January 1990.

The larger debt resulted in significantly higher debt-service levels peaking at a time when the automotive industry hit another major cyclical downturn. In fiscal 1990, the combination of dropping capacity utilization rates, high overhead costs, start-up facilities consuming inordinate amounts of management time and attention, and high debt-servicing requirements set the stage for disaster.

The result—in January 1990 Magna International defaulted on nearly Can$1 billion in debt; and for fiscal year ended July 31, 1990, the automobile parts supplier lost Can$224 million, or Can$8.06 per share, on revenues of Can$1.9 billion.

Magna's stock, which traded on NASDAQ as high as US$26⅜ per share in 1987, collapsed like a flat tire, dropping to US$2¾ per share in fiscal 1990 and hitting bottom below US$2 per share during the second quarter of fiscal 1991.

With no end to the recession in sight, investors had plenty of justification to shed Magna International stock like last year's automobile model. However, the turnaround investor needs to look beyond the immediate situation to see how the future will play itself out.

A little investigation would have uncovered a number of actions that Magna International had already taken as early as the second quarter of fiscal 1990 to turn things around.

For example, it reassessed the viability of every one of its operating units and decided to divest nonstrategic facilities, consolidate some operations, and shutter still others. This resulted in a Can$163 million write-down of assets in the second quarter of fiscal 1990, but more importantly the move eliminated some Can$50 million worth of future operating losses.

Cleaning up its financial act, Magna negotiated with creditors to restructure its debt load and gain some breathing room. Cost cutting helped reduce overhead costs and improve operating efficiencies. Management trimmed corporate and group office staff rolls by nearly 300 people, running a much leaner organization. Selling, general, and administrative expenses dropped to less than 8 percent of sales in fiscal 1991 from more than 10 percent in fiscal 1990.

By the end of fiscal 1991, Magna's long-term debt level was down to a more manageable Can$582 million with a corresponding decrease in debt-servicing costs.

Despite a decline in North American industry volumes, Magna International achieved its turnaround. For the fiscal year ended July 31,

1991, paced by higher utilization levels and improved operating efficiencies, Magna earned Can$16.5 million, or 58 Canadian cents per share.

Once again, the stock market "discovered" the completed turnaround. By July 1991, Magna's stock rose to nearly US$14 per share on NASDAQ. By the middle of fiscal 1992, Magna's earnings were solidly back on track. For that fiscal year's first nine months, the company earned over Can$2 per share, versus Can$0.18 for the previous fiscal year's first three quarters and the Can$1.32 per share analysts were previously projecting for the entire fiscal year. Impressed investors bid up the company's NASDAQ stock price to over US$26 per share.

Looking ahead to the economic recovery of the nineties, Magna should be well-positioned to increase its facility capacity utilization from the 70 percent it operated in early 1992.

Magna management had a strong interest in making the successful turnaround even more impressive. Chairman Stronach owned 54 percent of the class B stock, while an employees' profit-sharing plan controlled another 6 percent of outstanding shares.

Current Turnarounds

We searched for some potential turnarounds in process for evaluation. Assuming the turnarounds have not concluded before this book hits the streets, you can follow management's strategies and the results as well as track how the company reacts to outside forces such as the economy and competition. If the turnarounds have already been completed, these examples still serve as a valid historical reference for your turnaround analysis.

Westinghouse

"Westinghouse presents an interesting case. Sour loan problems in its financial group dragged down earnings and resulted in the quarterly dividend being cut nearly in half from the 35 cents per share paid in 1991 to 18 cents per share quarterly in 1992," says Bradley E. Turner, senior vice president with McDonald & Company Securities, Inc., in Cleveland, Ohio.

Severe deterioration in the economy caused Westinghouse's financial services operations to downsize, taking a $975 million pretax write-off against 1990 earnings. This extraordinary charge caused Westinghouse to slash its originally reported earnings $3.41 per share down to 91 cents per share.

Although management optimistically reported that the decisive action addressed the subsidiary's problems and enhanced the financial operation's value, the scenario repeated again in 1991 only more so. This time, the continued recession compounded the financial service's problem real estate loans, resulting in Westinghouse taking a whopping $1.68 billion write-down to cover the anticipated losses in liquidating assets of the financial services subsidiary.

As a result, Westinghouse lost over $1.08 billion, or $3.46 per share, in 1991. The company's stock tumbled along with earnings. From a high of nearly $39½ per share in 1990, Westinghouse's share price dropped to $13¾ per share in December 1991. Shortly thereafter the stock rose to the $20 per share level.

Obviously, Westinghouse management did not stand still. Efforts made to stem the losses and get earnings turned around included naming former Westinghouse chief financial officer head of the financial services segment, raising cash through a combination of an equity offer and asset sales, taking steps to reduce the risk posture of the financial services portfolio, reducing underperforming assets, and trimming the employment rolls by 4000 people.

Cost-cutting moves were expected to slash $200 million annually from company expenses. Despite the tough-minded Westinghouse measures, the overall economy may have as much, if not more, to do with the degree of success that Westinghouse enjoys in 1992 and beyond.

In addition to working to overcome recession-induced financial segment losses, Westinghouse also had to bear the brunt of the effects of two new accounting standards of the Financial Accounting Standards Board set to be put into motion in 1992. FASB No. 106, "Employers' Accounting for Postretirement Benefits Other Than Pensions," and FASB No. 96, "Accounting for Income Taxes," combined to create a one-time net after-tax charge of around $300 million in early 1992.

Be aware of the reasons for and the consequences of both accounting and restructuring write-offs. In many cases, they represent noncash charges and don't negatively, and often positively, impact corporate cashflow and future operational results. Look at the long-term results. While restructuring charges stem from past management mistakes, they represent a clear sign that management recognizes the seriousness of the predicament and is starting to put plans into action to correct the problems before they get even worse.

At this point, it's hard to tell whether or not Westinghouse's 1991 and early 1992 "clear the decks" strategy will pay off. As with any potential turnaround, it must be closely monitored to uncover the signs of a successful recovery in motion before the overall market anticipates the company's improving fortunes. In this way, you can beat the market to the punch and establish your investment position and enjoy the price surge as other investors arrive later to bid up the stock price.

Turnarounds: An Important Part of Putnam Voyager Fund's Portfolio

Matthew Weatherbie, vice president and fund manager for the Putnam Voyager Fund, uses a two-pronged investment approach blending a mix of small-cap stocks and blue-chip opportunity stocks in efforts to achieve above-average capital growth.

Seeking out common stocks in companies that possess the potential for capital appreciation significantly greater than the market averages, Weatherbie targets corporate turnarounds as one segment of Putnam's overall portfolio.

"We search for high investment quality in what we call `opportunity' stocks, those undergoing positive changes—changes that derive from such events as the introduction of a new product line, a rejuvenated management, or the selling off of losing divisions or operations," says Weatherbie.

While Weatherbie's investment horizon for the small-cap portion of the Putnam Voyager Fund's portfolio is typically two years or longer, his turnaround stock portfolio investment horizon typically lies within the 12- to 18-month range. As of January 31, 1992, the Putnam Voyager portfolio mix consisted of 66 percent foundation growth stocks (small caps), 7 percent cash and equivalents, and 26 percent "opportunity stocks."

The small-cap/opportunity stock strategy obviously works and has drawn attention. The November 1991 issue of *Morningstar Mutual Fund Values* described Putnam Voyager Fund as follows: "Its fine risk/reward profile makes it one of the most attractive aggressive-growth funds we cover."

According to Lipper Analytical Services, for the 10 years ended January 31, 1992, Putnam Voyager Fund ranked in the top 7 percent of the 42 capital appreciation funds tracked by Lipper and in the top 5 percent of the 367 equity funds in existence during that entire 10-year period. The fund's enviable performance also garnered an A rating from *Investor's Business Daily*. (See Chart 3-4).

Alcoa. Chosen as one of the "opportunity stocks" in Putnam Voyager Fund's portfolio as of May 1992, the Aluminum Company of America (Alcoa) saw earnings per share drop from a record $10.67 per share on revenues of $10.9 billion in 1989 to a dismal $0.71 per share on revenues of $9.89 billion in 1991. The 1991 results included a special charge of $217 million, or $2.56 per share, for costs involving environmental matters ($160 million) and restructuring business units ($57 million).

As a major supplier to the housing, construction, and automotive industries, Alcoa felt the impact of the prolonged recession entering the nineties. Further compounding the situation of the oversupply of aluminum and lower demand, the dissolving Soviet Union initiated the shipment of large quantities of aluminum into western markets.

"Looking forward, we anticipate the dumping of aluminum on the market to decrease, the United States and world economies to recover, and better pricing with increased unit demand," says fund manager Weatherbie.

He also views Alcoa as a world-class aluminum producer with a strong balance sheet and a lower cost structure than many of its competitors—all the elements required to take advantage of an economic turnaround.

"The dividend appears secure, and the stock trades around book value and at a low multiple to cashflow, definitely the signs of an `opportunity stock,'" says Weatherbie.

From a high of nearly $80 per share during the record year of 1989, Alcoa stock fell more than 37 percent to less than $50 per share in late 1990. Since then the stock had recovered to the mid-sixties range.

Your Choice

Now it's up to you to ferret out the next turnaround candidates. Contact the prospective companies and request to be placed on their mailing lists for financial reports and press releases. Also request copies of annual reports and 10Ks for the last three years. Simply call the director of investor relations or chief financial officer to get the reports flowing to you.

These will let you know how management assesses the situation, what actions have been taken to date, and what problematic operational and financial areas to be aware of in your analysis. Another required SEC report, the 8K, details information on specific occurrences such as the acquisition or disposition of assets, changes in the certifying accounting firm, director resignations, and other materially important items.

The financial reports often carry management's analysis and interpretation of industry trends and overall economic scenarios. Read the general business and financial publications and trade magazines to form your own opinion and to guard against management's wide-eyed optimism in the face of disaster. Remember, often it's the same management team who got the company into trouble that may be trying to execute the turnaround. It's wise to maintain a jaundiced eye in the world of turnarounds.

There's plenty of readily accessible information on companies. Check your public or university library for copies of *Value Line Investment Survey* and Standard & Poor's *The Outlook* for relatively current information.

Now, where to look. Since potential turnaround companies typically have suffered earnings declines and/or other financial or operational setbacks, start your search among depressed or cyclical industries in the midst of their economic downturn. Your continual perusal of business and trade publications will alert you to other turnaround prospects.

Recent examples of industries with companies with the potential for rebound include the banking, savings and loan, and insurance segments. Likewise, the traditional cyclical industries such as automotive and natural resource companies such as mining, paper, and retailing form fertile ground for the turnaround investor.

It's up to you. Do your homework and enjoy the substantial fruits that can be gained by beating the market to the punch.

10
Total-Return Candidates

Maximizing Yield and Capital Gains

Investors seeking both income and capital appreciation for an attractive total return have been faced with tough times in the late eighties and early nineties.

First of all, the number of companies declaring cash dividend increases dropped to 1086 in 1991, and only an estimated 1300 U.S. companies boosted cash dividends in 1992. The composite dividend for the S&P 500 rose a measly 1 percent in 1990 and an estimated 5 percent in 1991 to $12.80.

Second, yields on alternative investments such as certificates of deposit and government bonds have fallen to lows not experienced in decades. For example, by mid-1992 yields on 6-month certificates of deposit sank to 3.45 percent, compared with nearly 6 percent a year earlier, and since January 1991 to mid-1992 3-month Treasury bills slipped from 6.35 to 3.64 percent, 5-year Treasury notes from 7.86 to 6.6 percent, and 30-year Treasury bonds from 8.22 to 7.83 percent.

Finally, disappointing earnings surprises have sent many a company's stock price into a tailspin, slashing capital appreciation or even creating paper if not realized investment losses.

To be sure, investors fleeing from low yields offered by alternative investments have been flocking to stocks to improve their investment income and total return. The risk, of course, lies in moving from cash to trash. It's imperative that you maintain a quality investment focus. Sure, high-yielding stocks can be plenty enticing, but keep in mind that you only receive higher yields for taking on added risk. The two go hand in hand. There's no free lunch.

In the eighties, many investors were burnt by their greed for the lofty yields offered by high-flying savings and loans. Undoubtedly, history will repeat itself in the nineties with the flight to stocks. Don't get blindsided in the process. Do your investigative homework and seek out value.

Focus on Buying Common Stocks

From a historical perspective, common stocks have outperformed other traditional investments. From 1926 through 1991, common stocks delivered a total return of 12.4 percent versus 5.7 percent for long-term corporate bonds, 5.3 percent for intermediate-term government bonds, 5.1 percent for long-term government bonds, and 3.8 percent for U.S. Treasury bills.

As illustrated earlier in Chap. 3, "Small-Cap Gems," Chart 3-1 shows common stocks far outstripping inflation and competing investments in U.S. capital markets. From 1925 to 1991, $1.00 grew to $7.69 with inflation, while $1.00 invested in Treasury bills grew to $11.01, $1.00 invested in long-term government bonds grew to $21.94, and $1.00 invested in common stocks grew to $675.59.

It's evident that the total-return factor (dividends plus capital appreciation) makes investment in common stocks a perfect choice for building wealth over the long run. That doesn't set aside the need to diversify your portfolio among different investment classes, nor the need to invest in current income-generating assets outside of the common stock arena. Of course, the proportion of your investment portfolio in cash, money-market, or other liquid assets, in bonds, in common stocks, etc., will depend on several factors including what other sources of income you have, what your cash requirements are for expenses such as mortgages and college finances, how much readily available savings you have, and how close you are to retirement age.

Stake your claim on the ability of solid, well-run companies to increase their dividend payout and maintain revenues and earnings gains that translate into total-return-enhancing capital gains.

Bonds versus Stocks

A. G. Edwards conducted a bit of its own total-return research. Using a sample of five stocks that had increased their stock dividend for each of the 10 years from the end of 1981 through the end of 1991, A. G.

Edwards compared the returns from purchasing the companies' long-term bonds versus purchasing the companies' common stock.

While reinvestment of proceeds was not considered in the study (which would have made the difference in returns even more dramatic), the research showed that the best bond purchase (Philip Morris, Inc., 9.125 percent, July 18, 2003) increased the investors' wealth after 10 years by 217.96 percent (12.26 percent compounded annual growth), versus a gain of 1356.99 percent (30.72 percent compounded annual growth) for the best stock purchase (Philip Morris, Inc.). In fact, even the worst stock purchase (SCE Corp.), with a return of 382.40 percent (17.04 percent compounded annual growth), outperformed the best bond purchase by a considerable margin.

Another study, originally reported in the August 17, 1990, issue of *Value Line Selection & Opinion* and updated in the May 1, 1992, issue, demonstrated that utility stocks provided better total returns than bonds whether interest rates were rising or falling.

A number of factors account for the better performance exhibited by utility stocks. First of all, bonds carry fixed interest rates and yields, while dividend payouts for utility stocks can rise with improving operating results. Second, bonds often carry call provisions and have maturity dates that can prove detrimental to overall returns when bond proceeds must be reinvested at lower interest rates. Finally, the price appreciation of stocks traditionally outpaces that of bond value appreciation even as market interest rates fall and make higher-yielding bonds in the secondary market rise.

Even after excluding higher-yielding utility stocks that carry much higher risk exposure and lower-yielding utility stocks with too much market risk, the total return of the middle-ground utility stocks outperformed not only government bonds but also the average total return of all stocks under *Value Line* review.

Back in August 1990, a 30-year government bond with an 8 percent coupon rate purchased at a discount price of $915.90 for a $1000 bond yielded 8.8 percent. At the same time, the average yield for all utility common stocks covered by *Value Line* stood at 6.2 percent, while the Value Line Utility Stock Index stood at 187.

For the 20-month period following August 1990, the bondholder earned a total return of 23.5 percent consisting of 14.5 percent in income and 9 percent in capital gains as the price of the bond rose to approach par.

In comparison, the average utility stock returned a total of 25.4 percent, consisting of 12.0 percent in income and the 13.4 percent balance in capital gains. The average total return for all stocks under *Value Line* review came around 18 percent for the same time frame.

Buy High-Yielding Stocks

One way to beat the market and enjoy higher total returns lies in purchasing a package of the 10 highest-yielding Dow Jones Industrial stocks. Every 12 months cull out those stocks that have fallen from the top 10 yielding stocks and replace them with the newcomers. For 1991, this strategy delivered a total return of 34.4 percent, versus 24.3 percent for the Dow Jones Industrial Average as a whole. That occurred despite 2 of the top 19 yielding Dow firms (General Motors and Westinghouse) losing money in 1991.

The long-term record is even more impressive. For the 22-year period ending in 1991, the top 10 yielding Dow stocks generated 2134 percent in total return, versus only 545 percent for the Dow Jones Industrials.

According to John Slatter, senior vice president and senior portfolio manager with Hickory Investment Advisors in Cleveland, Ohio, and author of *Safe Investing: How to Make Money without Losing Your Shirt* (Simon & Schuster, 1991), over the past 31 years, $10,000 invested in the top 10 highest-yielding stocks would have returned $803,575, versus only $208,853 total return for all Dow stocks during that time frame. (See Chart 10-1).

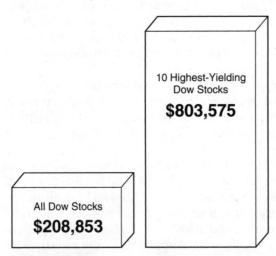

Chart 10-1. Ten highest yielding Dow stocks vs. all Dow stocks. Over the past 31 years, $10,000 invested in a portfolio of all 30 stocks in the Dow Jones Industrial Average provided a total return of $208,853 (includes appreciation plus dividends). The same $10,000 invested in only the 10 highest-yielding Dow stocks (eliminating the 20 lowest yielders) provided a total return of $803,575 or a 284% greater return. (*Source: John Slatter CFA*).

Table 10-1. Top 10 Yielding Dow Stocks versus
Dow Jones Industrial Average

Bear market year	Dow stocks	10 highest-yielding Dow stocks
1981	−3.6%	6.3%
1977	−13.2	1.1
1974	−23.4	−2.9
1973	−13.4	3.3
1969	−11.9	−10.8
1966	−16.0	−17.0
1962	−7.7	2.5
1960	−6.3	−3.3
1957	−8.2	−9.0
Average	−15.5%	−3.3%

Slatter's research also indicates that the top 10 yielding Dow stocks offer a degree of protection in bear markets, as evidenced in Table 10-1.

"If you follow this strategy, you should outpace the market by a considerable margin. There are no guarantees in the stock market, but this strategy comes as close to one as I can find," says Slatter.

Slatter cautions that the strategy won't work every year, but over the long run, you should be able to beat the Dow average by nearly 5 percent a year. Over a 20-year time frame, that 5 percent differential between a 15 percent return and a 10 percent return translates into more than $240,000 additional value on a $25,000 investment.

Overall, the 10 highest-yielding Dow stocks outperformed the Dow Jones Industrials in all but 7 years out of 32 and 14 times out of the last 16 years.

The Yacktman Fund Approach

"We employ our total-return approach with an emphasis on a big `G' (growth) and little `I' (income). If you can earn 15 to 20 percent or more, it just doesn't make much sense to want an interest or dividend check. Keep those funds fully invested to enhance your overall compounded return," advises Donald A. Yacktman, who piloted Selected American Shares to enviable investment returns before launching his own value-oriented growth and income fund, the Yacktman Fund, in 1992.

At Selected American Shares, Yacktman's value approach guided the growth and income fund to an annual average return of 15.6 percent for the five years ended 1991 and 18.8 percent for the ten-year period ended 1991. Even more impressive, during 1991, Selected American Shares gained 46.3 percent, versus only 29.3 percent for all growth and income mutual funds.

Rather than attempt to figure out where the economy and stock market are headed, Yacktman concentrates on uncovering value and purchasing it at a discount. He searches out good businesses with management dedicated to building shareholder value.

"I look for firms with a high return on tangible assets and management with a history of generating and utilizing corporate cashflow to increase the firm's value," says Yacktman.

He sees five options for the use of cash: protecting existing business through research and development efforts; making new marketing thrusts, for example, making acquisitions to add similar product lines or enhance the business; purchasing company stock (after all what business does management know better?); paying cash dividends; and sitting on it.

"I would hope management could find more creative and productive ways to use cash than sitting on it, and large cash dividend payouts could be better put to use increasing the value of shareholder's equity. Why pay out cash dividends that get taxed to the individual, who often then turns around and reinvests the tax-depleted funds back in the company via dividend reinvestment plans?" says Yacktman.

According to Yacktman, enticing low-price bargains exist for several reasons. First of all, a down stock market often creates undervalued situations. Second, potential threats to company earnings and cashflow cause psychological downward price pressure. Finally, real company problems, which can be easily corrected, currently depress the firm's stock price.

"Having the courage to make a purchase when a stock is low, and buy even more when the price declines, separates the men from the boys in this business," says Yacktman.

According to Yacktman, there's plenty of opportunity to get in on the low end. On average, individual stocks tend to fluctuate 50 percent in a single year from low to high. For example, if a stock fluctuates between $20 per share and $30 per share within a given year, Yacktman patiently waits until he can purchase the stock on the low end of the scale. These purchases typically coincide with the particular stock being out of favor for temporary reasons, as cited earlier.

Yacktman invests with a 10-year time horizon, providing plenty of time for the stock to rebound and post new highs. A fivefold-to-tenfold value increase is not out of the ordinary in Yacktman's portfolio over the 10-year span.

A classic example of Yacktman's search for value, he started purchasing Freddie Mac (Federal Home Loan Mortgage Corporation) in 1990 around $60 per share. Publicity over fraud occurring in its insured Atlanta and New York apartment mortgages, which accounted for only 3 percent of holdings, traumatized investors. The stock's price sunk to $50 per share and then $30 per share in a very short time.

However, in the long run value won out. In 1991, it hit a high of $138 per share (all Freddie Mac stock prices before the 1992 3-for-2 stock split).

More recently, Yacktman likes the prospects of RJR Nabisco Holdings Corporation. After two disastrous years in 1989 and 1990, the company is finally digging itself out of its highly leveraged hole with healthy cashflows. From record-high long-term debt of nearly $22 billion at the end of 1989, management has cut its debt load more than 40 percent by the end of 1991. The reduction of high-cost LBO debt reduced RJR Nabisco's first quarter 1992 interest expense by $225 million from 1991's similar quarter, a huge boost to the bottom line.

On the operations front, RJR Nabisco has proved itself adept at investing in markets with high profit potential. As domestic tobacco sales have dropped, increased market penetration in international markets has kept the international segment expanding at a double-digit clip. In the Nabisco food sector, new products and brand extensions combine to boost operating income.

To be sure, RJR Nabisco's still burdensome debt load, intense industry competition, and tobacco-cancer lawsuit challenges present significant hurdles for the near future. However, with Yacktman's 10-year investment horizon, RJR Nabisco has plenty of time to build shareholder value.

In March 1991, RJR Nabisco exchanged equity for debt, at which time the stock started trading publicly. In April 1991, the company sold 115 million shares of common stock to the public at $11¼ per share. Since then, the stock price hit a high of $13 per share in 1991 before treading lower to the $9 per share range in mid-1992.

Other growth and income mutual funds with decent track records include AIM Charter, American Mutual, Colonial Fund, Fidelity Growth/Income, and Vista Growth & Income.

Use Increasing Dividends as an Indicator

"Total-return investors must reinvest their dividends to maximize their compounded return over time. Look for companies that have consistently increased their dividend year after year," advises Geraldine Weiss, editor of *Investment Quality Trends* in La Jolla, California.

Increasing dividends sends out a strong positive signal of earnings gains, a healthy balance sheet and cashflow, and the board of directors' confidence of even better days ahead.

Table 10-2 lists companies that have increased their dividend payout for at least each of the past 15 years and possessed a dividend yield of at least 2.5 percent in 1991.

These stocks represent a wide range of industries, running the gamut from high-tech pharmaceuticals to low-tech check printing and from fi-

Table 10-2. Top-Dividend Performers

Company	Business	1991 average annual dividend yield, %
American Business Products	Office supplies	3.4%
American Home Products	Pharmaceuticals	3.8
American National Insurance	Insurance	4.6
Aon Corporation	Insurance	4.2
Ball Corporation	Packaging	3.8
Banc One	Banking	2.9
H&R Block	Tax preparation	2.7
Boatmen's Bancshares	Banking	5.2
Colonial Companies	Insurance	2.5
A. T. Cross	Writing instruments	5.0
Deluxe Corporation	Check printing	3.0
Diebold, Inc.	Transaction equipment	3.8
Dun & Bradstreet	Publishing	4.6
Emerson Electric	Electrical equipment	3.1
Gormann-Rupp	Pumps	3.5
John H. Harland	Publishing	3.8
Hubbell Inc.	Electrical equipment	3.0
Jefferson-Pilot	Insurance	3.5
K mart Corp.	Retail	4.1
Lance	Snack foods	3.8
Minnesota Mining	Tapes, adhesives	3.8
National Service	Lighting equipment	3.8
Thomas & Betts	Electrical Components	4.1
Universal Corp.	Tobacco, Ins.	5.6
UST	Tobacco	2.8

nancial service-based insurance firms to industrial manufacturers of electrical parts and pumps. Build your own diversified portfolio of top-dividend performers.

Dun & Bradstreet

Dun & Bradstreet has increased its cash dividend 25 times in the past 25 years. Since 1982, the dividend has jumped from $0.67 per share to an annual rate of $2.18 per share in 1992, up nearly 224 percent. After an earnings slump in 1990, Dun & Bradstreet appears back on track with favorable year-to-year quarterly earnings comparisons. An attractive 4.2 percent yield helps keep shareholders happy, while future earnings improvements should help boost the firm's stock price, adding to total investor return.

Other Companies with Total-Return Potential

Bristol-Myers Squibb

Weiss likes the prospects of Bristol-Myers Squibb for total-return potential. (See Chart 10-2.) She considers the sell-off in Bristol-Myers shares due to disappointing earnings comparable to the firm's undervalued situation 12 years ago when the company traded below $8 per share. Trading more than 25 points below its 52-week high of $90 per share, Bristol-Myers has plenty of room to recoup as earnings gains come back on stream.

In mid-1992, Bristol-Myers signed an agreement with an Italian company for the supply of raw material for its anticancer drug, Taxol. The new source is considered more plentiful and derives the raw material from the needles and twigs of the yew specie instead of from harvested bark which killed the rare yew tree.

"You need to keep a weather eye out for debt. In the Bristol-Myers case, you find a very strong company financially, with less than 4 percent debt and a good track record of dividend increases," says Weiss.

Utilities

In the utility arena, Weiss considers the segment to be in a long-term rising trend. She cites the following stocks with a long history of dividend increases: Allegheny Power Systems (35), American Water Works (24),

BRISTOL-MYERS SQ NYSE-BMY

RECENT PRICE **75**	P/E RATIO **16.9** (Trailing: 18.4 / Median: 16.0)	RELATIVE P/E RATIO **1.06**
DIV'D YLD **3.7%**		VALUE LINE **1263**

High: 14.7 14.4 18.5 23.9 15.25 ... Low: 11.4 12.7 15.6 20.5 ...

TIMELINESS **3** Average (Relative Price Perform-ance Next 12 Mos.)
SAFETY **1** Highest (Scale: 1 Highest to 5 Lowest)
BETA 1.00 (1.00 = Market)

1995-97 PROJECTIONS

	Price	Gain	Ann'l Total Return
High	185	(+145%)	26%
Low	155	(+105%)	23%

Insider Decisions / Institutional Decisions

Percent shares traded: 9.0 / 6.0 / 3.0

Relative Price Strength — 2-for-1 split

17.0 x "Cash Flow" p sh

Target Price Range 1995 1996 1997

Shaded areas indicate recessions

Options: CBOE

●VALUE LINE PUB., INC.	1982	1983	1984	1985	1986	1987	1988	1989	1990	1991	1992	1993	95-97
Sales per sh	13.31	14.36	15.25	16.08	16.89	18.76	20.76	17.49	19.66	21.48	22.80	27.60	42.00
"Cash Flow" per sh	1.51	1.74	1.98	2.24	2.50	2.87	3.33	3.11	3.80	4.43	5.25	6.10	9.50
Earnings per sh	1.30	1.50	1.73	1.93	2.14	2.47	2.88	2.75	3.33	3.95	4.60	5.45	8.50
Div'ds Decl'd per sh	.53	.60	.80	.94	1.06	1.40	1.68	2.00	2.12	2.40	2.76	3.00	5.00
Cap'l Spending per sh	.63	.52	.65	.75	.76	.63	.87	1.06	.98	1.21	1.15	1.25	1.75
Book Value per sh	6.26	6.94	7.77	8.84	9.88	11.20	12.31	9.67	10.34	11.15	14.25	16.75	23.00
Common Shs Outst'g	270.54	272.86	274.73	276.29	286.24	287.85	525.34	523.82	519.51			525.00	525.00
Avg Ann'l P/E Ratio	11.5	12.9	13.4	15.2	17.7	19.3	14.8	18.1	17.8	20.1			20.0
Relative P/E Ratio	1.27	1.09	1.25	1.23	1.20	1.29	1.23	1.37	1.32	1.28			1.55
Avg Ann'l Div'd Yield	3.6%	3.1%	3.5%	3.2%	2.8%	3.9%	3.9%	4.0%	3.6%	3.0%			3.0%
Sales ($mill)	3599.9	3917.0	4189.0	4444.0	4835.9	5401.2	5972.5	9189.0	10300	11159	11250	14600	22000
Operating Margin	17.5%	18.2%	18.9%	19.0%	20.9%	20.6%	22.1%	23.2%	25.6%	27.0%	27.0%	27.5%	30.5%
Depreciation ($mill)	60.1	66.6	74.0	86.4	104.9	115.9	127.9	196.0	244.0	246.0	250	275	400
Net Profit ($mill)	348.7	408.0	472.4	531.4	610.5	709.6	829.0	1440.0	1748.0	2056.0	2400	2875	4500
Income Tax Rate	42.5%	41.0%	39.5%	38.5%	35.8%	36.5%	35.5%	32.5%	30.7%	28.8%	30.0%	30.0%	30.0%
Net Profit Margin	9.7%	10.4%	11.3%	12.0%	12.6%	13.1%	13.9%	15.7%	17.0%	18.4%	19.2%	20.6%	20.5%
Working Cap'l ($mill)	1108.7	1231.3	1307.7	1505.2	1743.4	2164.3	2401.8	2893.0	2849.0	2815.0	3500	4500	10500
Long-Term Debt ($mill)	113.5	96.4	103.2	114.2	157.7	210.3	215.2	237.0	231.0	135.0	210	200	200
Net Worth ($mill)	1714.4	1907.9	2145.9	2451.0	2835.6	3229.3	3547.0	5084.0	5418.0	5795.0	6700	8000	15000
% Earned Total Cap'l	19.4%	20.8%	20.8%	20.9%	20.6%	20.8%	22.2%	27.2%	31.1%	34.8%	35.5%	36.0%	29.0%
% Earned Net Worth	20.3%	21.4%	22.0%	21.2%	21.5%	22.0%	23.4%	28.3%	32.3%	35.5%	36.0%	36.0%	30.0%
% Retained to Comm Eq	12.5%	13.2%	12.5%	11.5%	11.0%	9.5%	9.7%	14.1%	11.7%	13.9%	12.5%	16.0%	12.5%
% All Div'ds to Net Prof	39%	39%	44%	47%	49%	57%	58%	50%	64%	61%	60%	35%	59%

BUSINESS: Bristol-Myers Squibb Company manufactures proprietary medical products, household specialty products, ethical pharmaceuticals, diagnostics, infant formula, home specialty products, orthopedic implants, health and beauty aids. Major brand names include: Ban, Bufferin, Buspar, Capoten, Clairol, Comtrex, Drano, Enfamil, Excedrin, Isovue, Monopril, Nuprin, Paraplatin, Pravachol, VePesid, Videx, Windex. International represents 43% of sales (32% of operating profit); R&D, 8.9%. '91 depreciation rate: 5.2%. Estimated plant age: 7 years. Has about 100,000 shareholders, 53,000 employees. Insiders control 1% of stock. Chairman & C.E.O: R.L. Gelb. Inc.: Delaware. Address: 345 Park Avenue, NY, NY 10022. Telephone: 212-546-4000.

Chart 10-2. Bristol-Myers stock chart. (Copyright © 1992 by Value Line Publishing, Inc., used by permission. For subscription information to the Value Line Investment Survey, please call (800) 634-3583.)

Atlantic Energy, Inc. (40), Central & South West (41), Consolidated Edison (16), Florida Progress (38), IPALCO Enterprises (15), Northern States Power (17), TECO Energy (33), and Texas Utilities (45).

"It's great to have rising dividends and attractive yields, but don't forget to check for value before investing. Circumstances can change over time," Weiss warns.

Among quality utility companies that Standard & Poor's winter 1991–1992 issue of *The Outlook* recommended for superior total return over the next several years, the long-term prospects of the following electric and gas utility stocks look particularly promising: TECO Energy and Atlanta Gas Light.

TECO Energy.   On top of increasing dividends every year for 33 years, TECO Energy, based in Tampa, Florida, posted record earnings for the fifth year in a row. A number of factors contribute to TECO's bright future: A growing diversified sector already contributes nearly 30 percent of company earnings, increasing sales of wholesale power to other utilities benefits TECO with more efficient use of generating capacity, the firm's residential customer base continues to expand, and anticipated rate relief should come by late 1992.

Since 1988, TECO's stock has been on a fairly consistent upward path, hitting a high of $41¾ per share in late 1991. Continued earnings improvement and higher dividends in store bode well for an above-average total return for this well-run utility.

Atlanta Gas Light Company.   Incorporated in 1856, Atlanta Gas Light Company has boosted cash dividends for 29 consecutive years. Both its dividend payout rate and five-year dividend growth rate rank high in the utility industry at 82 percent and 10 percent, respectively.

Despite weather nearly 25 percent warmer than normal in 1991, Atlanta Gas Light raised earnings $0.05 to $2.07 per share. Atlanta, the nation's ninth largest metropolitan area, recorded the largest number of single-family housing permits in the nation in 1991. The pace of 1992 Atlanta housing permits in early 1992 ran nearly 30 percent ahead of the impressive 1991 figures. As the economy rebounds and weather returns to normal patterns, look for Atlanta Gas Light to return to the double-digit earnings gains previously enjoyed.

In the wake of a $4.9 million rate increase (only 15 percent of the amount requested by the utility), the company's stock dropped 15 percent. For the past two years, the company's stock price has traded between $30 and $37 per share. Once the earnings picture improves and additional rate requests take effect, Atlanta Gas Light will deliver impressive total returns in the 20 percent or more range. Until then, savvy and patient investors can sit back and enjoy its 6 percent yield.

Borden

Restructuring efforts, paydown of its heavy debt load, a rebounding industrial products sector, and an improving economy will help Borden recapture its earnings momentum in the years ahead.

Founded in 1857, the diversified food, consumer products, packaging, and industrial products company has paid dividends for 92 consecutive years and increased the dividend payout each of the past 18 years.

The company holds significant market-share position, with more than 40 of its grocery brands capturing either the number one or number two slots in the regional or national markets in which they compete. In addition, a rebound in the nation's overall economy and housing industry will add to already improving packaging and industrial products segments.

Trading near the low end of its price range over the past three years, Borden yields around 4 percent, quite a bit higher than other industry firms. As efficiencies from its restructuring take full effect in 1993 and beyond, look for Borden to make earnings gains in excess of 15 percent and deliver above-average total returns.

You don't have to forgo capital gains for income or vice versa. You can enjoy above-average total returns with strategic common stock investments firmly grounded in solid underlying valuation yet to be discovered by the market.

11
The Facts behind the Theories

You Can't Argue with History

There are all sorts of oddball theories floating around the investment community. They range from the sublime to the ridiculous and include everything from sports to fashion trends and from presidential elections to time-based predictions. Some work for a while and then fall out of favor, while others seem to defy all rational explanation but make accurate predictions of market moves. Still others have at least some basis in economic reality (such as the presidential election theory) if not a totally concrete foundation.

For the most part, nobody in their right mind should pay much attention to the majority of these "predictors"; however, as the old saying goes, "You can't argue with the facts."

Volumes have been written on the efficient market theory, the effect of price-earnings ratios, and stock market valuation and utility averages as a precursor of market turns. Now it's time to turn our attention to some of the more popular and unique theories.

In this chapter, we'll explore a number of the more esoteric stock market indicators and theories, their origins, and their track records. How you use this information to better your investment portfolio returns is up to you. The ball is in your court.

With the results of the nation's presidential election still fresh in our minds, it serves as an appropriate place to begin our discussion of oddball theories.

Presidential Election Theory

Despite the prospect of being punished with lengthy, boring political campaigns and superdull candidate speeches that fail to excite much enthusiasm, investors should look forward to approaching presidential elections if stock market history has any bearing. For the 12 presidential election years since the end of World War II and through 1992, the stock market, as measured by the S&P 500, rose 10 times, or 83 percent of the time. In comparison, nonelection years have been up only 65 percent of the time.

Taking a partisan approach to the theory, the only two declines occurred when Democrats won the election, with Harry S. Truman in 1948 and John F. Kennedy in 1960.

In reality, there are two parts to the presidential election theory. The first part deals with the preelection and election years themselves, while the second part looks at the results of the presidential election, in other words, which political party, Democrat or Republican, won the right to preside over our nation's highest office.

With past presidential elections and stock market performance as a guide, it's usually a safe bet that the stock market will rise in both the preelection and election years. Research performed by Kenneth T. Mayland covering stock prices from 1900 to 1986 reflected an average 8.7 percent rise in prepresidential election years and an average 9.6 percent rise in presidential election years. These results compare with an average rise of 2 percent in the two years following the election. However, no matter which party wins the election, stock prices tend to fall in the year immediately following the election.

The theory seems to be still on track. Prepresidential election year 1991 saw the S&P 500 Index surge 30.5 percent, and 1992 saw the market reach a number of new highs while closing higher than 1991.

Political actions clearly come to bear on the election and the stock market results. As the election draws near, the incumbent President goes to work using his power to improve the economy and preserve his job or the office of President for his party in the event he cannot or chooses not to run again.

Fiscal actions used by incumbents include stepping up the level of government spending to keep the economy moving or to get it off dead center in the case of a recession. On the monetary side, the President can exert pressure on the "independent" Federal Reserve chairman to stimulate the economy via loosened credit policies.

The record of the 12 most recent election years through 1992 clearly reinforces Wall Street's pro-Republican bent. As indicated earlier, the only two declines came on the heels of Truman's and Kennedy's elections. Truman's victory over Thomas E. Dewey not only confounded the political pundits of the day; it also shocked Wall Street. The 1948 stock market rose strongly for most of the year, right up to the day before the election, and fell sharply afterward, with the S&P 500 losing 0.7 percent for the year as a whole. Kennedy's election prompted the S&P 500 to lose 3.0 percent in 1960.

The market's single biggest gain during an election year came in 1980 with a 25.8 percent rise in the S&P 500 with the election of Ronald Reagan to his first term as President.

Some presidential cycle watchers contend that the market stands a better chance of moving up if there is a clear front-runner, thereby dispelling the uncertainty that financial markets abhor. They point to the declines in the Truman and Kennedy election years not as Republican-Democrat market indicators but as uncertainty indicators reflecting the narrow victories over Dewey and Nixon, respectively.

The fact that the Republicans have dominated the President's office over the past 46 years and the markets have also risen fairly steadily over that period gives fuel to the theory that a Republican administration is bullish for Wall Street.

Chart 11-1 shows the effects of presidential election years on the stock market from 1948 to 1988 as measured by the S&P 500.

A closer look at Republican administrations shows that, during the past 100 years, each Republican President's fourth year in office accounts for over half of the gains for the overall four-year period. Going back to 1832, Yale Hirsch, publisher of *Stock Trader's Almanac,* found a net market gain of 527 percent (ignoring dividends and compounding) for owning stocks in the latter two years of each administration (Republican and Democrat) versus the 74 percent gain for the first two years of these administrations.

Now, if you're looking for the stock market to predict who will win an election, Mayland's research indicates that if the Dow Jones Industrial Average is higher on the Monday before Election Day than it was at the beginning of the year, odds are the Republicans will win. Unfortunately for the Republicans and for President Bush, this prophecy did not work in the 1992 presidential election.

Fashionable Stock Gains

Moving from political foibles to high fashion, some investors swear by soothsaying styles when it comes to predicting market moves. Dating back to the 1900s, rising hemlines meant surging stock market values.

STOCKS AND PROFITS IN ELECTION YEARS

The stock market has a way of gathering steam as a presidential election approaches. In these examples, the S&P 500 Index is plotted at the beginning of each of the 11 presidential election years since World War II, six months before the election, the day before the election and at the end of the year. Figures for the year's gain or loss and earnings on the S&P 500 appear to the right of each chart.

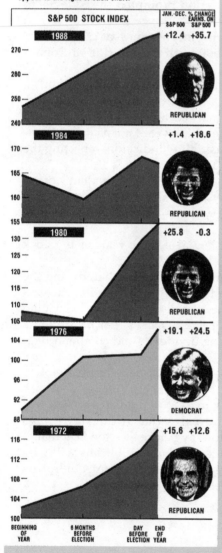

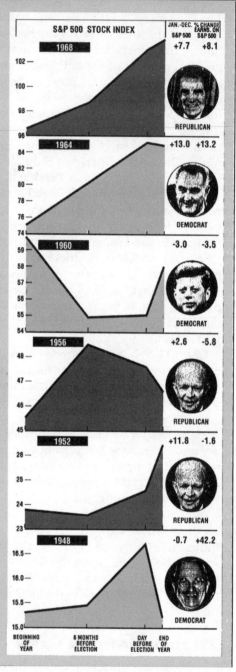

Chart 11-1. (*From* The Outlook, *Winter 1991. 1992. Reprinted by permission of Standard & Poor's Corporation*)

For example, women's dress fashions rose from ankle length around 1917 to shocking mid-calf around the late twenties, just in time for the stock market crash. By 1932, stocks had tanked and dress lengths were once again reaching for the floor.

More recently, the go-go sixties drove stock prices higher as miniskirts became the fashion. Later, hot pants became all the rage as stocks surged in the early seventies. Again, the bear market reasserted itself in the late seventies, driving both stock prices and hemlines south with the popular maxi style. The eighties saw the stock market post new high after new high and fashion took a new twist. Not only did hemlines once again begin their journey upward, but Madonna and others took to baring nearly all, by shedding outerwear for the sake of wearing undergarments as fashion statements. What this new fashion style portends for the nineties only remains to be seen.

Not to be outdone by clothing designers, avant-garde hair stylists introduced high hairdos to compliment market tops. The beehives of the sixties linked their fashion to the market top of the go-go years. Likewise, could the currently popular spiked hairdos, purple or any other color, be signaling another market top or just the decline of civilization in general?

Play Ball

In the world of baseball, technical analyst Robert Ritter of Ladenburg, Thalmann & Company in New York City likes to flaunt the New York Mets reverse market indicator. According to Ritter, every time the New York Mets get to the World Series, the stock market falls on its face the following year (see Table 11-1). For example, after the Mets made their World Series debut back in 1969, the Dow Jones Industrial Average bottomed out the next May 26 at its lowest closing since 1962.

The next Mets trip to the World Series in 1973 laid the groundwork for the Dow to drop a whopping 46 percent in 1974 from its 1973 high. For three strikes in a row, the Mets next trip to the World Series in 1986 cul-

Table 11-1. Mets Reverse Indicator

World Series	Year high	Next year low
1969	968.85	631.16
1973	1051.70	577.60
1986	1955.57	1738.74

Table 11-2. Athletics Reverse Indicator

World Series	Opponent	Winner	Games	Market
1905	N.Y. Giants	N.Y. Giants	4 to 1	Up
1910	Chicago Cubs	Philadelphia A's	4 to 1	Down
1911	Chicago Cubs	Philadelphia A's	4 to 2	Up
1913	N.Y. Giants	Philadelphia A's	4 to 1	Down
1914	Boston Braves	Boston Braves	4 to 0	Down
1929	Chicago Cubs	Philadelphia A's	4 to 1	Down
1930	St. Louis Cards	Philadelphia A's	4 to 2	Down
1931	St. Louis Cards	St. Louis Cards	4 to 3	Down
1972	Cincinnati Reds	Oakland A's	4 to 3	Up
1973	N.Y. Mets	Oakland A's	4 to 3	Down
1974	L.A. Dodgers	Oakland A's	4 to 1	Down
1990	Cincinnati Reds	Cincinnati Reds	4 to 0	Up

minated with the Black Monday crash on October 19, 1987. Luckily for
investors, the Mets' pennant race faded late in the 1989 season.

One word of warning. Don't believe everything you read regarding
sports investment theories (or any others for that matter). No less an in-
fluential publication as *Forbes* reported in its popular "Streetwalker
Column" that the Oakland Athletics (and predecessors Kansas City and
Philadelphia) had its own World Series track record pointing to declining stock prices.

According to "Streetwalker," the A's winning streaks and lousy stock
markets have "gone hand in glove" since before World War I.

Well, my research shows that not to be the case. As illustrated in Table
11-2, the market should have gone down in 1911 but it increased
slightly. Then again in 1914, 1931, and 1972, this supposed indicator
didn't live up to its billing.

They're Off and Running

Pulitzer Prize-winning sportswriter Walter W. "Red" Smith took his
eyes off the ponies long enough to discover the eerie correlation between Triple Crowns and Wall Street stumbles. If your favorite horse
wins the enviable Trible Crown (the Kentucky Derby, the Preakness,
and the Belmont Stakes) it's almost a sure bet that the stock market will
close out the year with a net loss.

According to William LeFevre, senior vice president and market strategist with Tucker Anthony in New York City, "Triple Crowns spell doom for the market."

The last Triple Crown winner, Affirmed in 1978, helped contribute to a 3.1 percent market decline. Before that, Seattle Slew`s 1977 and Secretariat's 1973 triumphs caused the market to falter 17.3 percent and 16.6 percent, respectively.

In 1948, jockey Eddie Arcaro led Citation to the winner's circle and the market dropped 2.1 percent. Two years earlier, Assault became the seventh horse to win the Triple Crown while the market slid 8.1 percent.

"All in all, in eight of the eleven years there has been a Triple Crown winner since 1919, the Dow Jones Industrial Average troughed for an average 4.2 percent decline for the period," says LeFevre.

But don't place any wagers for the Kentucky Derby winner to lose the Preakness. When the winner of the Kentucky Derby also wins the Preakness Stakes but then fails to win the Belmont Stakes, the stock market rises nearly 70 percent of the time, gaining an average 4.4 percent.

Don't forget, if a horse trots into the winner's circle at the Belmont Stakes in early June garnering the Triple Crown, you still have plenty of time to race to your broker and sell your holdings before the decline culminates at year-end.

Super Bowl: Bonanza or Buffoonery?

To be sure, savvy investors don't actually believe that the outcome of the Super Bowl impacts the stock market in one direction or the other, but it's harmless fun to watch the outcome of professional football's championship game and track the correlation with stock market prices. Unfortunately, this indicator, like many others, has lost some of its perceived clairvoyance in recent years.

Robert H. Stovall, president of Stovall/Twenty-First Advisers in New York City, pioneered much of the Super Bowl predictor theory, although a number of other investment pundits also follow Super Bowl results with some varying interpretations. According to Stovall, the theory contends that if an original National Football League (NFL) team wins the Super Bowl, the stock market will rise that year. Conversely, should an American Football League (AFL) team be lucky enough to beat the seemingly superior NFL contenders, the market will drop that year.

Included in the ranks of NFL teams as far as the predictor is concerned are such current American Football Conference (AFC) teams as the Cleveland Browns, Indianapolis Colts, and Pittsburgh Steelers, which originally derived from the NFL.

Stovall claims that between 1967, when the Green Bay Packers won Super Bowl I for the honor of the NFL, and 1984, the Super Bowl predictor proved fallible only once. The first failing occurred in 1970 when the AFL Kansas City Chiefs won the Super Bowl and the S&P 500 Index gained 0.1 percent. Adding to the confusion, while the S&P 500 and Dow both rose, the New York Stock Exchange Composite for 1970 did decline.

However, IDS Financial Corporation in Minneapolis, Minnesota, contends dividends accounted for the rise in the S&P 500 in 1970, thereby keeping the record intact. Both parties agree that the Los Angeles Raiders AFC victory in 1984 should have driven the market down, but it rose instead. There exists a plausible explanation for this aberration though. Despite the Raiders being clearly in the AFC camp, the franchise moved to an old NFL city, possibly causing the Super Bowl investment elves a bit of confusion. The Dow refused to be buffaloed and declined as it should have.

Another earlier blip in the theory did occur (ignored by Super Bowl indicator followers since most of them track the S&P 500 as the indicator benchmark) in 1978 when the National Football Conference (NFC) Dallas Cowboys triumphed. While the S&P 500 and NYSE Composite did rise as predicted, the Dow again refused to conform and declined.

In 1987, the declining NYSE Composite proved to be the naysayer as the NFC New York Giants won the Super Bowl and both the Dow and S&P 500 rose as expected. Up until 1990, the Super Bowl predictor accurately called the market direction based on at least one of the three stock market measures (Dow, S&P 500, or NYSE Composite). Despite a failure in prediction capability for 1990, the Super Bowl predictor regained its expertise in 1991 and 1992 with up markets following NFC wins.

Overall, since the first Super Bowl, the indicator has achieved an 88 percent success ratio. Not many other investment theories can claim that record.

Stovall advises against getting carried away with the results. He warns that the deck is stacked in the NFC's favor. For one thing, more football teams stem from the NFL than from its AFL counterpart. On top of that, in five of the Super Bowl games, both contestants were premerger NFL teams. Another factor contributing to the remarkable accuracy of the indicator—markets tend to rise more often than they decline.

For the record, Table 11-3 presents the facts. Make your own conclusions.

Table 11-3. The Super Bowl Predictor and the Stock Market

Year	Super Bowl	Winner	Loser	Predictor	Dow, %	S&P 500, %	NYSE Composite, %
1967	I	Packers	Chiefs	Up	15.2	20.1	23.1
1968	II	Packers	Raiders	Up	4.3	7.6	9.4
1969	III	Jets	Colts	Down	-15.2	-11.4	-12.5
1970	IV	Chiefs	Vikings	Down	4.8	0.1	-2.5
1971	V	Colts	Cowboys	Up	6.1	10.8	12.3
1972	VI	Cowboys	Dolphins	Up	14.6	15.6	14.3
1973	VII	Dolphins	Redskins	Down	-16.6	-17.4	-19.6
1974	VIII	Dolphins	Vikings	Down	-27.5	-29.7	-30.3
1975	IX	Steelers	Vikings	Up	38.3	31.6	31.9
1976	X	Steelers	Cowboys	Up	17.9	19.2	21.5
1977	XI	Raiders	Vikings	Down	-17.3	-11.5	-9.3
1978	XII	Cowboys	Broncos	Up	-3.2	1.1	2.1
1979	XIII	Steelers	Cowboys	Up	4.2	12.3	15.5
1980	XIV	Steelers	Rams	Up	14.9	25.8	25.7
1981	XV	Raiders	Eagles	Down	-9.2	-9.7	-8.7
1982	XVI	49ers	Bengals	Up	19.6	14.8	14.0
1983	XVII	Redskins	Dolphins	Up	20.3	17.3	17.5
1984	XVIII	Raiders	Redskins	Down	-3.7	1.4	1.3
1985	XIX	49ers	Dolphins	Up	27.7	20.5	20.6
1986	XX	Bears	Patriots	Up	22.6	20.2	19.2
1987	XXI	Giants	Broncos	Up	2.3	2.0	-0.3
1988	XXII	Redskins	Broncos	Up	11.9	12.4	13.0
1989	XXIII	49ers	Bengals	Up	27.0	27.3	24.8
1990	XXIV	49ers	Broncos	Up	-4.3	-6.6	-7.5
1991	XXV	Giants	Buffalo Bills	Up	20.3	26.3	27.1
1992	XXVI	Redskins	Buffalo Bills	Up	*	*	*

*Percentages were up when this book went to press.

The Times, They Are A-Changin'

As proponents of the efficient market theory are quick to attest, the stock market instantly processes all financial and economic information; therefore stock market prices should behave similarly whether traded on Friday, September 8th, or Monday, January 19th. The premise works great in theory, but it's flawed in practice.

Investors, being human for the most part, often act emotionally, and even irrationally, in response to economic and investment information. In addition, stock market history is strewn with anomalies in regard to stock market performance on specific dates, days of the week, seasons and other time references.

Being superstitious, it's appropriate to start this discussion with a review of Friday the 13th phenomena. Perhaps the most impressive Friday the 13th in recent memory, October 13, 1989, celebrated the date with a drop of nearly 200 points, or 6.9 percent, on the Dow.

How does that compare with other Friday the 13ths? According to two University of Miami professors who researched Friday the 13th stock market activity from 1962 to 1985, the market took a dive to the tune of an annual average 24.5 percent. It's even more impressive when you consider that other less notorious Fridays enjoyed an average annual gain of 27.9 percent.

It's said that trouble always comes in threes, and Friday the 13ths seem to confirm that notion. As Table 11-4 shows, whenever a year had the misfortune of having three Friday the 13ths, it coincided with the start of an

Table 11-4. Triple Friday the 13th Indicator

Year	Recession started	Length
1953	August 1953	10 months
1956	September 1957	8 months
1959	May 1960	10 months
1970	January 1970	11 months
1981	August 1981	16 months
1984	None*	0 months
1987	None†	0 months
1998	?	? months

*Economic growth slowed considerably even though there were not two consecutive quarters of declining gross national product.

†Dip in third quarter followed by rise in fourth quarter. Slow growth with quarterly declines through early 1992.

economic contraction or recession, at least until 1984. Fortunately, the next year with three Friday the 13ths won't occur until 1998.

Yale Hirsch, editor of the investment newsletter *Smart Money* and publisher of the *Stock Trader's Almanac,* also confirms that Fridays, not the 13th variety, bode well for stock market prices. Hirsch's research showed that during the 39-year period from 1952 to 1991, the S&P 500 Index rose on 57.8 percent of the Fridays versus declining on 44.5 percent of the Mondays during that same time frame.

Moreover, for the 35-year period from 1953 through 1987, the Dow fell a total of 2186 points on Mondays despite the average producing a net gain of 1647 points over that period. Fridays posted the second best trading gains with 1043 points, trailing the 1515 points gained on Wednesdays.

Holiday Treats

In addition to the gains attributable to Fridays, there are a bevy of pre-holiday trends that make investing before each of the eight stock market holidays a mouth-watering experience. Why not utilize the track record of preholiday trading activity and celebrate investment gains as well as a day or two off?

According to research for the classic book *Behavior of Prices on Wall Street* (written by Arthur Merrill of Merrill Analysis, Inc., in Haverford, Pennsylvania), going all the way back to 1897, the days before Labor Day work out to have the best track record with a price rise 81.2 percent of the time. The average day before all holidays is up 68 percent of the time, compared with the average trading day which rises 52 percent of the time.

"Next most accurate are the days before the Fourth of July and Memorial Day which deliver price increases 74 percent and 76 percent of the time, respectively. However, the day before the Fourth of July recently seems to have fallen off the wagon with only 6 increases out of the past 17 years," says John McGinley, who took over from Arthur Merrill as editor of *Technical Trends* (P.O. Box 792, Wilton, Connecticut).

Should you take the days-before-a-holiday-price-gains theory to heart, it could make good sense if you're bullish to purchase stocks on Monday before the onrush to buy stocks.

Autumn Leaves Drop

During autumn, the leaves aren't the only things to drop. During the past 17 years, September markets declined 13 times, or over 76 percent of the time. In fact since 1897, September markets headed south 56 times versus only 39 advances. In the past 23 years through 1991, the market has risen only five times in September. While there does not appear to be any rational explanation for September's inconsiderate behavior, it's hard to argue with history. One of the few things in September's favor lies in the fact that the stock market saw fit to wait until October before embarking on its recent infamous crashes.

Summer Sizzle?

Moving to warmer weather, proponents of the summer rally theory contend that on balance summer months prove to be bullish for the market. In theory, the summer rally should give the Dow Jones Industrial Average a boost from a May–June low point to a new high during the three-month span from July through September.

During the 22-year period from 1964 to 1985, the Dow rose in excess of 10 percent during 7 of those years. That translates to a 300-point jump based on today's market level. Moreover, the Dow rose at least 5 percent during 17 of those 22 summers.

The summer rally, like most other investment theories, also has its detractors. In this case, Yale Hirsch plays devil's advocate. His research shows that while the Dow did average an 8.8 percent increase during the so-called summer rallies, the Dow averaged from 9.4 to 11.7 percent gains during the other seasons over the same time frame.

When it comes to picking which month to avoid when investing in stocks, we turn to no less an authority on the American scene than Mark Twain in *Pudd'nhead Wilson.* "October. This is one of the peculiarly dangerous months to speculate in stocks. The others are July, January, September, April, November, May, March, June, December, August and February."

The January Effect

On Mark Twain's somber advice, we'll take a look at the widely publicized January effect. Among early research, Donald B. Keim of the University of Pennsylvania tracked January action from 1963 to 1979. Keim ranked firms in order of market value, segmenting the universe into 10 stock portfolios.

His research concluded that small-cap stocks, those with a capitalization up to $100 million, outperformed large-cap stocks by a margin of 8.2 percent during the first five trading days of January.

As a group, small-cap stocks have risen in 37 of the last 40 Januarys.

Table 11-5. NASDAQ January Effect

Year	NASDAQ Composite, January change	S&P 500
1987	12.4%	13.2%
1988	4.3%	4.0%
1989	5.2%	7.1%
1990	−8.6%	−6.9%
1991	10.8%	4.2%
1992	5.8%	−2.0%

For the past 40 years, the January effect has added in excess of 6 percent to small-cap company stock prices.

Table 11-5 illustrates how the January effect impacted NASDAQ stocks and the S&P 500 for each year from 1987 through 1992.

That doesn't mean that large-cap stocks get left out in the January cold, however. For the years 1980 through 1990, the Dow increased in 7 Januarys out of 11. While the NASDAQ Composite rose 38 percent during those 11 years, the Dow turned in a respectable performance with a 27 percent gain.

Some January effect supporters even go so far as to state that a gain in January sets the pattern for the whole year. Likewise, a decline in January spells lower stock prices by year-end.

Yale Hirsch claims that during the 41-year period from 1950 through 1991, his research reflects that the year ended in the same direction as indicated by January stock market performance 36 of 41 years, as measured by the S&P 500.

A number of reasons are offered to account for the January effect. First of all, year-end tax selling artificially depresses stock prices, resulting in a January rebound. This makes good sense since end-of-the-year tax-loss selling typically occurs more often in secondary issues, setting the stage for small-cap stocks to outperform their larger brethren in January. However, it does not explain why the January effect also occurs in Europe where tax considerations don't enter year-end-selling decision making.

Second, attempts by portfolio managers to window-dress their holdings and move closer to the S&P 500 benchmark as the year winds down lead them to shed secondary stocks and depress their market price. After the prior year's performance numbers are history, they shift again to a more aggressive stance, bidding up the shares of the more thinly traded secondary issues.

Third, a renewed interest in investing begins after the year-end holiday season, with investors concentrating on bargain hunting.

Fourth, as usual, politics get into the picture with the President's State of the Union address, giving a boost to public morale and visions of better times ahead.

Benefiting from the January Effect

Here are a few investment strategies to help boost your overall return. Pay close attention to the timing of your sales and purchases to take the most advantage of the January effect. Don't wait till the last minute to get the lowest possible price and risk missing the boat altogether when demand from other bargain hunters forces up stock prices.

Don't forget the fundamentals. Ferret out small-stock funds or individual small-cap issues with a good story and proven track record but beaten down by year-end selling pressure. Of course, choosing the right stocks or funds may prove to be tricky. Don't get enamored with the January effect. Pick stocks you would want to own at any time of the year. Remember, the January effect could falter, leaving you with losses to recoup the rest of the year or providing you with unwanted tax-loss selling opportunities the next December.

Compare current stock prices with 52-week highs and lows as well as the prior two months' worth of price movement to get a sense of the stock's potential. The greater the drop from its 52-week high, the greater the rebound potential. If the majority of the stock's price drop occurred closer to the end of the year, the more likely it reflects year-end selling pressure rather than underlying financial and operating problems. Again, remember to study the stock's investment fundamentals.

Steer clear of thinly traded stocks with unreasonable quote spreads. No matter how low the price, it's no bargain if you can't get out of the stock without taking a big hit when you decide to sell later on.

Instead of purchasing the stocks themselves, you can purchase call (buy) and put (sell) options on index options. These options give you the right to purchase or sell the stocks in the index at predetermined prices within specified time periods. In reality, however, the options are settled in cash instead of stock shares.

For example, you could purchase call options on the Value Line Index that expire on the third Friday in January and also purchase puts on the S&P 500 that are due to expire on the same day. If stocks in general rise, the Value Line call option should rise by more than the S&P 500 put falls. If the market drops, the S&P 500 put should rise more than the Value Line call declines. Your risk is limited to the cost of the respective options.

Table 11-6. January Futures Trading Strategy*
Strategy: Purchase March Value Line futures†; sell March
S&P 500 futures‡

Year	Entry date	Entry price, $	Exit date	Exit price, $	Spread profit, $	Profit per spread, $
1983	12/16	17.10	1/07	21.50	4.40	2200
1984	12/16	30.00	1/09	32.90	2.90	1450
1985	12/17	11.95	1/09	15.55	3.60	1800
1986	1/03	2.80	1/09	4.50	1.70	850
1987	12/16	−22.00	1/09	−16.90	5.10	2550
1988	12/16	−53.15	1/08	−44.45	8.70	4350
1989	12/16	−34.80	1/09	−31.40	3.40	1700
1990	12/18	−60.15	1/09	−58.80	1.35	675
1991	12/17	−88.55	1/09	−80.60	7.95	3975
Average profit on trades					4.34	2172

*Entry and exit prices based on the difference in closing values of the March Value Line futures and the March S&P 500 futures.

†Value Line futures trade on the Kansas City Board of Trade.

‡S&P 500 futures trade on the Chicago Mercantile Exchange.

SOURCE: Moore Research Center Inc., Eugene, Oregon.

For the more advanced investor, futures offer a unique way to capitalize on the January effect. According to Steve Moore, founder of Moore Research in Eugene, Oregon, it works like this: If investors had concurrently purchased, say, a March Value Line futures contract and sold a March S&P 500 futures contract in each of the past nine years, they could have earned average profits in excess of $2100, based on closing prices at the optimal entry and exit dates.

The optimal entry date to initiate a position has typically occurred between December 16 and December 18 in each of the past nine years, while the optimal exit date to close out the position occurred between January 7 and January 9.

"This investment works because the Value Line Index is more heavily weighted in secondary stocks, representing the small-cap sector, while the S&P 500 Index represents the large-cap sector," says Moore.

As long as the January effect, with secondary issues outperforming the large-cap stocks, continues to work, the Value Line/S&P 500 futures strategy should continue to deliver trading profits.

Table 11-6 illustrates the success of the above futures trading strategy from 1983 through 1991.

Cycling to Profits

Ironically, one of the original and most prominent cycle proponents came not from a free-market economy but out of a state-controlled environment. Nikolai Kondratieff (of the Kondratieff wave fame, K-wave for short) was a Russian economist in the 1920s who contended that nations' economies move in broad cycles extending between 48 and 60 years each in length. Kondratieff's original theory was boiled down to 50-year cycles with alternating 25-year-up and 25-year-down periods.

Followers of the K-wave theory cite recent evidence that the Russian's observations are still valid. Since the Great Depression trough in 1932, the United States experienced its worst recession in 1982, fitting the 50-year cycle time frame. In addition, the stock market tanked in both 1937 and 1987, 50 years apart.

Charting the K-wave, you can locate economic lows between 1720 and 1740, 1780 and 1800, 1840 and 1860, 1880 and 1900, and 1940 and 1960. Likewise, economic peaks occurred around the 1760s, 1810s, 1860s, 1920s, and 1970s, with approximately 50 years between peaks. Based on this information, some K-wave enthusiasts predict that a major downturn is in the making.

Turning to the action in stock prices, R. N. Elliott developed the Elliott wave theory based on market-cycle research between 1934 and 1948. Elliott observed a repetitious pattern in market price averages and a lesser repetitive pattern in individual stocks. He laid out his wave theory into an eight-leg pattern made up of three rising waves followed by intermediate pullbacks, followed by two declining waves divided by one intermediate rally.

The basic premise of the Elliott wave theory is that both bull and bear markets are governed by underlying natural law expressed in market-cycle waves that repeat themselves over time. Elliott based his own theory on the Fibonacci number series theory that each number in the series equals the sum of the two numbers that precede it—for example, 1-2-3-5-8-13-21-34. Fibonacci, a thirteenth-century Italian mathematician, found this series to occur in numerous natural phenomena such as the arrangement of leaf buds on a stem and the spiral design in sunflowers.

The Elliott wave theory appears to be more reliable in predicting longer cycles rather than short-term movements.

Robert Prechter and Dave Allman of the *Elliott Wave Theorist* newsletter in Gainesville, Georgia, are on record predicting that we are on the verge of a major down cycle with the possibilities of the Dow plummeting to the 1100 level or lower. Time will tell.

A Bevy of Other Theories
Things Astrological

If economic cycles don't turn you on, you can look to the heavens for inspiration and market predictions. Take the Sunspot Indicator, for example. Heightened sunspot activity (dark spots appearing in groups on the sun's surface) occurs in approximate 11-year cycles and is associated with strong magnetic fields. The Sunspot Indicator was originally developed by nineteenth-century astronomer Sir William Herschel to correlate sunspot activity and the price of wheat.

Sunspot activity affects climate, which affects the success of agricultural endeavors, which in turn affects the market prices of commodities. Herschel found that abundant sunspots created wheat gluts and drove wheat prices down. Conversely, low sunspot activity resulted in wheat scarcity and higher wheat prices.

Expansion of the theory now predicts that peak sunspot activity precedes a bear market.

Turning from the sun to the moon, Dr. Arnold Leiber in his book *The Lunar Effect: Biological Tides and Human Emotions* (Anchor Press, 1978) argues that human emotions drive financial markets and that the moon's tidal effects on water transfers to humans since we are composed of 80 percent water. So don't make investment decisions without first consulting your moon chart.

The Name Game

In 1988, a New York City corporate identity consulting firm measured the financial performance of more than 50 firms with letter names such as TRW and CSX versus "name-name" companies over the five-year period 1983 through 1987. According to the study, letter-name companies performed worse than name-name companies on a number of financial benchmarks such as earnings per share, sales growth, and return on equity.

All in all, in most industries letter names underperformed the group averages on all three benchmarks. Only in the insurance industry did letter-name companies outperform the group averages on all three performance measures. Letter-name companies averaged 7.4 percent sales growth versus the 9.2 percent group average. Likewise, letter-name companies' return on equity of 10.5 percent and earnings per share growth of 1.3 percent trailed group averages of 12.8 percent and 6.9 percent, respectively.

Ads and Fads

Back in 1985, Harold W. Gourgues, Jr., newsletter editor from Atlanta, Georgia, devised the Gourgues Ad Index. Using advertisements in *Financial Planning* as a database, Gourgues measures the percentage of full-page ads devoted to each of 10 investment categories. According to Gourgues, heavy advertisement in a category month after month foretells doom for that investment category.

Using data going back to 1979, Gourgues argues his data predicted trouble ahead for tangible investments in 1980–1981 and real estate in 1984–1987. The tangible index peaked at 82 percent in February 1980, shortly after gold prices peaked at around $800 per ounce. Since then, gold prices have drifted to the mid-$300 per ounce range.

The real estate index reached its high-water mark at 64 percent in April 1985. Returns on real estate investments averaged in excess of 14 percent but declined to just over 5 percent by 1987. The dire real estate markets in the late eighties and early nineties seem to add additional credence to the Gourgues Ad Index.

In the stock, bond, and mutual fund arena, the ad index peaked at 39 percent in April 1987, just months before the October 1987 market crash. Later, insurance products accounted for some 30 percent of the ads, accurately predicting trouble ahead for the insurance industry and certain products such as annuities which may be killed by congressional action.

According to Gourgues, his ad index is relatively quiet at the present, not signaling any warnings on the high side. But on the low end of the index, real estate ads appear to be bottoming out, perhaps indicating some buying opportunities in that segment.

Military Markets and Other Crises

The prospect of war usually results in U.S. markets taking a nosedive for a few days or weeks, according to research prepared by Ned Davis Research in Nokomis, Florida. After the initial plunge, stocks tend to rebound, regaining all their losses within one to three months.

There are several ways to play the war or crises markets. First of all, if the specter of war raises its ugly head and creates fears of higher prices for oil and other commodities, sending up yields on long-term government bonds, it may be a great time to lock in those higher yields for better investment returns over the long-term horizon.

Adept stock buyers willing to make fast trades could also take advantage of short-term price declines caused by overpessimistic sellers. Obviously, the steeper the initial decline, the greater the opportunity

Table 11-7. Market Crises

Event	Date	Reaction dates	Initial change	One month after low
Pearl Harbor	DE 7, 41	DE 6–10, 41	−6.5%	+1.4%
Korean War	JN 25, 50	JN 23–JL 13, 50	−12.0	+9.0
Cuban Missile	AG 24–OC 28, 62	AG 23–OC 23, 63	−9.4	+15.6
Grenada invas	OC 25, 83	OC 24–NV 7, 83	−2.7	+4.9
Libya bombing	AP 15–16, 86	AP 15–21, 86	+2.6	−4.3
Panama invas	DC 17–JA 4, 90	DC 15–20, 89	−1.9	−3.2
Iraq War	DC 26–JA 16, 91	DC 24–JA 16, 91	−4.3	+17.5

SOURCE: Ned Davis Research Inc.

to make substantial gains as war jitters dissipate and stock prices rebound.

Ned Davis Research evaluated 18 market crises over the past 50-plus years, including 11 military conflicts. By far the steepest decline came with the panic of 1987 with a drop of 34.2 percent, followed by the 1973–1974 Arab oil embargo that pushed the market down 18.2 percent. Of war-related Dow Jones Industrial Average declines, Germany's 1940 occupation of France sent the Dow reeling 17.1 percent. Other notable Dow drops were sparked by the Hunt silver crisis (−15.9 percent), the outbreak of the Korean war (−12.0 percent), *Sputnik*'s launching (−9.9 percent), the Cuban missile crisis (−9.4 percent), and the Japanese bombing of Pearl Harbor (−6.5 percent).

As noted earlier, postdecline rallies helped the stocks recover over a six-month period. The average rally boosted the Dow from its low up 5.1 percent after one month, up 6.8 percent within three months, and up 11.8 percent after six months. Table 11-7 illustrates market moves associated with various crises.

The Ticker Test

For my own money, I've developed the Stock Ticker Indicator. It doesn't involve a lot of research, but it does take some time—the amount of time it takes for you to drive or walk to your broker's office. Check out the quote machine. If more than five people are lined up to obtain quotes, it's time to sell out your holdings because every Tom, Dick, and Harry is getting into the market, bidding up prices to ridiculous levels. On the other hand, if the line only contains one or two people, it's a safe bet that bargains are to be found in the market. Get in early before the herd stampedes again.

While not all-inclusive, I've provided you with a wealth of stock theories to contemplate—some oddball, some unexplainable but obviously successful, and still others deeply rooted in economic realities. I hope you find the information profitable.

Table 11-8 provides you with a handy, quick reference guide to each indicator.

Table 11-8. Stock Market Indicators

Indicator	Prediction
Presidential election	Stocks will rise in preelection and election years.
	Stocks will decline in postelection years.
	Tendency to do better with Republican President.
Hemline	Higher skirts, higher prices.
High hair styles	Higher prices.
New York Mets	Mets win World Series, market dives.
Oakland Athletics	Don't believe it.
Triple Crown	Triple Crown winner, market dives.
Super Bowl	NFL victory, market up.
Weekend effect	Fridays up, Mondays down.
Friday the 13th	Market down.
Preholidays	Market rallies.
September lull	Market decline.
Summer rally	Market rise.
January effect	Market rise.
	Small caps outperform large caps.
K-wave	Predictable economic cycles.
Elliott wave	Predictable market cycles.
Sunspots	Sunspot peak, bears in sight.
Lunar attraction	Markets tied to lunar activity.
Names	Letter-name companies don't make grade.
Ad fad	High ad percentage predicts downfall.
War	Brief decline, then recovery.
Ticker time	Over five, take a dive.

Glossary

Annual report: The Securities and Exchange Commission–required report presenting a portrayal of the company's operations and financial position. It includes a balance sheet, income statement, statement of cashflows, description of company operations, management discussion of company financial condition and operating results, and any events that materially impact the company.

Asset play: A stock investment that value investors find attractive due to asset undervaluation by the market.

Basis price: The cost of an investment used to determine capital gains or losses.

Bear market: A period of months or years during which stock prices decline.

Bond: A long-term debt security that obligates the issuer to pay interest and repay the principal. The holder does not have any ownership rights in the issuer.

Bond ratio: The measure of a company's leverage comparing the firm's debt to total capital.

Bottom-up investing: An investment strategy starting with company fundamentals and then moving to the overall economic and investment environment.

Bull market: A period of months or years during which stock prices rise.

Call option: A contract providing the holder the right to buy the underlying security at a specific price during a specified time period.

Call provision: A provision allowing the security issuer to recall the security before maturity.

Cash equivalent: A type of asset with maturities of less than one year.

Cashflow: The flow of funds in and out of an operating business. Normally calculated as net income plus depreciation and other noncash items.

Cashflow-Debt ratio: The relationship of free cashflow to total long-term indebtedness. This ratio is helpful in tracking a firm's ability to meet scheduled debt and interest payment requirements.

Cashflow-Interest ratio: This ratio determines how many times free cashflow will cover fixed interest payments on long-term debt.

Cashflow per share: The amount earned before deduction for depreciation and other charges not involving the outlay of cash.

Cash ratio: A ratio used to measure liquidity. It is calculated as the sum of cash and marketable securities divided by current liabilities. It indicates how well a company can meet current liabilities.

Common and **preferred cashflow coverage ratios:** Ratios that determine how many times annual free cashflow will cover common and preferred cash dividend payments.

Common stock ratio: The relationship of common stock to total company capitalization.

Contrarian: An investor seeking securities that are out of favor with other investors.

Convertibles: A security that is exchangeable into common stock at the option of the holder under specified terms and conditions.

Current ratio: A liquidity ratio calculated by dividing current assets by current liabilities.

Cyclical: Referring to industries and companies that advance and decline in relation to the changes in the overall economic environment.

Debt-to-equity ratio: The relationship of debt to shareholder's equity in a firm's capitalization structure.

Defensive investments: Securities that are less affected by economic retractions, thus offering downside price protection.

Diversification: The spreading of investment risk by owning different types of securities, investments in different geographical markets, etc.

Dollar cost averaging: An investment strategy of investing a fixed amount of money over time to achieve a lower average security purchase price.

Dow Jones Industrial Average: A market index consisting of 30 U.S. industrial companies. Used as a measure of market performance.

Earnings per share: Net after-tax income divided by the number of outstanding company shares.

Economic value: The economic worth of a stock as represented by the anticipated free cashflow the company will generate over a period of time, discounted by the weighted cost of a company's capital.

Efficient market: A market that instantly takes into account all known financial information and reflects it in the security's price.

Exercise price: The price at which an option or futures contract can be executed. Also known as the *striking price.*

Expiration date: The last day on which an option or future can be exercised.

Federal reserve: The national banking system consisting of 12 independent Federal Reserve banks in Atlanta, Boston, Chicago, Cleveland, Dallas, Kansas City, Minneapolis, New York, Philadelphia, Richmond, St. Louis, and San Francisco.

Fiscal year: The 12-month accounting period that conforms to the company's natural operating cycle versus the calendar year.

Freddie Mac: The nickname of the Federal Home Loan Mortgage Corporation.

Free cashflow: Cashflow determined by calculating operating earnings after taxes and then adding depreciation and other noncash expenses, less capital expenditures and increases in working capital.

Free cashflow–earnings ratio: The percentage of earnings actually available in cash. It is the percentage of free cash available to company management for investments, acquisitions, plant construction, dividends, etc.

Fundamental analysis: An investment strategy focusing on the intrinsic value of the company as evidenced by a review of the balance sheet, income statement, cashflow, operating performance, etc.

Gap: The occurrence of a trading pattern when the price range from one day does not overlap the previous day's price range.

Growth investments: Companies or industries with earnings projected to outpace the market consistently over the long term.

High-tech stock: Securities of firms in high-technology industries such as biotechnology, computers, electronics, lasers, medical devices, and robotics.

Hybrid security: A security that possesses the characteristics of both stock and bonds, such as a convertible bond.

Indenture: The legal contract spelling out the terms and conditions between the issuer and bondholders.

Index: The compilation of performance for specific groupings of stocks or mutual funds such as the Dow Jones Industrial Average and the S&P 500.

IPO (initial public offering): The first public offering of a company's stock.

Insider: Anyone having access to material corporate information. Most frequently used to refer to company officers, directors, and top management.

Institutional investor: An investor organization, such as a pension fund or money manager, which trades large volumes of securities.

Intrinsic value: The difference between the current market price of the underlying security and the striking price of a related option.

Junk bonds: Bonds with ratings below investment grade.

Leading indicator: An economic measurement that tends to accurately predict the future direction of the economy or stock market.

Leverage: The use of debt to finance a company's operations. Also, the use of debt by investors to increase the return on investment from securities transactions.

Liquidity: The degree of ease with which assets can be turned into readily available cash.

Listed: Investment securities that have met the listing requirements of a particular exchange.

Maintenance margin: The minimum equity value that must be maintained in a margin account. Initial margin requirements include a minimum deposit of $2000 before any credit can be extended. Current Regulation T rules require that maintenance margin equal at least 50 percent of the market value of the margined positions.

Margin: The capital (in cash or securities) that an investor deposits with a broker to borrow additional funds to purchase securities.

Margin call: A demand from a broker for additional cash or securities as collateral to bring the margin account back within maintenance limits.

Mutual fund: An investment company that sells shares in itself to the investing public and uses the proceeds to purchase individual securities.

NASDAQ: National Association of Securities Dealers Automated Quotation System providing computerized quotes of market makers for stocks traded over the counter.

Net asset value: The quoted market value of a mutual fund share. Determined by dividing the closing market value of all securities owned by the mutual fund plus all other assets and liabilities by the total number of shares outstanding.

Oddball theories: Esoteric investment theories not readily explained by rational investment behavior or analysis. Examples include the Super Bowl, New York Mets, and lunar investment theories.

Option: A security that gives the holder the right to purchase or sell a particular investment at a fixed price for a specified period of time.

Out of the money: An option whose striking price is higher than the underlying security's current market price for a call option or whose striking price is lower than the current market price for a put option.

Payout ratio: The percentage of a company's profit paid out in cash dividends.

Portfolio: The investment holdings of an individual or institutional investor; includes stocks, bonds, options, money-market accounts, etc.

Price-earnings (P/E) ratio: The ratio determined by dividing the stock's market price by its earnings per common share. Used as an indicator of company performance and in comparison with other stock investments and the overall market.

Put option: A contract giving the holder the right to sell the underlying security at a specific price over a specified time frame.

Quick ratio: The ratio used to measure corporate liquidity. It is regarded as an improvement over the current ratio, which includes the usually not very liquid inventory. The quick ratio formula is computed as current assets less inventory divided by current liabilities.

Range: The high and low prices over which the security trades during a specific time frame such as a day, a month, or 52 weeks.

Relative strength: Comparison of a security's earnings or stock price strength in relation to other investments or indices.

Risk: The financial uncertainty that the actual return will vary from the expected return. Risk factors include inflation, deflation, interest rate risk, market risk, liquidity, default, etc.

Secondary market: A market where previously issued securities trade, such as the New York Stock Exchange.

Short sale: The sale of a security not yet owned in order to capitalize on an anticipated market price drop.

Short squeeze: A rapid price rise forcing investors to cover their short positions. This drives the security price up even higher, often squeezing even more short investors.

Special situation: An undervalued security with special circumstances such as a management change, a new product, or a technological breakthrough, favoring its return to better operating performance and higher prices.

Spin-off: The shedding of a corporate subsidiary, division, or other operation via the issuance of shares in the new corporate entity.

Split: A change in the number of outstanding shares through board of directors' action. While shareholder's equity remains the same, each shareholder receives new stock in proportion to his or her holdings on the date of record. Dividends and earnings per share are adjusted to reflect the stock split.

Standard & Poor's (S&P) 500: A broad-based stock index composed of 400 industrial, 40 financial, 40 utility, and 20 transportation stocks.

Striking price: The price at which an option or future contract can be executed according to the terms of the contract. Also called *exercise price.*

10K, 10Q: Annual and quarterly reports required by the Securities and Exchange Commission. They contain more in-depth financial and operating information than the annual and quarterly stockholder's reports.

Technical analysis: An investment strategy that focuses on market and stock price patterns.

Top-down investing: An investment strategy starting with the overall economic scenario and then moving downward to consider industry and individual company investments.

Total return: The return achieved by combining both the dividend/interest and capital appreciation earned on an investment.

Trading range: The spread between the high and low prices for a given period.

Turnaround: A positive change in the fortunes of a company or industry. Turnarounds occur for a variety of reasons such as economic upturn, new management, new product lines, and strategic acquisition.

Underlying security: A security that may be bought or sold under the terms of an option agreement, warrant, etc.

Undervalued situation: A security with a market value that does not fully value its potential or the true value of the company.

Uptrend: An upward movement in the market price of a stock.

Volume: The number of units of a security traded during a given time frame.

Warrant: An option to purchase a stated number of shares at a specified price within a specific time frame. Warrants are typically offered as sweeteners to enhance the marketability of stock or debt issues.

Working capital: The difference between current assets and current liabilities.

Yield: An investor's return on an investment in the form of interest or dividends.

Index

The author of *Stock Picking* invites you to examine these two special offers:

- *Gaming & Investments Quarterly*
  Covers the gambling, hotel, and entertainment industries with in-depth analysis of unique common stock investment opportunities. Regular $75 annual subscription; special price, $25 annual subscription.

- *Utility & Energy Portfolio*
  Includes investment ideas, discussions of where to find higher yields and safety, plus coverage of major industry trends and key players. Includes annual investment roundup of every major U.S. utility. Regular $95 annual subscription; special price, $35 annual subscription.

Richard J. Maturi

BONUS Either subscription entitles you to a free copy of *Wall Street Words: The Basics and Beyond*, a $14.95 value.